CAUGHT IN THE ACT

With a sigh of recognition, I pick up the trail and begin the march in. I am at the limit of my endurance. I've been concentrating all night and am by this time mentally bushed. I was missing everything off the side of the trail; we were passing right by mortar shells rigged to drop and explode. We spot an old Belgian Gate booby trap that is no longer functional, and keep moving farther and farther into the jungle.

Then I step on a Bouncing Betty.

A Bouncing Betty is an explosive booby trap that is placed in the ground in a pipe, tin can, or wide piece of bamboo, immediately off the side of a trail. As you step on it, the charge is propelled straight up into the air about four to six feet before detonating. They are usually lethal.

I watch as the Bouncing Betty rises into the air, sailing above my head. I will never know why, but I instinctively reach out and catch it as it is falling.

It fails to detonate! All of this transpires in a few seconds, and I'm left standing in the middle of the trail with the Bouncing Betty in my hand. I turn to look back at the rest of the squad, and they are moving very quickly back down the trail. Now I realize—standing there holding this explosive—that if somebody approaches me from the front, I'll have to think very quickly. . . .

SEAL!

From Vietnam's PHOENIX Program
to Central America's Drug Wars:
Twenty-six Years with
a Special Operations Warrior

Lt. Cmdr. Michael J. Walsh, USN (Ret.)

with Greg Walker

POCKET BOOKS
New York   London   Toronto   Sydney   Tokyo   Singapore

Insert photos are from the author's collection, unless otherwise noted.

An *Original* Publication of POCKET BOOKS

POCKET BOOKS, a division of Simon & Schuster Inc.
1230 Avenue of the Americas, New York, NY 10020

Copyright © 1994 by Lieutenant Commander Michael J. Walsh, USN, and Greg Walker

All rights reserved, including the right to reproduce this book or portions thereof in any form whatsoever. For information address Pocket Books, 1230 Avenue of the Americas, New York, NY 10020

ISBN: 0-671-86853-5

First Pocket Books printing January 1995

10 9 8 7 6 5 4 3 2 1

POCKET and colophon are registered trademarks of Simon & Schuster Inc.

Cover photo courtesy of the author

Printed in the U.S.A.

ACKNOWLEDGMENTS

First off, I wish to thank Greg Walker, my old friend, blood brother, and co-author. His guiding hand is throughout this book. This is but our beginning. "All passengers will please fasten your seat belts."

My many friends, listed here, contributed in one way or another to the successful completion of this book. I am truly grateful for all of them.

Mr. Morris Rowe and his wife, Shirley, for sound advice, wise counsel, and most of all, steadfast friendship. LCDR (Dr.) Greg DeMarco, CHC, USN, for his eternal friendship and manuscript review. Mr. Sheldon Kelly, *Reader's Digest* senior editor, and best "writing sea-daddy" a man could ask for. Mr. Raymond Ashe Sr. for providing me a quiet place to write the majority of this book at kill Devil Hills, North Carolina. His son, "Dickie" Ashe, another old and trusted (inner circle) friend for the instant feedback. Mr. Mike Carter, for instant feedback. Thanks, guys.

Others who helped significantly in one form or another are: GMGC (Chief Gunners Mate) Barry "The Bear" Enoch, USN (Ret.), CDR Tim Gilchriest, USN (Ret.), Lt. Col James R. "Jim" Stephan, USAF (Ret.), CDR Rich Finley, USN (Ret.), and SGT Les Stiles, Bend, Oregon, Police Dept., for manuscript accuracy, review, and maturing friendships. LTC (SF) Geoff Barker, USA (Ret.), a trusted adviser and old friend. Thanks also to the former and retired brothers from SEAL Team ONE who helped in many different ways: former Chief Warrant Officer Wayne Boles, Gary L. Harrawood, HMC Wayne "DOC" Jones, USN (Ret.), HMC Terry "DOC" Bryant, USN (Ret.), Lou DiCroce, EM1 (Electricians Mate) (Ret.), and MM2 (Machinist Mate) Fletcher "Bill" Wright, USN (Ret.). Master Chief James Matthews, USCG (Ret.), and his son John, for manuscript review and honest feedback. Mr. Douglas B. Ragsdale, for "the chop" and renewed kinship. Captain William Hawkins, USN (Ret.), for the straight talk, always.

My thanks to others who honored me by their comments, reactions, and patient reading of manuscript and/or moral support: Ms. Diane Grentzer, one of my oldest friends in this world, CDR Dale R. Klugman, USN (Ret.), and his devoted wife, Natalia, LCDR Greg Legore, USN, EWC (E-7) Nick Gaster, USN, Harold and Diana Price. My neighbors Al and Christy Morris, who befriended and fed me regularly. Tom and Renay Meyer, for always being there. My ministers, Tom Taylor, Alan Taylor, and David Bradley, for more than mere words. Mr. Dennis J. Cummings, for research help and commonsense advice. And my sincere appreciation to Wendy DeMarco and Julie Callas, two of the strongest Christian women I know, who have stood by me no matter the weather! And a special thanks to Rich Peters, who came back into my life at a time when it really counted. We both know who really planned that move. Thank you all.

There are two men whom I believe personify the true nature of a United States Navy SEAL: Captain Tom Richards, USN, and Chief Petty Officer Matt Lewis, USN. You two guys have done well, and I'm very proud to know you both!

Tom Richards, recently selected for rear admiral, has lost neither his bearing nor his compass. In the new world of political correctness he has remained loyal to his school, and more importantly to his beliefs. I look forward to your ascension to gold shoulder boards, old friend, and wish you every success and happiness. Our community needs you and will prosper through your leadership.

Matt Lewis is everything a Navy SEAL enlisted man should be. When we were together in Grenada and Lebanon, he made my job as his platoon commander easier simply by doing his. When things looked bleak, and everyone around me was doubting, this man kept his head and resolve. I don't forget things like that. Matt, any officer fortunate enough to have you as his platoon chief ignores your advice at his peril.

The common denominator in both of these fine men is their continued quest for excellence—in everything. Thanks, Tom. Thanks, Matt. When the next "contingency" crisis goes down and you run out of real operators . . . give me a call.

Finally, many thanks to my sister, Patricia. She provided me the "space" to write the closing chapters of this book in New England, in the family setting I truly miss sometimes. Thanks, Trish. To my wonderful brothers and sisters for always *being there* all those years I spent running all over the world, my love and eternal thanks. God bless you all.

SEAL!

勇猛无畏

忠

毅

1

Targeting the New Left

"I would think that, if you understood what communism was, you would hope, you would pray on your knees that we would become communists."

—*Jane Fonda*

"We felt empathy for those . . . of the other side, spokesmen for the communist world in Prague and Moscow, Peking and Hanoi. After all, we call ourselves in some sense revolutionaries. So do they."

—*Tom Hayden*

It was early 1972. I was twenty-four years old, had been a U.S. Navy SEAL for four years, and had recently finished my fourth tour of duty in Vietnam. The war was by then no longer in full combat bloom, and four years in what is still known simply as "the Teams" was a lifetime. Everyone in the Navy SEAL business was preoccupied with going back and forth to Vietnam. Nothing else mattered. I had recently finished a combat tour in a place called Soc Trang. Then my platoon moved to My Tho and I was wounded in Ben Tre. All in the same tour! My friend Don Barnes and I were visiting with X-ray platoon in Ben Tre, and when one Navy SEAL visited another platoon in Vietnam we went into the field and operated together. It's part of the continual bonding process. With us, the bonding process never stops —never. Operating is important to Navy SEALs. That's where all the training and hard times are put to the test.

And combat is the toughest test there is.

The wound I received in Ben Tre still troubles me. A B-40 rocket hit our small boat and wounded everyone aboard. The B-40 had an 88mm warhead and when it hit the boat it went right through eight inches of armor plate. I took shrapnel in the back of the head, back, buttocks, and legs and lost my left eardrum, but I was alive. Others were not so lucky. The stench of severed legs, ripped-open bodies, and burning flesh filled my nostrils. Human debris littered the bottom of the boat.

With all this behind me the command decided to put me in the SEAL Team ONE intelligence department at Coronado, California. Coronado is the West Coast base of operations for the Navy SEAL community; Little Creek, Virginia, near Norfolk, is the East Coast base of operations. "Mikey, you need to rest for a while," the commanding officer gently said to me.

I hate it when people tell me that.

Every Navy SEAL develops a specialty, much the same as members of our Army Special Forces colleagues do. I chose to specialize in the intelligence and weapons areas. As a petty officer second class, I was assigned as a leading petty officer, or LPO. I decided to throw myself into the job and learn all I could. I had just become engaged to a girl I met the day I returned from my most recent Vietnam tour, and we were married six months later, after I finished intelligence school in Denver. I was beginning to see my life change from the constant combat stress of Vietnam to that of a married man with a career to build. I have always enjoyed intelligence work, and my first peacetime assignment never bothered me to the degree other peacetime assignments might have.

As SEAL platoons began trickling back from Vietnam, it became obvious there were going to be difficult times ahead. This was especially true for those of us who didn't have another tour of the war to look forward to. I remember trying to understand the coming uncertainty by asking questions of older and wiser men. I'd enrolled in college, and I was determined to make the transition from warrior to peacetime sailor. I'm still trying to make it! Frankly, as the war in Vietnam came to a close, we Navy SEALs who had fought it were more than just a bit uncertain as to how to approach the future. The navy was downsizing, operating budgets were shrinking, and the world around us was changing rapidly.

Personal and professional relationships among us were very intense. The collective mood of SEAL Team ONE was intense, as was our nearly unreasonable animosity toward those who had opposed the war. As a young man and a Navy SEAL I had early on elected not to concern myself with politics. Being a warrior was all I cared about, all I lived for. So I buried my feelings about the war as I was experiencing them in the deepest recesses of my soul. I would not and could not think about it as anything other than my job. I was going to prove myself as a Navy SEAL warrior or die trying. The commitment was etched in stone as well as in my mind and spirit.

War brings out two distinct aspects of human behavior—the very best a man can be and the very worst. War is also a simple way to exist. For many, its very nature tugs at our most basic primordial instincts. The path into the heart of war demands that you ignore its objectives and its politics, as these have no place on the battlefield where warriors meet. To understand war, you must first view it from its most basic level, where the rubber meets the road.

The simplicity of just pure living and dying appeals to the remnant of animal instinct and human savage that lives inside all men, to one degree or another. Some men find they like taking this course, as all other challenges in life get left in the rearview mirror. Marriages end with the regularity of autumn leaves falling, bills cease to have importance, outside relationships flounder as the war overtakes them. Everything becomes insignificant when one is totally consumed by the bright fire of combat over an extended period of time. Certainly this was happening to me, despite my efforts to secure a berth in the supposedly normal society of the time.

Life back at Coronado, California, was certainly not life as I had known it in Vietnam. Most of us had not been on a long-distance ocean swim for so long that our wet suits had dry-rotted in their storage lockers. The nightly forays across jungle streams and rivers in the 'Nam were not the same as our beloved ocean conditioning swims, so we reentered the sea again with gusto. Vigorous physical exercise became a substitute for some of what we had left behind in Vietnam, and besides, there weren't any leeches in the salt water off Coronado's silver sand beaches.

Team humor was another outlet for our frustration with Stateside duty. One constant ceremony was the Monday morning inspection. During one Monday morning inspection a teammate who had failed to get his uniform out of the cleaners over the weekend decided to attend the ceremony anyhow, despite being on crutches due to an injury. It is still common in the Teams to see any number of folks on crutches. Sonny stripped himself naked except for an issue woolen watch cap, his ever present issue Rolex watch, and a pair of Tony the Tiger socks with red felt claws! Hobbling out to our surprised formation he took his place in ranks like everyone else and waited for the inspection to begin. As the executive officer (XO) came face to face with Sonny, he gave the nude SEAL the professional once-over and kept his expression professionally deadpan. "Shine up the bright-work on that crutch, boy," was his only observation about Sonny's definitely nonregulation condition. Nowhere but in the Teams could you do something like this and have it so wonderfully appreciated.

Peacetime also meant we had to attend dress uniform inspections, something I had not done since learning to become a navy sailor. I remember watching our XO, Bruce Van Heertum, attempting to conduct just such an inspection where most of our uniforms were two different tones of white, much to his dismay. When Bruce asked the chief to give the command to pull up our trouser legs to ensure everyone was wearing black socks, the entire exercise became a three-ring circus. One SEAL was wearing red socks, and Dan Cerigoni had white holes showing on both ankles. Turned out that Dan didn't own any socks, period. To pass inspection he'd gone into the engineering shop and dyed his ankles black. As he walked to inspection his trousers had rubbed against his ankles, wearing the dye off, leaving him with two pasty white full moons for Van Heertum's inspection. Yep, we were well on our way to a peacetime environment.

On a far more serious level we didn't want to lose our fine-tuned edge as combat SEALs or our ability to both plan and conduct operations. Physical training, inspections, and the other droll activities normally associated with being stationed at the flagpole just didn't jibe with the reality we'd come to embrace as veterans of the war. One of my particular specialties was the ability to construct target folders, a skill I'd learned as a Navy SEAL with the Phoenix program in Vietnam.

A target folder is essentially a file that contains the latest intelligence about whatever target is going to be attacked. Photos, background information, narrative support from the various intelligence agencies and theater intelligence centers will all be found in a target folder.

Target folders come in three categories: hard targets, soft targets, and human targets. Hard and soft targets are normally facilities such as petroleum pumping and storage stations or telecommunications or command and control facilities. Direct action missions are designed so that such facilities can be neutralized by limited destruction, usually to render the facility inoperable. To accomplish this, a critical node related to the site must be determined, which will ensure its being inoperable for at least seventy-two hours. Such attacks normally take place before a U.S. or Allied assault or during its early stages. Special Operations Forces carry out such attacks after training for them using the target folders assembled during peacetime.

Human targets are a different matter.

No one still on active duty in Special Operations will, or can, discuss this aspect of our business. In actual practice, very little of this form of targeting is done these days, but the capability is still alive and well. Certainly the hunt for General Manuel Noriega during Operation Just Cause made use of a formal target folder compiled on the general. Capture or termination is the goal of such a folder. Termination is an option that requires total commitment on the part of those carrying out the mission.

As SEAL Team ONE's Intelligence LPO, I decided after much discussion with selected teammates that we would use the resources of our intelligence department to help us retain our hard-earned ability to build a file on human targets. There was another reason: terrorism. Now that the Vietnam War was just about over, I could see terrorism on a global scale looming ahead. We discussed the vulnerability of our national military and political leaders to an undefined Middle Eastern group with unlimited resources who could enter the United States and kill a key figure or steal nuclear weapons. The term "low intensity conflict" was in the process of being coined to replace "insurgency" and other like terms of the Vietnam War. Another aspect of our experiment was to ascertain just how much information a terrorist could acquire about a public figure from open sources.

The intelligence department chief petty officer was Roger Thompson. He was assigned to the command from the regular navy and was an intelligence specialist. This meant we had a professional from the fleet who knew how things were supposed to work, and that was how we learned the navy way of doing things. The rest of us on Roger's staff were all qualified SEALs. Chief Thompson proved to be an easy man to work for, and only once would I see him appear rattled by the activities taking place in his shop.

My closest supporter and friend at the time was Gary Harrawood. Even for a SEAL, Gary was an unusual character in a sea full of other unusual characters. A former Franciscan monk, he was rumored to have left the missionary's life for one of clandestine operations. After turning in his monk's robes for a Navy SEAL breast insignia—known as the Trident, or the Budweiser—Gary joined the brotherhood of the navy's elite. I never pushed Gary for the particulars of his past, content to know that he was as solid as New Hampshire granite in both body and spirit, and one heck of a SEAL operator. And well he ought to have been, given that his father was a former UDT (Underwater Demolition Team) frogman who'd hit the beaches at Iwo Jima during World War II.

The targeting project started out simply and innocently enough, even by our standards. Our subjects were to be notorious public figures who were in the news all the time. We originally discussed picking names out of a hat. Then Gary and I explained to Chief Thompson that we'd need subscriptions to five newspapers: the *Los Angeles Times, New York Times, Washington Post, San Francisco Chronicle,* and the local *San Diego Union.* As an afterthought we subscribed to *Time* magazine, which seemed (to us) to keep fairly good track of the American leftist activists we despised even more than the Vietcong or North Vietnamese. Our goal was to see how much intelligence we could gather on these folks and then see if we could target them with a high degree of certainty. If we could do it, then it followed that a foreign terrorist could as well.

Gary and I spent hours deciding on the time frame and time sequence we would rely on to fix our exact target in place. Fixing a target implies that the target has been surveilled, a pattern has been established, and all that remains is to finalize the mission. Finally we returned to the tried and true Phoenix targeting process known in the trade as the Figure Eight. This method of targeting is based on the assumption that human beings will act out their lives as creatures of habit. After you have established a surveillance of the target, you simply track and record the subject's daily routine until a pattern emerges that can be relied upon: where the subjects go, what they do when they arrive, how long they stay, whom they see, and so on. Once a pattern becomes apparent, you must confirm it. When this is done, you have the individual's figure eight pinpointed. This means you know where your target's day begins and where it ends, with any and all minor deviations taken into account.

Jane Fonda, Joan Baez, Tom Hayden (who would later marry Jane Fonda), and pro-communist activist Angela Davis were adamant in their support of the New Left movement in the United States. They were among our subjects. Also included in our targeting process were the Students for a Democratic Society. The SDS advocated the overthrow of the U.S. government, and as members of our nation's military we'd taken an oath to protect the Republic and our Constitution from its enemies, both foreign and domestic. Certainly the SDS qualified for the top ten on our hit parade.

At this point in the targeting process we began evaluating what we had learned so far. The target folder's sponsor looks for critical nodes in the target's life where more time might be spent verifying particulars. Once these are established, we begin the second surveillance track, which will firmly fix the target in place for what will come next, capture or termination. This is all the theory behind targeting, and it works. If it didn't, terrorists wouldn't use it.

With over fifty such missions under my belt as a Phoenix operator in Vietnam, I returned to SEAL Team ONE with some of my own theories. My rule as a Phoenix adviser was to act on the third go-around, or surveillance track. Surveillance is your best weapon if you have the patience to conduct it properly. Terrorists take their time when targeting because they have all the time in the world. Employees of the U.S. government don't have this advantage, as Uncle Sam wants everything done yesterday. So time is a serious constraint. It makes you perform under pressure, which I and my fellow SEALs were very, very good at.

With Hanoi Jane, as Jane Fonda became known, at the top of our list, we began the process of tracking and targeting. In Vietnam we knew exactly what we were doing. We could tap into all of the intelligence sources we needed for a complete target folder. But now we were back home, back in the United States, and the process was far more challenging. After reviewing the newspapers over several weeks, our tiny committee decided we had only a three-day margin of error, plus or minus one day, to fix a specific target on the list. The three-day margin of error was simple. No one but the three of us even knew what we were contemplating overall, and only Gary Harrawood and I knew what was really in our hearts, so it followed that this would have to be the most meticulously planned operation either of us ever attempted. Taking leave could have tied us to the operation if Murphy's Law became a factor. So the operation would have to occur over a weekend. Getting a Monday or Friday off was relatively simple. All one day off required was permission and not necessarily paperwork. At least that was how it was then. Now it's all paperwork.

Chief Thompson said that everything seemed simple enough, but he was unaware at this early stage of the identity of our targets. With the chief's blessing, we plunged headlong into the planning phase with all the passion of young men dedicated to mission accomplishment.

From the newspapers we began clipping articles containing anything at all about the folks on our list. We never posted the list anywhere public, and its content was discussed only inside the secure confines of the intelligence department. The master list was secured in the first drawer of our number one file cabinet, and a select few SEALs in the command were made aware of what we were up to. In time, we accumulated so much data that we had to order more file cabinets, each carefully numbered as it was delivered to our "war room."

Television can, at times, also be of tremendous help to the inquiring mind, and we began watching TV in the shop to see what information might come our way. If a tidbit was broadcast, either Gary or I jotted down a quick narrative, which we inserted in the growing file. The first in-progress review, or IPR, was scheduled to take place ninety days after we'd begun the project.

That IPR told us a lot about the challenges facing us. This was not Vietnam, and we couldn't just query "the system" and expect to get an intelligence report confirming or denying whatever we were asking for. Operating in the United States demanded a whole new approach to the targeting process, so we became highly innovative. The public library became a resource option, but the city of Coronado's was simply too small and inadequate for our needs. We turned instead to the San Diego library and to the University of San Diego. Every good intelligence officer understands the value of the U.S. public library system. It is one of the best sources of information in this country. We elected to do all research on scene and never use a library card; we wanted nothing traceable to come back on us. Now our efforts began to move ahead at a rapid pace. Yet another file cabinet was added, and our target's folder began to assume epic proportions.

After the first four months of gleaning items from the daily papers Gary and I didn't care about Joan or Tom or Angela or even the SDS anymore. Our work now centered on Jane Fonda. She had made her infamous trip to North Vietnam, and the picture of her sitting on a Soviet antiaircraft artillery gun and smiling incensed me.

Building a target folder began to occupy much of our time. We chose not to work on it during most weekends, as Gary and I felt we needed the time to keep our focus sharp. Also, I was a newly married man and working over the weekend would have been unpopular on the home front. Furthermore our operational security during the project was tight, and spending too much time on base at the intelligence shop would surely have raised eyebrows. One of the more effective methods we used to gather information revolved around phone calls made to various Hollywood press agencies. We called them release agencies because they would release information to us if they thought we were professional Hollywood types or journalists. The amount of information we were able to gather surreptitiously surprised us, so we kept expanding our effort. Gary and I created a simple code system when discussing our project, based upon the military phonetic alphabet. For example, Hotel Juliet stood for Hanoi Jane.

About six months into the project Chief Thompson began to sense that our efforts were more than a class project. Still, he allotted us the extra file space we needed, advised us regarding the finer points of intelligence gathering and analysis, and gave us some pointers on satellite photography and its capabilities. We were learning a lot, but we soon noted that the newspapers were redundant and the information they provided was limited, though certainly useful. Magazines were good for recent photographs, and we sought out those with identifiable backgrounds. Often public figures will have their picture taken at home, and despite the address not being given, the background is useful to the professional in this business. If you can pinpoint the background, then you can find out where the picture was taken. It is a very slow process, but it works. All it takes is one distinguishing feature that can be matched to a location and . . . gotcha!

As a young man of some intense passion, I held a deep professional dislike for Ms. Fonda. It is safe to say I was not alone in this feeling, as it was a time of high anxiety for everyone whose life had been touched by the Vietnam War. The conflict was tearing away at the fabric of our society, dividing families, races, and the American people as a whole. Respect for authority was declining, and disorder was everywhere. It grieved my heart and soul to see my country in moral turmoil. And all the while I had to wrestle with what my mother had told me when I was a little boy: "Hate is wrong, Michael, and God will punish you if you hate." No wonder I was so intense and somewhat confused.

Still, with all that in my mind, when Gary and I were alone I confided to him my vision of justice where Jane Fonda was concerned. This was a woman who'd used her fame as an actress and as the daughter of a famous actor to lead the antiwar movement, a woman whose own status as a public figure gave credence to what I and many of my friends considered a warped and dangerous political agenda for the United States. A far worse action took place when she visited North Vietnam and, as an antiwar activist, donned a North Vietnamese helmet and allowed herself to be photographed by the world press. That photo became an instant communist propaganda success around the world. It was a knife violently twisted into the guts of every U.S. veteran of the war. Most who fought in Vietnam left part of themselves there—whether it was a friend, a family member, or a portion of their physical, mental, or emotional selves.

My access to the command's extensive array of photographic equipment gave me access to a camera nearly all the time. I became an expert in taking surveillance pictures and developing my own film in the privacy of the intelligence department photo lab. I also took advantage of the lab to print up numerous eight-by-ten photos of Jane Fonda. In the beginning I practiced my photo-surveillance skills on people I knew. I got a few surprises there, as you might imagine. Then Gary and I did local surveillance jobs on people I'd selected at random, which allowed us to work together as a team.

Chief Thompson began getting anxious at our zeal and continuing preparations. He must have sensed the change in the project's flavor, but he didn't stop us. After all, this was fascinating stuff for someone not used to this kind of activity. This was not the standard fare for an intelligence specialist from the fleet. Those folks are more concerned with photographic intelligence and working from aircraft carriers. Their focus is in technical things. This was human intelligence and we were SEALs. The chief was somewhat dazzled by the project, always assured by Gary and me that it was nothing more than a training exercise.

After about nine months Jane Fonda's life had come into focus for us. I developed a master file I could take home and read at night. I had a large blowup of the photo of her sitting on that antiaircraft gun, and we were sure enough of her daily pattern to begin planning.

We'd prepared a graph of her education record and known addresses. There was a good photograph of where she presently lived—her local chamber of commerce had happily, and unknowingly, provided us with everything we needed in terms of street maps and such. Most of our brainstorming sessions took place in the intelligence shop behind locked doors. No one questioned our presence or activities. After all, intelligence work was always off limits to all but a few.

During one of these sessions, however, we realized that it was impossible to target anyone with a high degree of accuracy and certainty using only newspapers and other open source documents. We needed to do a personal reconnaissance of the Fonda neighborhood. So we took a weekend drive up the coast on I-5 to Los Angeles and from there to where Jane Fonda was living. The ride up the coast was beautiful, and the time in my car gave us time to think and try to resolve the moral dilemma in our souls.

Once we had the Fonda residence pinpointed we would execute our drive-by only once. I was using a 400mm telephoto lens for the job. Our exposure in the neighborhood had to be limited so as not to draw attention to our presence. Whenever operations are in the planning stages, security considerations are a constant. When working in an urban area there is always someone who has nothing better to do than sit and stare out the window. I was driving my own vehicle, a white Camaro with black roof. Looking back on it today I can see that we should have rented a car, but I was only a petty officer second class, and this whole operation was on the economy plan.

Targeting someone means paying meticulous attention to detail. It doesn't matter whether the mission is a kidnapping, a hard target, or an assassination. We were using the most effective targeting procedure we knew at the time, the Phoenix figure eight method.

Arriving in our target's community we began by scoping out the town and all its possible exits. We used what is called the circle, or clock, method—that is, we did a 360-degree driving reconnaissance of the entire area and then gradually worked our way into town and into the target neighborhood. Using the city map and a pencil we marked areas of note and jotted down little details that could make all the difference. The California hill country adjacent to the area is latticed with secondary and back roads, and we avoided the main highways during the post-operation phase for obvious reasons. Casually driving back to San Diego via the countryside seemed the appropriate manner of accomplishing this portion of the plan.

In this kind of work the psychological factor is important. You don't want anyone to remember you when the hunting party is called out. If you wish to remain invisible in a modern city it is best not to make direct eye contact with anyone. Why? Because the chances are that the person you made direct eye contact with will remember you later. Thieves, criminals, and others who are used to the psychology of disguise understand this principle well. So do some in the special operations business. I wore a baseball cap and sunglasses to alter the shape of my head and to hide my military haircut. Time was also a critical factor, since we had only the weekends to accomplish this mission. In addition, using the tradecraft taught us during the train-up for the Phoenix and other programs I was privileged to attend, I was carrying a second wallet containing a complete false identity, which I had been nurturing for some time.

We made contact with a local man who knew his way around. He was to be our diversionary dupe. He had his own vehicle. We nicknamed him simply Dupe. Not incredibly intelligent, he had the forty-fathom stare of someone who had seen a little too much combat and now had a *baaad* attitude. His job would be to drive a diversionary vehicle past the target's house at the precise moment it was being taken down in order to mislead people about what was happening. He would lead the high-speed chase in another direction and buy us time should that become necessary. We knew the heat would be intense on this mission, given who the target was. We had a method of communicating with this man using our false identities, and we were frankly stunned to find someone living so close to Jane Fonda who would gladly betray her.

Looking back on it today I can only wonder how Gary and I ever got so caught up in this thing. I knew in my heart what we were contemplating was wrong. But we convinced ourselves our act would avenge every prisoner of war as well as our teammates and fellow American warriors who'd given their lives while Jane Fonda was mugging for the camera.

We weren't playing any longer. We were in it, and events were moving more and more rapidly out of our control.

We considered taking Fonda down in a crowd, but dismissed that idea for two very good reasons. One, it was too difficult, given the available escape routes. Secondly, there was the martyr complex to consider. We didn't want another revolutionary hero to emerge from her ashes who might further fan the flames of America's increasingly violent New Left movement. Approaching her as she returned from work was the only viable option open to us. We concluded that if we could discern this avenue of attack, a terrorist or terrorist group could reach the same conclusion. So we proceeded along those lines.

Late afternoon or evening is a good time to catch someone off guard. (When folks are leaving for work in the morning is also good.) In the evening most people are trying to get through rush-hour traffic or are preparing for supper, the day's work done, the family in familiar surroundings. We could live with the somewhat uncertain schedule Jane Fonda maintained with respect to coming home from work or play, and we knew it always varied. Vietnam operations had taught us patience. So we would wait for her with a casualness born of battle.

We continued training. Any number of guys went out to the Chocolate Mountains desert area during the weekends. The SEAL training camp was located near a small town called Niland on the Salton Sea in the California desert. It would draw no eyebrow upward to see someone working out with one of our weapons systems on a weekend. Weapons control in those days was casual at best—some guys even brought their girlfriends—and I took full advantage of that.

Using the photo lab I had printed many eight-by-ten photos of Ms. Fonda. I would take them to the desert and staple them on posts, bushes, and anything else I could secure them to. I varied the range to see how good my distance judging was. I learned quickly that I needed a lot of work here.

The whole project unraveled for Gary and me one Friday afternoon, though, when the intelligence department received a surprise inspection by the XO. Earlier that morning

14

he had announced that there would be a department inspection that day, but we weren't worried; our department had slid out of these inspections regularly. Our small committee was happily working away when the XO popped his head in the door. I'll never forget the look on the chief's face when the XO made his presence felt in our small office. Roger was a heavy smoker, but I had never seen him chain-smoke before. He was now, and his hand began to shake. As usual, the intelligence officer responsible for all of us was nowhere to be found. Coincidence?

The XO went about the usual cleanliness routine, commenting on missing lights and such. We all nodded our heads like good sailors, diligently writing down the XO's remarks in our wheel books, as we knew he liked such attention to his comments. Then he asked to see the map and chart files. No problem there. We gladly displayed these for him in the hope the inspection might end at this point. It didn't.

"What's in these file cabinets?" he quietly asked. We possessed no less than five file cabinets filled to capacity with targeting intelligence.

"Nothing important, sir," we answered in unison.

"If they're not important, what are they here for?" Moving to the unlocked drawers the XO began going through our carefully constructed files. His face began to show the dawning of recognition and understanding, and his features at that specific moment are burned into my mind's eye forever.

"Is this training stuff, Walsh?" he asked.

"Sure is, XO," I responded, trying to keep my expression deadpan. He wasn't smiling. In fact, a bright red hue began to stain his features with blood red intensity. Gary and I made eye contact with each other while the chief lit up another cigarette. We attempted to put on our best face as the charade fell down around our collective knees. I was scared, and my stomach began to ache. Now I felt blood rushing to my head, and I wasn't sure what to do next.

As one we tried to convince the XO about our theoretical targeting class. We stressed our intention to preserve the skill level learned in Vietnam in hitting hard, soft, and human targets. Such information couldn't be allowed to

15

disappear just because the war was drawing to a close, could it? The XO's circuit board fairly popped when he heard our lame rationale. He was clearly scared.

"This isn't training stuff, Walsh!" he screamed at me.

I didn't budge an inch. "Of course it is, XO," I calmly replied. The impromptu interrogation continued, but we couldn't be broken down. The Chief backed us up, something I have never forgotten. Of course, we never would have betrayed him either. The XO looked me square in the eye, his own now so narrow they reminded me of twin cannon. His mouth was drawn tight, his whole being so tightly coiled I was afraid he might explode if we gave him one more lame excuse.

"You know better than this, Walsh," he finally blurted out. I remember thinking how odd it was that he was no longer screaming at me. He simply looked disappointed. "I know you take this job seriously, but I thought I knew you better than this," he continued. Somehow those words hurt me more than any amount of invective he might have fired in my direction. I'd let him down. I'd failed him in his professional expectations of me. My abilities were never in question, but my character now was. That moment has become one of the bittersweet lessons of my rather active life.

Then another big question from the XO. "Who else knows about all this?" he asked.

"No one else, sir, not even the intelligence officer," I replied.

He looked a little relieved. You could have cut the tension in that room with a knife. Our personal and professional lives were now clearly in this man's hands, and we didn't have a clue what his next move would be. The XO did after all have a reputation for extremely strict discipline.

We were ordered to collect and burn every shred of evidence, along with anything having to do with our project, and so we burned every article, picture, synopsis, and file. The XO asked if anyone present had any material at home. I confessed I did. I was ordered to bring everything in the next day, Saturday, and burn it. Just to make sure we didn't cheat, the XO told the chief to "make sure every shred of paperwork is destroyed."

Roger gave the XO a quiet "Aye-aye, sir." Since Gary and

16

I were sharing an apartment at the time, such a visit would kill two birds at once. We didn't object to the home search. We all knew what the XO could have done. The next day, Saturday, we committed every bit of information to the funeral pyre.

In reality the only give-away of my suspected involvement was the large blowup picture I kept on the wall of Jane Fonda looking through the sight of the antiaircraft artillery gun. That picture has haunted hundreds of thousands of Vietnam veterans and other patriotic Americans.

Of course, with the passage of time and the growth of my professional and personal maturity, I have reevaluated my thoughts about Ms. Fonda. My recent embrace of Christianity is perhaps the final cleansing of the brutal and destructive actions I once considered acceptable. I thank God for His divine intervention via the XO's unexpected visit. Today my thoughts regarding Jane Fonda and that terrible time for our country are in much better perspective.

Like most Vietnam veterans I have a difficult time forgiving Ms. Fonda for her Vietnam era protest actions. But when I put the entire war into twenty-twenty hindsight I'm not at all sure I can continue to condemn her any longer for opposing the war. What I cannot support were her personal actions in support of the North Vietnamese, actions that she committed while my teammates and many other American men were fighting, bleeding, languishing in POW camps, and dying in Vietnam.

I never discussed the exercise targeting of Hanoi Jane from the day all evidence of its existence was destroyed until now. As I advanced to the rank of a commissioned naval officer, Ms. Fonda became, and remains, an insignificant speck in my life's rearview mirror. I could never have imagined that I would retire as the deputy director of intelligence in a joint special operations headquarters doing targeting—among other things—on a global scale.

Life, as they say, is full of surprises.

2

So Ya Wanna Be a Navy SEAL?

As with every story there is a beginning. For me, and for every other sailor who volunteered for the Teams, that beginning was BUD/S training. The Basic Underwater Demolition/SEAL course is the beginning of the process that molds us into elite underwater warriors called Navy SEALs. Our BUD/S training will stay with us until the day we die. The course is designed to turn navy machinists, boiler technicians, damage control specialists, electronics wizards and other tradesmen into SEALs. The challenge is to convert the trainees' academic and technical skills into the skills and dedication demanded by Navy Special Warfare. This is why it is necessary to subject trainees, or tadpoles, to freezing cold mud baths in January. It is also why we're expected to conduct ocean swims in fifty-five-degree weather. During future missions SEALs will look back on BUD/S and remember that "the only easy day was yesterday," and they'll get on with accomplishing the mission. Because of this rigorous training, however, the attrition rate at BUD/S has remained constant at roughly fifty percent since the end of World War II.

UDT/SEAL history began during the invasion of Tarawa in the Pacific on November 20, 1943. Upon disembarking from their landing craft, many U.S. Marines were forced to wade slowly toward the beaches under full equipment loads and with no cover. The water was deep, and the ocean's bottom was a mass of holes and crevices. Many marines drowned, still more were wounded by small arms fire, and others were trapped when their armored vehicles floundered and sank. The tide rose very, very quickly and caught them by surprise. It, too, claimed many lives as the marines

battled their way toward Tarawa's sandy shoreline. Had accurate beach intelligence been available, precious lives could have been saved.

Reeling from the tragic loss of American lives at Tarawa, the navy began studying the need for near-shore beach intelligence. No one wanted another Tarawa, and thus UDT Teams were established.

In 1975, while working with the marines in the Philippines, I found out what it was like to sink when our landing vehicle went to the bottom during a training exercise. Someone yelled, "Don't panic—wait till we reach the bottom and we'll swim straight up to the surface." Yeah, right. You haven't seen panic until you're aboard a tracked amphibious vehicle going straight down with a squad of armed marines whose eyes have become as big as tea saucers. In the SEAL trade a moment like this is known as the super big pucker factor. We all got out of the LVT okay, but it reminded me of how the underwater demolition training (UDT) program began and why.

What gets you through the UDT/SEAL training program is willpower—and teamwork. No one goes through training alone; you either learn to work as part of a team to survive or you fail alone. I remember standing alongside twenty-eight other SEAL candidates in the surf zone at Coronado in January 1968. The water was freezing! The water temperature during that time of year is in the low fifties. Cold water will always get your attention. Our rubber boats were lined up on the beach drying under a warm sun while our instructor sat in a lounge chair reading the paper. Occasionally he looked out to sea, noting our attempts to stay in formation as the waves assaulted our bruised and battered bodies. Noting our inability to hold a proper military course he picked up his bullhorn and instructed us to "straighten out those lines!" As we attempted to comply he rubbed tanning oil on his arms, hoping perhaps to impress some of the East Coast women vacationing at the exclusive Hotel Del Coronado just up the beach from us. We were dying— or thought we were—and he seemed totally unaware of our peril.

Being up to our necks in ice-cold seawater, was only the beginning of the training prospective SEALs were expected to endure. The real challenge of the exercise made itself evident after an hour or so. First, the shivering started; then the color began to drain from our faces. We were huddling together, trying to share our warmth, trying to keep the sound of our teeth chattering down to a dull roar. Someone started talking about quitting—not what I wanted, or needed, to hear. Many men during the early phases of training wanted to quit, but they wanted someone else to quit with them. When you're cold and tired and all you can think about is getting warm again, your judgment is easily impaired because you're listening to your body, not your mind.

This rational insight was not at all apparent during our ocean formation, however. All we wanted to do was kill our instructor and then get warm. I didn't listen to the man next to me urging anyone interested in joining him to quit. I closed it out, concentrating on hanging in there for just a while longer. Everyone around him did the same thing. During BUD/S, if you want to quit and go back to the fleet you merely have to fall out and toss your helmet liner down on the ground. Otherwise, you shut up and suffer with the rest of the herd. It's that simple—pass or fail, victory or defeat, life or death. There is no in between in the Teams. There's a saying painted on the wall at SEAL Team TWO: "Defeat is worse than death . . . you have to live with defeat." Understand this, and you are well on your way to becoming a Navy SEAL.

BUD/S is divided into three individual phases. Phase One was the hell week phase, meant to get us into shape and to weed out the frogmen from the fleet sailors. Phase Two centered on learning how to dive, and Phase Three concerned itself with demolition and land warfare training. When I went through the course there were still UDT teams as well as SEAL teams. The SEAL teams went on to take a six-week land warfare course at the Chocolate Mountain bombing range in the desert east of San Diego. Today, everyone is a SEAL, as the missions have been unified under one concept.

I will never forget showing up for training with class forty-four. The class ahead of mine (class forty-three) was going through the daily drill, running to the chow hall for breakfast. You'd eat, do physical training, then go for the post-breakfast training and run. Before anything, though, there was the early morning inspection. This is a daily routine in BUD/S. As I would learn, your boots had better be well shined at the day's beginning or there was hell to pay. Sound easy? Not if you'd been thrown into the ocean the day before! There's no mistaking the salt residue around the sole of a military boot. I would learn to soak my boots in fresh water the previous evening so they'd still be wet . . . and clean . . . the next morning. The truly wily tadpoles kept several extra pairs of boots in their lockers, just in case. I ended up with four pairs of jungle boots and a stack of white T-shirts in my stash. And boot shining became a way for me to save money during training.

It was during BUD/S that I first began drinking beer on the weekends. Every Friday afternoon, the instructors would march-run us down to the navy piers at the end of the amphibious base where we trained. From there one could look across San Diego Bay and see the Thirty-second Street naval base, where all the ships were tied up. We'd be ordered to take a good look at the ships, and then the order would come: "Hit the bay, bananas!" We had thirty seconds to get the entire class in the water, which meant moving twenty-nine men down a one-man finger pier mighty quickly. Naturally we ended up devising a system to get the mission accomplished. After several futile attempts to get the whole class down the finger pier, we simply jumped off the quay wall in unison into the water. Took only five to ten seconds to make it happen. The faster and better you can get things done in training the less pain you suffer, singularly and collectively. That was the point—working as a team to accomplish the impossible. Everything in training had a purpose, every single thing. The term "banana" has a special meaning to most SEALs. Bananas are soft on the outside and soft on the inside. So SEAL instructors address trainees as bananas during the first weeks of training. As the class begins to pull together, toughen up, and work as a team, the use of the term subsides. "Hit the bay, banana!" will always bring a smile to my face, although perhaps a pained one.

Anyhow, the tadpole officers among us absolutely hated to shine their soiled boots on the weekend. After all, the instructors told us to take it easy during these two days and most officers took this to mean chasing stewardesses over in San Diego. I began charging a six-pack of beer for each pair of officer's boots I shined. This kept me in beer for the weekend, after my routine 6- to 8-mile run in the morning, that is. I'd finish my run, get cleaned up, then begin drinking with the boys after lunch. Today the SEALs' reputation for being heavy drinkers is nearly a thing of the past. In my mind, this is a good turn of events, as alcohol has ruined too many SEAL careers, individual lives, and families.

My first day in training was anything but pleasant. It was December 1967 and I'd just returned from the Philippi s, my first tour of Vietnam completed. I'd fired twin .50 caliber machine guns in combat as a member of a swift boat crew, thrown hand grenades at VC sampans, and sent rounds down-range with the XM-148 grenade launcher with the very real intention of killing folks. I was twenty years old, five feet four inches tall, and 120 pounds soaking wet! I was a cocky little guy, but I'd "been there." To be honest, I thought I was a pretty tough character, and then I met a man we'd only heard rumors about: BM1 Vince Olivera.

Boatswain's Mate First Class Olivera was one of the few true sailors left in today's navy. They're deck apes, meaning they do everything from underway replenishment line handling to driving small craft to operating ship cranes to standing watch on the bridge. They are the most versatile men in the navy, and the navy could not function at sea without them. Olivera was a tall man, very lean, very mean, very crude, and most of all, very cunning. His smile was an evil sneer, which for some odd reason, many women found attractive.

Olivera was of Mexican and Indian stock. His skin was the color of well-burnished brass. He had legs like coiled springs and was a meticulous dresser even by military standards. He wore a navy blue baseball cap with the instructor logo displayed on its front. His blue windbreaker had the word "God" emblazoned in huge white capital letters above the left breast. His nose had been broken so many times it was hooked. His green military shorts were tailored to his body, the diving socks rolled carefully a precise three times so they rested just atop his spit-shined combat boots. Seeing him struck immediate fear into our tadpole-like hearts.

Olivera's eyes were the worst. They were a demon's eyes and they burned right through your soul. When I first met Vince I made a true error in judgment by approaching him. I asked what time it was as an icebreaker, wanting to follow up with more questions about training.

"What do I look like, information central, you short little pissant?" Vince fired back at me. "You got legs in those drawers—what are you talking to me for? You ain't even a banana yet!" All the time he was moving closer and closer to me, intimidating me with his greater height and his overpowering presence. For a moment I thought I was standing still, but then I noticed that the people around me, including the officers, were the ones who weren't moving. I was the one edging backwards, stuttering with every unsure step, "I'm sorry, sir, very sorry, sir . . . I was just . . ." I never got to finish that sentence.

Olivera screamed at me. "Shut up, banana! Get out of my face! Do I look like a puke-soaked officer? Do I look like I don't work for a living?" It went on and on, but never once did he swear at me. The instructors in BUD/S almost never swore in training; that would have brought them down to our level. They established psychological control over us using this simple technique, and Olivera was the best.

I survived this encounter with Vince Olivera, and he eventually left quite a mark on the young man who thought he knew it all. Vince was striving to instill the right combat ethic in us, to make us into warriors.

Pretraining was pretty informal in those days and was run by Chief Petty Officer Bernie Waddell, a ruggedly built and handsome black man with a dignified demeanor. He was forty-something and in superb shape. Waddell conducted our physical training, and I remember asking him question after question about what was to come. Unlike Vince, Bernie was the "good guy" instructor who could be approached by a self-doubting tadpole.

The grinch inside me hadn't really come into his own yet, but he was there. Today I doubt anyone on the Teams who was close to me ever suspected his existence. He was the little man inside me who never allowed my spirit to be dominated—not by my father, not by anyone who wanted to own my soul. The grinch—as I named him—is the axis of centrality vis-à-vis my determination when threatened. Every time I got into trouble I had only to look inward to find this little guy, his beady eyes and half-angelic, half-demonic smile telling me that we would prevail. The grinch eventually took more and more control over my helm, and miraculously seemed to show up just when needed. Today I've learned he was misnamed in my youth. The true spirit of this force will be revealed at the end of my story.

I passed the PT test expected of every tadpole, but I was always being harassed because of my lack of height and muscle mass. My two weeks with Chief Waddell passed uneventfully. Bernie was very proud of the fact that he was among the first from the Teams to graduate from the U.S. Army Ranger course. As it turned out, the honor of being the first Navy SEAL to finish this grueling light infantry-patrolling course was Chief Gunners Mate Barry Enoch, one of the Teams' most highly decorated operators. For Bernie, being both a black man and a SEAL must have made that little journey hell on earth, but in true UDT/SEAL tradition, he accomplished his mission. The Teams are filled with guys like Barry and Bernie, non-quitters and overachievers.

Day one of our formal training began with the director of training informing us that most of our class would probably be gone in short order. He would be proven right. Out of the 1,510 sailors who took the screening test for BUD/S, thirty-four passed and then chose to actually show up for the course. Five of these quit before the sun rose on day one, and we began with twenty-nine tadpoles. Lieutenant Commander Wilson, the training director, was one inch shorter than me . . . and I am quite short enough. In this business an inch might as well be a mile, and Wilson now had my number because I was taller than he. When we ran the obstacle course he would point out that he could accomplish each obstacle better than I. That was true: he could run it perfectly almost every time, whereas I would struggle with specific challenges on the course, which only brought extra harassment my way. What I did discover, though, was my ability to run like a gazelle. It would be a lifesaver.

Another character was Chief Allen. He and Olivera were a

24

team, and they were tough on us tadpoles. Dick Allen was a huge man, a former navy boxer whose arms and legs reminded me of telephone poles. With Allen and Vince in charge, our lives ceased to belong to us.

Every phase of training has a purpose. Commands are to be obeyed, but not without thought. A SEAL cannot behave like a trained animal, as this will get him killed in combat. We had to stay alert no matter how tired, pissed off, hungry, thirsty, or injured we were at the time. Every time the instructors caught one of us off guard, not listening, we would all be punished. Mostly this meant running with a full head of steam into the bay and then finishing PT in wet boots and trousers. Running four miles in wet boots is murder. A special treat was getting our legs sandblasted. We would all sit at the edge of the water holding our trouser legs open as the surf rushed up around us. Deposits of sand were left inside our pants, all the way up around our butt. A nice run along the beach would complete the sandblast effect, which could only be held in check if we were smart enough to buy and wear silk underwear, which saved our private parts from becoming like ground round from the effects of the wet sand. One of the traditions upon successfully completing BUD/S was for the class to burn all their silk underwear. After all, "Frogmen don't wear skivvies."

I suppose to many this kind of treatment sounds cruel, but war, as I would be reminded during four more tours of Vietnam, is far more abusive of both the human body and spirit. SEALs learn by virtue of their training at BUD/S that no matter what, you don't quit. In fact, we hate quitters . . . passionately. Regardless of the conditions, you as a SEAL will overcome.

The hell week phase is the most intense in every respect. The instructors never let up, not once, not ever. The unexpected becomes the expected as each day unfolds. The price of failing to perceive, to correctly understand and do, resulted in physical, mental, and emotional misery. If one of us screwed up, the whole class suffered for it. The word "team" began to take on a new meaning. It began to figure prominently in our thought process, because we knew that failure to operate as a thinking member of the Team could result in injury or even death.

BM1 Olivera is inspecting the troops. We tadpoles are

lined up in three ranks, Lieutenant Loma returning his salute as the class proctor arrives. Halfway down the first rank Olivera notes a glitch in Kaneakua's uniform but says nothing. As he comes to Frank Willis at the opposite end of the rank he promptly gets in Frank's face and yells, *"Drop,* pineapple!" Willis assumes the lean-and-rest, or push-up, position without thinking. Then he realizes that Olivera was in fact yelling at Kaneakua—even as "Pineapple" catches on to the game at the other end of the rank. "Stay down there, banana. It'll help you stay awake!" orders Olivera, and the inspection continues. This is yet another example of how we are taught to stay awake and alert. In BUD/S they can keep you in the lean-and-rest forever if they want to. When the pain—and there's a lot of pain in becoming a SEAL—becomes severe the rallying cry is "hoo-ya!" Every service has its own battle cry. It's a code, a means of bonding that soon becomes a greeting, a means of voicing agreement, a means of expressing group displeasure but determination to get the job done, and finally, a battle cry.

There is no difference in training between the officer and enlisted ranks. Officers and enlisted men undertake the same regimen. Lifelong friendships are made, and some men become enemies. By the time graduation rolls around you know pretty much everything about your classmates— their strengths and weaknesses, their likes and dislikes. The common working unit in training is the boat crew, which is usually seven men, six guys who paddle and one coxswain. The standard rubber boat used in training is the IBS, or inflatable boat, small. It is twelve feet long and weighs just 250 pounds inflated. The IBS becomes a part of you in BUD/S; you live with it and in it. Lose your IBS and you may as well lose your soul.

My boat crew was made up of guys all six feet tall and taller. When the order, "Up boat" was given, all members of the boat crew pick up the rubber boat and balance it on their heads. When that happened, the boat was a foot above my head! No problem. The instructors simply ordered me to grab all the paddles and fall in behind my crew. Now my teammates were pissed off at me because they had to carry that much more weight. I tried to say something encouraging to them, but when I did, I wished I hadn't. With the torrent of curses and other suggestions of more than impending pain coming my way, I had visions of being ax-murdered in my sleep. This kind of development is constant in our business, even after training. When you sit down and analyze it, you realize that no matter how tough or fit you are physically, the mind is truly the master of the body. If the mind is not tough, the body will not obey a simple command from the mind to ignore cold or pain.

Log PT is another example of team spirit. Seven men hoist a shortened telephone pole and begin rolling it around, transferring it from shoulder to shoulder. If someone starts faking it, the rest of us can tell immediately. You never fake it with your teammates, because in training everyone is punished and in combat someone is going to die. Falling asleep in class was another no-no. Fall asleep and they'd send you running into the Pacific Ocean to wake up. Return to class, soaking wet of course, and you get to clean the classroom floor because you got it wet. In BUD/S, everything leads to something else.

The sixth week of training, known as hell week, completes the first phase of training, which everyone must pass to continue on to the next phase. However, before we can begin hell week there is the IB run—a ten-mile or so jaunt from Coronado straight down the beach to the Imperial Beach pier. This run is conducted on the Thursday or Friday prior to hell week, kicking it off. From start to finish in training there exists a goon squad, made up of those poor souls who have difficulty keeping pace during the long runs. These are not the guys you want to hang out with. As different instructors conduct the runs, each man's pace is different. The idea is to be able to follow any man at the pace set. This is tough to do, but it teaches you a great deal. For example, in combat you will be able to move only as fast as the slowest man in your squad. This kind of conditioning teaches us how different people accomplish different things. No one in the Navy SEAL business is a lone wolf. You either become a team player or you play by yourself.

I clearly remember our class IB run. We couldn't see Imperial Beach from the start point, it was that far away, and the usual haze that hangs over San Diego was present. Olivera strode out to us in his usual uniform. He adjusted the ball cap slightly, the "God" windbreaker snapping lightly in the breeze. Doc Heatherington gave him a baseball-size chew of tobacco, which he stuffed into his mouth. Then he lit a wicked cigar after settling the evil wad somewhere along the inside of his distinct jawline. The fighter pilot sunglasses were positioned, and the double-time arm signal was given for the run to begin. We never stopped until we reached the IB pier. As we arrived, Olivera turned the column around toward Coronado, called a halt, and orders us to do two minutes' worth of "deep breathers, you bananas!" I never remember seeing that cigar leave the man's mouth during the entire exercise.

Halfway to the IB pier, the instructors ordered the goon squad into the surf zone and made them sit at the edge of the water with their pants rolled up. It was a sad sight to see. As the waves roared in, sand and crushed seashells were driven up inside their trouser legs. This brutal mix bead-blasted even the most sensitive areas of their lower bodies. The goon squad was then ordered back on their feet. They ran in circles, their chafed and bleeding groin areas causing immense discomfort in addition to the pain already being endured. Olivera demanded, "Motivation, men, motivation." As I looked back I suddenly heard my name. "Walsh! If you like what you see back there you can join them," offered Olivera, in a tone I couldn't mistake. I started the run in the first rank behind the officers, and I stayed there until we reached the IB pier.

On the way back we ran headlong into our classmates in the goon squad. We were ordered to run in big circles until they caught up with the group. But then the goon squad was again broken off. "Their little cookies have been turned into hamburger!" puffed one man, and he was right. We made it back to the beach at Coronado, and headed for the chow hall, where a meal and a few moments of rest were waiting. Once inside and seated, we witnessed one of those events that made SEAL training legendary in the navy.

Frank Willis, a member of the goon squad, literally crawled into the chow hall. His face was as red as a Washington apple, his eyes bloodshot, his uniform soaked with sweat, covered with sand and salt stain. He was gasping, his hair was plastered to his skull, and his eyes were glazed like those of a madman. Willis tossed his helmet liner into the pile by the door and continued crawling up to the water cooler. Everyone but us was trying to help him. We were gulping down juice and milk as fast as we could. Frank asked the master-at-arms to pour water over him until he could stand and drink for himself. Nearly three hundred sailors standing in the chow line were watching this, their mouths hanging open as they witnessed Frank Willis coming back to life.

Hoo-ya, Frank!

Hell week is the essence of the SEAL business. Though it is physically exhausting, it is primarily a mental game from start to finish. How much difficulty can you put up with, how many obstacles can you overcome, how much personal discomfort can you ignore, and how well can you perform despite the mental and physical exhaustion? Remember, you can quit anytime. Today they offer counseling for those who opt out of the program. How nice. We in the SEAL business do not have the option of quitting or failing when things get real. We can only reach down into the deepest pit of our gut and continue. We've built a strong legacy of both physical and mental prowess to negotiate impossible obstacles, and we didn't do it by seeking counseling when the going got so tough we wanted to quit. Nonetheless, hell week usually began on Sunday evening with instructors assaulting the barracks with guns blazin'. It didn't take long before the class was in the water and the fun started. On Tuesday the demolition harassment took place. This was where we crawled through a barbed-wire obstacle field while half-pound blocks of TNT were detonated in the sand dunes on both sides of the course. This is where the numbness and ear ringing began. The exercise was designed to simulate the stresses and conditions of combat. By Tuesday evening the first signs of hallucination began to creep in. While paddling late at night we all saw weird things. I saw a train cutting across our path, and it was a pretty pink train, too! The rest of the week was one disappointment after another on top of the physical and mental hardship. Our training produced SEALs who were highly competitive, especially with each other. The only safe thing is another SEAL. Everything else is up for grabs. During hell week we began drawing hazardous duty pay, which is a nice addition to the paycheck.

One of the more interesting events during hell week was

the TJ paddle. It began at the west end of the base and extended all the way to the south end of San Diego Bay, with Tijuana, Mexico, just next door. A very subtle part of training is the encouragement to cheat, if only just a bit. The adage when I went through BUD/S was "Cheat, steal, lie, even kill . . . but don't let us catch you!" Our boat crew decided to try to outsmart the instructors during the paddle.

After taking off we seized the first opportunity to beach our IBS just outside the base and adjacent to the highway. The ensign ran back to the base—fairly easy to get away with as the event took place at night—and phoned up his wife. Several minutes later she arrived with two bags of chow and two six-packs of beer. We deflated the IBS, loaded it atop the car, and headed for Tijuana! Two sips of the beer put me to sleep; that's how tired I was. Just north of the halfway point, we resumed the drill. Back in the bay—our stash of food hidden aboard someone's pleasure yacht—we paddled like crazy to the check-in point. Why all the concerned looks on the instructors' faces when we arrived? It turned out we'd missed the check-in point located at the end of the navy housing area that juts out into the bay. We sleazed our way out of that one, but we ended up having to paddle our asses off to get back because now we'd drawn attention to ourselves in a big way.

We had failed to realize that we actually lost more time and expended more effort trying to trick the system. We'd let one man persuade us he had a better idea, a better way to do it. This same man would later plague my entire career, and more SEALs would pay with their lives for his "better ideas." When we got back from our little boat trip, Ensign Sandoz was ordered to take us into the bay for "some rest." We had to squat in water up to our necks while an instructor lectured us on safety, just waiting for someone to drift into sleep. It didn't take long. The sound of a human head hitting the water was a dead giveaway that someone had fallen asleep in the squatting position. My head was the second to hit the water. We lost out on two hours' sleep that night. The rest of our class had three whole hours of sleep. Now we were mad as hell at each other and at the man we had allowed to talk us into this in the first place. It is at times like this that keeping one's focus can become lost in a sea of anxiety which is precisely what all this training was about: maintaining combat focus.

My swim buddy through most of BUD/S was a courageous man named Rocky Cocklin. During our ocean swims, Rocky would sometimes fall asleep and we'd end up swimming in circles. Surface swimming becomes quite mechanical and more than once I saw men fall asleep while swimming. Rocky is an example of the guts it takes to survive hell week and the rest of training. The boots we were issued back then were not the best. I remember Rocky having blisters so bad that his feet became infected and after a few weeks he had deep holes in the outer quadrants of both heels. Not once did he complain or discuss quitting. He cut the heels off all his duty shoes and kept his feet as dry as possible at night to stay in the program. Today BUD/S offers a roll-back meant to keep injured men in training. This is a wise idea, and something that should have been done long ago. It was guys like Rocky, however, who motivated the rest of us.

One of the most eventful moments of hell week occurred on the mud flats, another period in my young SEAL life I will never forget. The mud flats were actually an old sewer field that is now the foundation for the overpriced luxury community known as Coronado Cays. The mud flats were significant because by this point in hell week we had lost our sense of humor. Animal instinct was getting me through every minute. There was no hint of civilization evident in my psyche any longer. I was surviving, period.

It was a bright, cold January day with the water temperature an even fifty-five degrees. Wind was at about twenty miles per hour. We all had our faces in the mud as BM1 Vince Olivera literally danced across the flats, leaping from head to head in order to keep his polished boots clean and dry. If you'd given Vince a reason—any reason—to become displeased with you as an individual he'd hesitate for a split second after landing on your head. "Eat mud, you banana!" and he'd be gone.

Lunchtime in the mud flats. I was covered in the filthy mud, and I barely recognized some of my classmates. My nose was filled with its cloying stench, as were my eyes, ears, and mouth. My tongue was coated with liquid grit; the taste was enough to drive me crazy. I could not get it off me, only move it from place to place. No canteens of fresh water were allowed, nor rags to clean ourselves up. We ate lunch in the mud.

Then came the real mental killer. The instructors ate lunch with their girlfriends! They were all sitting on the bank of the mud flats above us. One woman opened her blouse and flashed us. She had nothing else on. We were snorting through our meal like lions on a fresh kill, and she was mocking us, teasing us with something we all wanted but couldn't have. This was part of the plan to mentally kick us when we were really down, and really feeling sorry for ourselves. The hotter heads among us began mouthing off. Tempers flared, and then someone was roaring out of the mud flat with every intention of killing an instructor. The emotion was real, the instructors knew it, and they were prepared.

Dick Allen simply looked up as his attacker reached him and with one punch sent him back down into the mud. Not a word was said. Nothing needed to be. Survival instincts carried us all through, and I relied on mine 100 percent. Some men got through BUD/S out of pure determination, as in my case. Others by hatred, and some . . . well, I still haven't figured out how they made it, but they did. The process is extreme, and some consider it cruel, but not a man I know would make it any less than it is. Hell week is the separation process.

A Navy SEAL, in combat, does not have the option to quit. Most who do quit, do so during hell week. During my entire career as a SEAL I've never seen a teammate give up until the mission or task at hand was accomplished. Say what you will, the program works. And because it does I am alive today.

If you were to photograph every face that comes through that door before BUD/S training and then do the same before graduation you'd note a remarkable difference in each man's countenance. We learned to huddle together in freezing water for warmth, and we slept next to each other, an old parachute canopy our only protection from the elements. We were force-fed mud together, paddled a rubber boat together, ran into exhaustion together, and shored each other up to make it through just one more day of training. We went from meal to meal, always wet, like wild animals.

I kept thinking to myself, "Keep it simple, finish it . . . just get to the Teams!" I did anything I had to just to make it past hell week. No one ever forgets that our physical being is beyond exhaustion, and now we all rely totally upon the mind to take the next step.

At one point during the last night of hell week we were taken to the base swimming pool. By this time I was on edge, wary, looking for the trap I knew was ready to be sprung. This was the first time in my life that I had experienced extreme mental and physical exhaustion. There were no freebies during hell week. We paid for everything. Soon we were jumping in and then out of the pool. It was a tiring exercise, mindless, meant to push us to our physical limits. Suddenly we were ordered out of the pool and in came a man in a wheelchair with two useless legs.

Every instructor became very still. We all noticed the respect being given to the individual before us. One of the instructors moved forward to help the man into the pool. His arms and shoulders were huge! Around his skull were rows of scar tissue. His neck was thick and powerful. Chief Allen brought us to attention. "Gentlemen," he intoned, "allow me to introduce you to Lieutenant Pechacek." The chief told us how the sailor now holding himself steady in the pool was wounded the previous year aboard the Mighty Mo, an amphibious assault craft, known as a Mike 8. The lieutenant (j.g.) was the officer in charge of a SEAL platoon operating in the Rung Sat Special Zone when the Mighty Mo he was riding in was ambushed by the Vietcong. The VC fired B-40 rockets into the craft, ripping it from stem to stern with hot shrapnel. The lieutenant's brains were literally blown out of his skull onto the deck! His teammates scooped the tissue up, shoved it back into his bleeding head, and wrapped a compress around it before returning to the fight. Everyone thought he was dead, but he beat the odds and survived.

And now he was here, at the base pool, preparing to begin his physical therapy program for the day. The purpose of hell week suddenly became clear to all of us as we watched him. We later learned the instructors were as surprised as any of us at his appearance, but they made the best of the moment, as any good SEAL will do. The wounded officer knew who we were, and in great, graceful strokes he swam from his end of the pool to where we were standing at attention at our end of the pool. When he reached us he looked up and studied us very carefully. I could see his legs below the water's surface. They were suspended there like useless ropes—his feet like lead weights attached to his ankles. He was treading water very slowly, appearing to use only minimum energy to remain at the surface. I remember becoming very emotional at that point. It must have shown on my face as the lieutenant glided in front of where I was standing and for a long time just looked dead into my face. There was no sadness or self-pity written on his face, just fire, steel, and a mischievous gleam in his dark eyes. Then he raised one arm out of the water, his fist clenched, and erupted with a mighty "Hoo-ya!" I remember this moment as the pivotal point in hell week for me. I knew right then that no matter what, I would survive this course. I can still see the unconquerable fire that burned in Pechacek's eyes. Any doubts I'd had about finishing BUD/S evaporated under his stare. I would face other challenges as my career unfolded. But the challenges of this courageous SEAL officer with whom I exchanged so much without a word being spoken has stayed with me ever since.

Teamwork. It rarely exists outside of the military, and in my judgment it is one of the things our country needs to correct itself from the top on down. Hell week made us a team of thinking, functioning individuals who would never quit and never let each other down.

I survived hell week intact and much stronger than when I'd arrived at BUD/S. The cocksure Vietnam combat veteran had disappeared. There was no doubt I'd earn the SEAL trident. They couldn't throw anything my way I couldn't handle. My career as a warrior was set in stone, and combat would soon become a way of life for me that would not cease until I retired from the Teams I love so much.

3

Becoming a Frogman

First phase and hell week are now behind us. We moved into the second phase, which I was greatly looking forward to. Learning to scuba dive, military style, my true communion with water began. During the first phase of BUD/S training we'd undertaken ocean swims up to a mile or so. It's the "or so" that gets you. The ocean swims in phase two would be much longer, up to two miles. When I first arrived at training I didn't have a great deal of confidence in my swimming ability. I was good enough to pass the screening test, but I lacked finesse. I was also slower than a rock, and that bothered me.

At nine years old, I had been a troublemaker and would harass the girls, most of whom could swim. It was all the usual nine-year-old high jinks like stealing their towels, throwing them off the pier, and on and on. All this was going on as my family was vacationing at our cottage on Buzzards Bay, Cape Cod. We went there often, up until I joined the navy. Unable to swim at that time, I entertained myself by jumping off the pier at nearby Buttermilk Bay beach, sinking nine to twelve feet to the bottom, kicking off the floor, and springing to the surface where I could once again feel the sun on my face and catch a breath. I always stayed close enough to the pier to grab something in case of trouble. It was a great game, and eventually I would bounce my way back to shallow water and the safety of the shore. Along the way I'd continue to harass the girls. They got even with me one day by enlisting the aid of an assassin.

I'd gone out on the pier and was preparing to jump into about ten feet of water. Pretty deep stuff for a little kid who couldn't swim. The assassin caught me unprepared and pushed me off the pier, much to the delight of the girls on the beach. I can still hear their applause as I tumbled into the water. The luminescent green surface closed over me, becoming a darker green as I sank, then black as the depth overtook me entirely. I began to panic. No one was coming in after me. Apparently no one understood I was in serious trouble.

The world around me began to narrow as water forced its way down my throat. I was drowning! My arms were moving wildly, almost violently in an effort to regain the surface. I began entering a kind of tunnel, my movements slowing, my vision blurring, the bottom now reality. I remember not being sad at my coming death. I was actually calm! Then suddenly I was free of the bottom, breaking the surface, with cold, wonderful oxygen rushing into my starved lungs. A large boy who had hold of me was punching my abdomen like crazy, and water was spewing from my mouth in a torrent. We were still in deep water and I begged my savior to get me to land. When he'd finally succeeded in dragging me ashore, the girls were standing in a neat little rank, arms folded across their flat little chests, their smirks betraying their conspiracy.

I vowed to myself I'd learn how to swim. The lesson I learned that day was that I could die, by someone's else's hand or desire, and no one would notice or care. Strangely enough, this same thought would cross my mind years down the road when I was operating in Lebanon. It is a sobering bit of self-realization.

During the next two summers I learned how to swim in the freshwater lake near my parents' cottage. There was no one who could teach me. My mother could swim, but with four other children to care for at the time, taking time out for swim lessons was out of the question. My dad couldn't swim a stroke. So I simply dog-paddled until I began to relax in the water and experiment with different strokes. I watched others as they swam, and I copied their actions. One day it finally happened. I was afloat! At eleven years old I was swimming. I was scared, but I fought back the fear and carried on. Displaying fear was something my father did not tolerate very well. He expected strength of his sons. He would tell me, "Don't be afraid of anything . . . or I'll beat you harder!" And he did. In this less than satisfactory manner he instilled an inflexible iron discipline in me that I carry to this day, for better or for worse. On that day, though, I used it to swim to the tiny dock that bobbed about a hundred meters off shore. It was as if I'd conquered Mount Everest.

When I told my dad about what I'd accomplished, he was unimpressed.

I remember how I learned to multiply by three. I was having a dickens of a time with multiplication at school, much to my own displeasure. My father's reputation as a strict disciplinarian was known to the nuns, who were no slouches themselves when it came to ruling by the rod. My troubles came to my father's attention and I found myself sitting down at the dining room table where we began our "learning session."

"Take your shirt off," he told me. Then he asked, "Now, what is three times three?"

"Six?"

Whack! The ruler would crack itself across my back or the side of my head when the answer was wrong. After two weeks of this I learned the threes table, but my animosity toward my father and the nuns at school was more firmly embedded than ever before. It wasn't important that I learned as far as my father was concerned. He wanted absolute control over my thoughts, my feelings, and my spirit. There was little father-son dialogue between us. He was not adept at discussion with his children where life was the subject. I figured out early on I would have to be a self-taught human being. To survive at home, with a minimum of beatings, I adopted the policy of listening to the current edict and then figuring out how to work around it. Sometimes I was successful; sometimes I got beaten. This technique would follow me into the SEAL profession, and more often than not, I would come out on top.

It may sound strange, but when I finally entered the military I was surprised my commanding officers didn't beat me when I screwed up. I discovered I loved the military life, and in fact I'd found a new home. The discipline was less painful than what I'd been used to. It took many years for me to purge myself of those feelings created when I was just a toddler, though. Nearly drowning and then forcing myself to learn to swim was the beginning of the drive that lives in the breast of every Navy SEAL today. The conquest of fear . . . and doing what must be done.

The first thing we learned in the diving phase of BUD/S was drownproofing, naturally. Every Navy SEAL must pass this test, no exceptions. You float on your belly, face down in the water, for an hour, wearing your working uniform and boots. Need air? Raise your face slowly and inhale. At the same time do a long, slow modified breast stroke, then place your face back in the water. You sink just a bit, but the air in your lungs refloats you. With control you can float like this for quite some time.

In 1967 a SEAL had drowned in the Rung Sat Special Zone of Vietnam. His platoon had been preparing to conduct a body snatch (military chatter for kidnapping), and they were rehearsing for the operation aboard a river patrol boat. The operator was sitting on the side of the boat with his hands tied behind his back, playing the role of the captured VC. A wave created by a smaller passing craft struck the patrol boat, and the SEAL went into the water. No one noticed, as the others were busy with preparations and were distracted. He went to the bottom and drowned because he hadn't learned the simple technique of drownproofing.

That was our wake-up call. So we learned how to drownproof ourselves, thanks to the training team. Naturally, the SEALs improved upon the original technique, adapting it specifically to our needs. After I'd mastered the initial phase, I found myself face down in the water with my hands tied behind my back. Everyone gets the creeps doing this at first. But the name of the game is mastering your fears. I was dumped in the deep end of the pool, and heard the catcalls as I sank toward the bottom. When your hands are tied behind your back, you rely on your legs for forward motion to assist in raising your head to catch a breath. When your legs are tied, you propel yourself by employing a dolphin-style stroke. It is all done very slowly and methodically to conserve energy. Life was repeating itself, but this time I was much better prepared. I beat the fear and pushed the Cape Cod experience out of my mind. Even when they tied my feet and threw me back in, I overcame the fear and stayed calm in the water for over an hour. I'd made it.

Another trainee, who was six feet four and exceptionally strong, went another way. During the hands-feet portion of training he panicked, actually breaking the ropes that bound him. Instructor Messenger was at the edge of the pool, leaning over and harassing this man when suddenly two great huge hands exploded from beneath the surface, reaching like brittle talons for Messenger's exposed throat. I caught sight of this as I was surfacing at the deep end of the pool, the look of sheer terror on the instructor's face leaving me with a good feeling. We were afraid, and now our tormenter was getting a bit of payback. Down beneath the surface I went, a bit of a smile plastered across my face, I'm sure.

This simple technique can ensure a SEAL's survival. During the war in Vietnam we had two men in the water a considerable distance from shore. They were to link up with a submarine that would locate them via periscope. The two SEALs would access the periscope, snare it with the rubber boat bowline, and enjoy a brief ride farther out to sea where the sub could safely surface and bring them aboard.

But if a military operation can go wrong, it will. The sub located the rubber boat and they tied up with each other. Not taken into account was the submarine's speed and what it would do to the rubber boat being towed. The rubber boat was ripped to shreds within minutes, and the two swimmers were left far behind, forced to employ their drownproofing training for nearly eight hours! After a great while someone aboard the sub had the good sense to check the periscope for an update. No SEALs were in view, and panic hit the conning tower. Executing a very tight Williamson turn, or an immediate about-face, they began searching for the men.

It wasn't until the sun was coming up that they spotted our SEALs off in the distance, waving like crazy. As the sub pulled alongside, one SEAL mooned the periscope up close and proper just to show there weren't any hard feelings. The other, taking his cue from his moon-man teammate, stuck his face right up against the scope, made monster faces, and bared his fangs. It was all done in good fun, to break the tension when things were looking grim. Their lives were saved because they had both the will to live and the training to accomplish the mission. A SEAL will always get the mission done or die trying.

Drownproofing out of the way, we moved on to the more fun business of SCUBA. Early PT, runs up to four miles, running the obstacle course in faster and faster times, and demanding ocean swims made up our days in second phase. The obstacle course consisted of twenty-one obstacles designed to test one's endurance, agility, balance, and self-confidence. Like many difficult things in life, the O-course takes time to master. The "dirty name" obstacle became my nemesis. Every time our class went to the O-course Commander Wilson would be there. It was only near the very end of training that I was able to make it across from one telephone pole to the next without having to retry it. The object of this particular obstacle was to jump across from a standing start from one horizontal pole, land on your stomach on the second pole, which was three feet higher, pull yourself up to the next level, and jump to the ground from a height of ten feet. Commander Wilson made it look easy, and I took the heat every time I fell off. I found myself truly enjoying the runs as they allowed me to collect my thoughts and to further resolve never to give in, regardless of what was coming next.

SCUBA training progressed nicely but it was hydrographic reconnaissance that I truly enjoyed. Again, this specialty came about in the aftermath of Tarawa, where so many fine Americans perished due to a lack of environmental intelligence. The process is remarkably simple and accurate. Each SEAL makes up what we call a lead line, which measures at least thirty-three feet. Knots are tied at one-foot intervals for the first ten feet. After this, the line has a knot every two feet. Prior to an amphibious landing the task force commander is concerned about the three-and-a-half fathom curve to the high-water line.

A fathom measures six feet. So, from the twenty-one-foot depth to the high-water line is critical where navy landing craft are concerned, with the exception of the air-cushion vehicles. The twenty-one-foot depth limitation satisfies the need for the larger landing ships to have enough room to keep the stern in the water and keep the propellers from fouling. Propellers in the navy are referred to as screws. The object of a hydrographic survey is to extend a swimmer line perpendicularly from the beach. Range flags are used to line up the swimmer line so it is as straight as possible. Then each SEAL takes a sounding with a lead line. The depths are then recorded with a number two pencil on a plastic slate hung around the neck of each SEAL. All swimmers are twenty-five yards apart and are expected to maintain that distance so that an accurate reading can be taken. Of course, in a combat recon, everything is done at night, in silence, and with red-lens flashlights. All the while the cartographer is drawing as accurate a sketch as possible of the backshore. Once the swimming portion of the reconnaissance is completed, the cartographer records the readings taken by each swimmer. His work is now just beginning. Virtually every beach reconnaissance chart going all the way back to World War II is stored at the Defense Intelligence Agency. Our rule of thumb is that a chart should be good for about ten years. No beach anywhere in the world stays the same. Some just evolve faster than others. It's nice to have the record, however, as old intel is better than no intel.

The intelligence provided by these reconnaissance missions is vital, as the marines need it to off-load landing craft as quickly as possible and take the high ground. The information provided by SEAL survey parties designates likely avenues of approach for the marines' vehicles, whether wheeled or tracked. Any defenses or obstacles are also noted and recorded, to include roving security patrols.

The beauty of beach reconnaissance is that we can conduct these operations in any country we choose, whether enemy or friendly. Why? Because no one ever knows we've been ashore. Beach recon is carried out during those intervals between conflicts, since we can never say where we might go ashore. Despite all the advances in satellite technology, there is still nothing more accurate than a Navy SEAL in the water with his lead line.

It was during this phase of BUD/S that I learned the difference between clandestine and covert operations. In a clandestine operation you want to hide the fact that the action committed ever took place. In and out, with no one the wiser. Covert ops, on the other hand, conceal the true sponsor of the action. Why covert operations? It allows the president the option of "plausible deniability" once the action is carried through to its conclusion (or is blown). Like it or not, this is the real world of governments and global agendas, and we are a major league player in every respect.

Since BUD/S, I have come to believe in the merits of such operations, and I trust that the national leadership will continue to rely on the special warfare community to execute them. Sadly, far too many at the top level of our government lack the guts to do so despite the very real hostility that is aimed against our country by many around the world. Much of SEAL training is geared to operate in either the clandestine or covert mode. In BUD/S, we learned to expect to be wheels up and on our way within four hours of being alerted for a mission. Yes, we do make house calls!

The SDV (swimmer delivery vehicle) program really captured my imagination in BUD/S. SDVs are small submersible vehicles that can carry a pilot, a copilot, and four SEAL passengers. The first of these vehicles carried only one passenger who rode astride the vehicle while the operator rode on top of it. I've watched these vehicles develop over the course of my career into the best clandestine weapons platforms we have. Training for the SDV program is long and arduous. For example, hard-hat diving is done by professionals who work primarily underneath ships. Explosive Ordnance Disposal folks also fall into this category of diver. Only the Navy SEAL community is chartered to conduct combat swimmer operations that use the water primarily for concealment. The SDV has increased our ability to travel great distances underwater carrying heavier, more deadly loads. Particulars of SDV performance are classified at the SECRET-NOFORN level. The term "NOFORN" means no foreign dissemination. As much as I would enjoy discussing this fascinating aspect of naval special warfare, it is simply outside my purview to do so.

The SDV is designed to operate from a mother ship, normally a nuclear submarine, referred to as an SSN. Fitted to the back of the SSN is a dry deck shelter that weighs about fifty tons. Inside the shelter is one SDV. Today we rely on both the MK-8 and MK-9 SDV for such operations. The MK-8 is a seagoing bus that can carry up to four SEALs from the ship clear to the shoreline. Once near their objective—a harbor, for example—the swimmers exit the vehicle and conduct their mission on either water or land.

The MK-9 SDV carries two torpedoes that will sink any known ship afloat today. The trick is to get close enough to hit the target. The MK-9 relies on stealth, approaching its target on the water's surface. This is a naturally buoyant craft and very difficult to see, even in daylight. On sonar it's a bear to pick up, much less track. A good MK-9 SDV crew can get well within striking distance of a ship before letting its fish fly. Sadly, in my opinion, the MK-9 will soon be out of the SEAL inventory. Replacing it will be the Advanced SEAL Delivery System, which is much larger than anything we've seen before—over thirty meters in length! It will allow the crew to remain perfectly dry during operation. This is a tremendous advancement in SDV technology as the wet aspect of the MK-8 and MK-9 vehicles does have a restraining effect on crew endurance and safety.

My first dive in the ocean using SCUBA is one I'll never forget. We were within sight of migrating gray whales just off the coast of San Diego. Chief Shultz, one of our instructors, was yelling and screaming at everyone to get suited up *now*. We were on the fringe of the kelp forest west of Point Loma where all the action is. Sea creatures abound in such a place. No zoo I've seen can rival the beauty and wildness of a kelp forest. Now, the trick is to swim down about ten feet and get underneath the vegetation lying on the surface. As I descended the water became darker. It was as though I had some feel for how a bird must fly through the trees. Only this was water and there were more forces at work here. I'd remembered all the academics. I told myself, "Breathe evenly, don't hold your breath, relax." The descent was gradual, and at forty feet I was on the bottom. It was then that I discovered that kelp anchors itself to rocks and the amount of bottom life is incredible. Being in the company of whales made my first ocean dive that much more memorable, even with Chief Schultz yelling and screaming.

SEALs train with both closed and open SCUBA. Open circuit systems mean you breath air from bottles, or tanks, then expend the used air into the water. This is the kind of diving most civilians are used to. In closed-circuit systems, the air you breathe is scrubbed with a CO_2 absorbent with pure oxygen being fed into the system. The problem is, you can't dive below twenty-five feet without suffering what is known as O_2 toxicity, or oxygen poisoning. But the rig allows over two hundred minutes of air, and it leaves no bubble trail on the surface. Great for long-range infiltration and exfiltration work.

Finally we worked on compass swims. This requires that the swimmer take a bearing on the objective and then dive beneath the surface and begin swimming toward it. If the water is a little rough you have to kick to gain some height so as to get a good fix on the target. If you're smart you have a swimmer slate available with your swimming track, or course, laid out. Now it's only a question of distance and time. You can cover roughly one hundred meters underwater every three minutes. SEALs navigate at fifteen feet below the surface, and despite this shallow depth the water is dark, especially at night. Your face is glued to your attack board, which houses the compass, a watch, and a depth gauge. A swim buddy is the timekeeper while your job is to navigate. You always feel you're swimming in circles, which means you must have faith in yourself, your buddy, and your equipment.

I made it through the diving phase of training without much trouble, although I was kidded a great deal by my teammates for being a far better runner than swimmer. Over the years I sought to increase my ability in the water and to keep my skills fresh.

Anyway, from the second phase of our training to become Navy SEALs we graduated to the meat and potatoes of the SEAL ethos: land warfare, where the rubber meets the road.

4

San Clemente Island

San Clemente Island is located roughly seventy-five miles off the coast of California. Its waters teem with marine life that local abalone fishermen plunder without remorse. The island is primarily a naval gunnery range whose primitive state offers wild goats and still wilder hogs. It's also where maturing tadpoles such as SEAL trainees put much of what they learn to the test. In fact, Russian submarines used to lurk around its shores hoping to spy on our navy's comings and goings. In addition, they could monitor our unguarded communications in relative safety. San Nicholas Island is even farther out to sea and fairly bristles with electronic toys that our former cold war enemies were curious about. SEALs play on San Nicholas every once in a while, but it's San Clemente that receives the most attention.

In the old days we lived in used trailers on the island. Today they have been replaced with some very nice structures that make the tiny camp look more like a recreation getaway. The work we did was challenging as well as interesting, with the additional water work further binding us together as a team. The sea, I learned, will take your life if you are not careful. It doesn't care how it hurts you, and if you're careless or stupid, it will bite. I began to think that the sea was like a senior chief. The wise officer will listen to such a person and heed his warnings and take advantage of his experience. The fool will ignore the chief, with the result being the needless death of those under his command. It is this way with the ocean, and it is this way with men who pursue the warrior's path.

San Clemente is also where the long-awaited ocean swim to end all ocean swims is conducted. SEALs must pass this test to graduate. It begins shortly after breakfast from Wilson Cove and only finishes at Northwest Harbor, and the only real requirements are that you don't lose your swim buddy and that both of you arrive at the camp before dark. The current runs against you all the way. The current out there can run from one mile per hour to more than three miles per hour, depending on where you are offshore. It's a five-mile haul, and a real gut-buster.

My swim buddy was Rocky Cocklin, the same Rocky whose feet had blistered so badly during first phase training. He never quit, and I've always admired him for this. Rocky had a knack for falling asleep during a swim. I'm quite serious! During hell week more than once someone would fall asleep while paddling in a rubber boat and paddle himself right into the water. Roger could sack out at any time, and I'd have to nudge him awake as he drifted into me. He nudged me awake more than once on a long swim. To the uninitiated this may seem strange, but to a SEAL in training, it's just another day at the office. We used the sidestroke on long swims. For tactical approaches it is very quiet and hard to detect from shore or a boat. In rough seas, a swimmer so moving can pass right by you using the sidestroke and never give himself away. I know, I've done it. It's also the preferred stroke for swimming, as it is the best method of conserving energy over the long haul, and we've gotta be able to fight if we have to when we get there.

From Wilson Cove, Rocky and I swam straight out to sea for about a mile, hanging a left at a specific buoy and heading for Northwest Harbor. Our confidence level was sky high by this point in training, so we simply slipped into a steady rhythm and enjoyed the view. Falling back on the Lie, Cheat, Steal, Kill formula, we took a vote and elected to try to cut a mile off the overall distance by hiding in a kelp bed till the chase boat filled with instructors went by. We would then make a diagonal dash across the kelp bed, and save some time and energy in the long run. Seemed like a good plan at the time.

The chase boat spotted our little game from the get-go but allowed us to play the string out. Just as Rocky and I were chuckling about how smart we were, the kelp bed nearly behind us, an instructor slipped a gaff hook up through the back of my UDT life jacket. We never heard the boat

46

slinking up behind us, but now we were their prisoners and totally at their mercy. "Get in the boat, you bananas" was all I heard. The boat took both of us back to the buoy and we swam the entire distance again. We swam all day against the current.

One of the most enjoyable aspects of swims at San Clemente was the dolphins that cut and glided like sea-borne ballerinas along with us. They swam around us, took a good look, then dived beneath the surface leaving a slim trail of air bubbles in their wake. I often wondered if they thought we were bananas, too. This was not just being in the great outdoors; this was truly communing with the natural environment.

Just as the sun began to set, Rocky and I crawled up on to the beach. My right armpit was rubbed raw from the swim. We'd later learn to use Vaseline to solve this problem and cornstarch at night to ease pain and promote healing. Salt water speeds up the healing process, but infection is a real worry. The point is to ignore the pain and focus on the job. I adhered to this policy throughout my career in the Teams, even when on crutches a few times.

With the swim out of the way we began our demolition training. We laid detonation cord along the beach at Northwest Harbor and watched it explode at four miles per second! Very impressive. To this day when I smell burned cordite I am reminded of those days on the beach on San Clemente. I would later come to associate the smell of cordite with close combat in Vietnam. That odor became stimulating for me, very powerful, and very motivating.

I enjoyed San Clemente immensely. Even daily PT took on a new face while we were isolated from the urban sprawl of Coronado and Imperial Beach. Running, working out, and learning my craft surrounded by nature was invigorating to the body and soul. There was just the sea, the rocky terrain, the sparse vegetation, and the constant wind in your face or at your back. With morning PT out of the way our attention turned to learning war fighting. We fired our small arms, studied patrolling and small unit tactics, ran land navigation courses, paddled our rubber boats, and blew up more beach with a variety of demolitions. All of this was conducted in full mission profile mode, meaning it was as real as we could make it. It is potentially dangerous training, and we've lost men because of human error or Murphy's Law. You don't play with explosives.

Two trainees in the class before mine were killed during an underwater demolition exercise. In that exercise the obstacles to be demolished were placed on the ocean floor, and a hydrographic reconnaissance was conducted to find and plot the obstacles. Then a UDT hydrographic chart was drawn. The next phase was to plan the demolition of the obstacle field using live explosives. After one swim pair had placed their charge on an obstacle, the two swimmers were preparing to tie their explosive haversack into the main trunk line. One man was on the surface keeping watch over his swim buddy. When the man on the bottom had tied in his obstacle he began his ascent to the surface, but the knife on his belt caught on the main trunk line. He panicked and he ran out of air. In this particular situation we don't rely on SCUBA; we hold our breath while placing the explosive charge then ascend to the surface for air. When the trapped man's swim buddy realized something was wrong he free-dived down and was about to free his swim buddy's knife handle from the trunk line when the trapped man grabbed his rescuer and held on with super-human strength. Both men drowned.

Our hardest lessons are written in the blood of our own.

On the lighter side, it was at San Clemente that I learned about Garcia's Outpost. Remember the story of the man assigned to take a message to Garcia during the Spanish-American War? Well, in BUD/S training, tadpoles get to deliver messages to "Garcia," whose outpost is situated about a mile from the base camp. To get there, you are encouraged to "fly," and wooden pallets are provided for passengers. To fly you merely have to pick up a pallet and balance it across your shoulders. Then you double-time, or fly, up to Garcia's Outpost and check in with the instructor. If he doesn't like your looks you are put in a holding pattern around the outpost, and to keep everyone happy you're encouraged to sing as you zoom around and around awaiting permission to land. One does not run out of fuel, and in fact, you'd better have a no-sweat look on your face or it's going to be a long day. Permission is finally given for the return "flight" back to camp where you must once again check in and request permission to land. By this time the crimp in your neck is sheer murder, but you let out with a thunderous "Hoo-ya!" and fall back into training as if nothing ever happened.

My first rifle in BUD/S training was the venerable M-1 Garand. We didn't see the M-16A1 rifle until we got to the Teams. I swam with the Garand, slept with it, ate with it nearby, and kept it wonderfully clean at all times. Not once did I ever put a round through the M-1 during training, but we did fire the .45 caliber M-3 grease gun and the Swedish K 9mm sub-gun while we were working with the variety of small arms found in special operations armories. The basics of small unit tactics were covered in depth. Using the most simple equipment we conducted all types of amphibious raids, reconnaissance patrols, ambushes, and hydrographic surveys. We learned to plan combat missions, with the officers doing the majority of planning and briefings while the enlisted folks did the mission equipment preparations. All were involved in the process, and carried their load equally. This was an intense time in training, but there was now more dialogue between instructor and student. It was also at this point in training that we began to look toward life in the Teams. Though the patrol orders were basic, they were thorough. Time was everything, and by design, there was never enough time. The first time we went out on a reconnaissance we blundered into a cactus patch and someone began screaming as he made direct contact. Mother Nature had drawn first blood, and we had flunked the stealth portion of the exercise. When debriefed we learned just how much detail we'd missed relative to the San Clemente airfield. The debriefs were great learning tools for us, as the experience of each individual instructor really came through. I was no longer respecting them simply as instructors. I was realizing that I could very well find myself in the field with one of these men in Vietnam, and soon. I paid close attention.

Forgetting to bring an item that was briefed prior to a mission can be costly in combat. To imprint this upon us we often paid dearly when screwing up in training. One time I failed to bring some line and a rubber boat patch kit. We pulled the training mission off without it, and nothing was said afterward. I thought I'd successfully skated out of that one until two days later, when Roger Sick, an instructor, approached me and told me to remove my wet suit. "No midgets in wet suits today," he offered. I looked over at Frank Sparks, the other "midget" in our class and shrugged with that all-knowing look which translates as "Misery loves company." Sick caught the exchange and added, "Frank, you can keep yours on," and then he walked away.

This particular training exercise was a hydrographic reconnaissance. The weather was sunny, wind balmy and the water in the usual fifties. Our officers were now extremely well versed in playing the SEAL instructor-student psyche-out game. So it was decided to leave me on the beach to hold the bitter end of the flutterboard. A spool of nylon line is played out from the flutterboard man to each swimmer to keep the swimmer lines straight in the water. Along came Sick who immediately grasped their plan of attack and ordered me into the water. And in I went, of course. By the time the swim was over, I was going into hypothermia. The wind was brisk, which only made things worse for me, but the sand had been warmed by the afternoon sun. My teammates lowered me to the earth and buried me in warm sand. It was all they could do, but they did it. Frank Sparks and a man named Cleary took over the Sand Wrapping of Mikey operation. Not a whole lot was said, save the constant, quiet encouragement of Frank. Frank was a tremendous athlete, an attribute that has served him well: Today he is a successful stuntman in the film industry. Instructor Sick was standing over me now, telling me I could quit any time. The look in my eyes told him I'd quit when I died in his presence. He walked away after a while, muttering about what a tough little s.o.b. I was.

After about thirty minutes beneath my quilt of sand, I felt warmth starting to filter through my body. I was alive. There was no sympathy shown me by the cadre, and if you're expecting kindness during SEAL training, you're in the wrong business, and on the wrong planet. Although my teammates had taken care of me they weren't gonna hang around and wait on my freezing tail. I had to recover quickly and get back into the program. Once they know you're alive and kicking, you're on your own.

I lay there until my pulse became regular again, and my body temperature rose back to normal. After everyone had left and gone back to camp I dug myself out and headed for home, looking forward to getting dry and even warmer. This is the name of the game. It may sound cruel to some, but I wouldn't have it any other way. In the Teams we don't need quitters, nor do we need deadweight. Most of all, there's no room for self-pity, which is the worst trap a man can fall into. So I shambled back to the trailers gloating over how I'd just triumphed over Roger Sick. Bottom line: You want to wear the name? Then play the game. Special warfare is not a job, it's a commitment. You have to live it every day, body, mind, and spirit.

5

A Real Deal SEAL at Last

After graduating from eighteen weeks of BUD/S training I took a thirty-day leave before entering SEAL indoctrination training. (The BUD/S course runs twenty-six weeks these days and is much more comprehensive.) Before heading out the gate I'd made sure my assignment request for SEAL Team ONE was properly submitted as I wanted to stay on the West Coast at Coronado. It was interesting to me that all the odd-numbered teams were West Coast based, whereas the even-numbered teams were situated at Little Creek, Virginia. Back then both coasts ran their own training in many areas, which contributed to the friendly rivalry you find today. When training was finally consolidated in the mid-1970s, all SEALs finally began coming out of the same mold.

With no place to go, and still a bit shy of the opposite sex, I elected to hang out with UDT ELEVEN. They were preparing for their operational readiness inspection, so we went right back out to San Clemente island for three weeks of tune-up work. One platoon rode out on a diesel submarine that, after surfacing, suffered a serious accident when a rogue wave washed both the men and the equipment overboard. The men came to the surface, spitting, sputtering, and swearing as only sailors can, but the equipment went straight to the bottom. It took them two days to locate and recover the gear, which only made the pressure greater where the inspection was concerned. The rest of the exercise went without incident except for a stuck bow gate on the LST, which was quickly repaired.

"Leave" was essentially a great on-the-job training program for me, and when it was over, I reported to SEAL Team ONE on a bright Monday morning. There was a big difference between the UDT and SEAL teams of this era, a difference as clear as night and day. I was told before reporting that I'd better not have a smile on my face when I showed up or I'd be seeing pavement. SEALs were serious players, first and foremost. The proctor for our class as we prepared to learn about becoming SEAL operators was a former army man by the name of Guy Stone. He was tough, weathered, and obviously responsible for making us ready for Vietnam.

While I was standing in formation I heard Stone ask for a teammate named Farmer. The man raised his hand, and Guy asked him if he'd been in a fight in the club the night before? "Yes," responded Farmer.

"You'd better not let anyone squeal on you if it happens again," offered Stone. "Even if it means you gotta kill 'em, you understand?" I was both surprised and shocked, but this was the ideal that we would come to embrace over the next six weeks of training. Now, if something like that was said today the repercussions would be immediate. Different times, different philosophy.

The interesting thing about SEAL basic indoctrination instruction, or SBI, was that it first made us feel as if we were losing our navy identity. In a sense we were, as our entire military world now consisted of small arms, land warfare, map and compass work, other weapons systems generic to SEAL operations, and learning about the Vietcong and their infrastructure. My uniform for the day consisted of green fatigues when inside the compound, and camouflage fatigues when on exercises. The goal of SBI was to teach us just enough to keep us alive so we could develop street smarts on our own. We'd then get assigned to a platoon and shipped off to Vietnam as quickly as possible.

General Westmoreland, the commander of all U.S. forces in Vietnam at the time, had put in an urgent request for more SEALs. He wanted five hundred of us in-country so as to stalemate expected VC and North Vietnamese Army (NVA) offensives during their early planning stages. We could do this because we worked in the enemy's backyard, the only place he could plan and train away from the bulk of the fighting going on throughout the south of Vietnam. The five hundred mark was never reached, with just under three hundred operators taking the war to Uncle Ho's forces at the height of the conflict. At no one time were there ever more than fourteen platoons operational in Vietnam. But Westmoreland's emphasis on our importance had a profound effect on the entire community.

This pressure to produce more SEALs as quickly as possible led to the number of BUD/S classes being increased from four to eight a year. Then the unthinkable happened. The bureaucrats, who continue to plague special warfare to this very day, ordered hell week to be dropped! This order was in effect for about one year, and then this critical period of training was reinstated. The psychological effect of this ill-founded edict was profound within our ranks. It was on everyone's lips and everyone's mind. It allowed some men to become frogmen and SEALs who never should have made the grade. In my mind it was a contributing factor for some of our dead and wounded in Vietnam. Hell week taught us to act, not ponder, and to never quit. Combat is unmerciful, yet taking out hell week showed mercy. Once again the admin weenies killed us with their misplaced kindness. I can only hope history will not repeat itself. That effort to achieve General Westmoreland's goal was misdirected. In fairness to the bureaucrats, they failed to realize that each Navy SEAL produced must be a Cadillac, not a Chevy. This takes time. You can mass-produce soldiers and sailors, but not special warfare people.

During the first week in SEAL Basic Indoctrination I worked with small arms and was introduced to all the areas an infantryman becomes expert in. We emphasized traveling light and moving fast, as the environment of Vietnam was unforgiving in every respect. Our instructors were strict, without humor, but very, very good at their jobs. Wounded and injured SEALs returning from the war were brought out to address our class and to give the instructors the latest poop regarding enemy tactics and weapons. This was all passed on to us, and I can't recall anyone ever falling asleep in class.

It was during SBI that my teammates and I began deciding what we wanted to do as part of a combat team. Some wanted to act as rear security, carrying the important and devastating M-60 light machine gun. Others were content to be riflemen, and a few chose to pursue the important but very dangerous job of radioman, or RTO (radio telephone operator). I elected to become a point man, a position considered exclusive only because so few wanted the responsibility involved. The point man's job was to guide his team to the objective safely. He looked for booby traps, spotted the bad guys first, and generally could expect to make hostile contact first. For this reason, he often got hurt or killed. I wanted the challenge, and perhaps I needed to prove something to myself.

Two weeks at Coronado passed quickly. From our seaside "resort" we were taken inland to the SEAL training camp at Niland, California, the small town beside the Salton Sea that's near a bombing range which later became yet another important SEAL training site. At Niland we lived on the edge of a corn field in old trailers, just like on San Clemente. The heat was intense. I mean it flattened you! It was here we took on our corpsmen—operators like Fat Mac and Bo, Stoney and Doc Jones. At the time these guys often weren't fully SEAL qualified because they weren't required to be. They came in from the fleet or the Fleet Marine Force, and found themselves working with us. Two notable exceptions to this were Doc Jones and Hetherington. Both men had graduated from BUD/S before the navy Bureau of Medicine went ballistic and forbade the practice of sending its corpsmen through a "killer" school. Today, all of our corpsmen must be SEAL qualified and are subject to further intensive training on the medical side of the house if they are to play in the special warfare sandbox.

Some SEALs gave the corpsmen a bad time because they hadn't been through our qualification course, but I didn't give it much thought. We had other guys like Doc Johnson and Bob Sell who distinguished themselves in every environment we worked in. These two, in particular, were as good as any fully qualified SEAL I've ever served with. Terry Bryant was another cool operator under any conditions. One time we were pinned down under heavy fire and Terry never lost it . . . not for one second. I recall watching him lying there close to me, smiling like he was going to eat someone for breakfast. Doc Bryant was lethal, and deadly accurate with any small arm. Bob Sell is another combat medic whose performance was outstanding. He was an expert at gathering and working with battlefield intelligence. Legendary SEAL Gary Gallagher and Bob Sell were the most effective—and scary—intelligence team ever produced by naval special warfare. Those commanders who came to SEAL Team ONE during the Vietnam War always had to reckon with Gary and Bob, if they wanted to be successful.

At Niland I paid attention to every instructor's class. They were specialists, experts at their trade. After class, during breaks, and during the infrequent downtime allowed us, I picked their brains. Bohannon was an artist with the Stoner weapons system, and Doc Jones was a top flight medicine man. I learned from all of them because I wanted not only to survive but to excel at SEAL warfare.

Weapons training was our number one priority during the Vietnam era. We were training in the heat of the desert at our Chocolate Mountain camp. All tactical training maneuvers were accomplished using live rounds; no blanks and no blank firing adapters were fitted to our weapons. I learned while moving quickly through the desert scrub to always know where my teammates were and which way they were firing. When we screwed up, the instructors were all over us. We worked day and night, until we were mentally wrung out and physically depleted. This was where I learned the value of a simple thing like wearing a T-shirt. It worked. I was able to maintain my body temperature without having to take a salt tablet. Never believed in that theory anyway. Keep it simple, I kept telling myself. But don't quit or lose the animal edge being grafted to us. Remember hell week?

Our instructors continued to make each day rewarding with new knowledge. The only hardnose was Guy Stone, known as Stoney. When he got upset he liked to make threats. I remember when this tactic backfired on him, though. Our class had been having trouble with night ambushes, and so we found ourselves out in the desert scrub again, forming up in the classic V shape for an ambush. Guy Stone walked out into the middle of the killing zone and began chewing us out, telling us how stupid we were and how we'd better get our act together where ambushes were concerned. Then Stone started in with his "When I was in Korea" stories and we'd had enough. Lieutenant Gray took his weapon off safety. The loud click it made was clearly audible and one by one the rest of us did the same. Fat Mac then suggested terminating the exercise, and Guy got the message. The lecture stopped. We returned to training without having to listen to any more of his tall tales about how tough it was in Korea.

The Navy SEAL warfare business was only seven years old at this time. Every day the awareness in us grew that we would soon be in Vietnam and that what we learned there would be put right into training when we returned to the States. I can still hear Fat Mac saying, "We're still writing our own book, people, so pay attention." Our drills, although foreign to the conventional Navy way of thinking, were taken from standard U.S. Army infantry doctrine. Everything I learned during SBI went with me and was put into practice in Vietnam. Later on, when I was working with Chinese mercenaries during a tour with the Phoenix program, these simple techniques and tactics proved invaluable. Only the simple succeeds in combat. That fact will never change or go out of date.

As SBI drew to a close, we began getting our platoon assignments. I went to Charlie platoon as their point man. The platoon was already in the mountains east of San Diego, which we called Cuyamaca. When I arrived I was greeted by the man who would become my "sea daddy," where SEAL operations and my success in them were at stake. Chief Warrant Officer Wayne Boles was the assistant platoon commander, and I owe him more than can ever be repaid. We were assigned to act as aggressors for a class preparing to join the Phoenix program as advisers to the Provincial Reconnaissance Unit (PRU). To better play our roles we learned more about the Vietcong and their infrastructure, as we would play the enemy for our teammates heading for this important, highly classified program in Vietnam. Needless to say, as a young SEAL I was excited!

My excitement was tempered by the knowledge that I was the FNG, which is old navy vernacular for a new man in the platoon. Everyone was watching me closely. They had to have confidence in me as their point man, as sooner or later we'd be heading overseas ourselves. Along with our support of the PRU advisers, we'd conduct our own training as well. It was during one of these times I encountered the liberal attitude regarding SEAL training methods. In short, anything goes, as long as it makes sense and works.

Preparing for an urban ambush exercise we noted a Camp

57

Fire Girls' summer camp across from our mountainside position. Wayne, the warrant officer, asked me if I thought I could guide us down to the camp so we could ambush the Camp Fire Girls who were enjoying their summer away from home. "No sweat, sir," came my eager reply. As a departure from the norm, we were using blanks, although the box-shaped red blank-firing adapter that fitted over the end of our rifles had been modified. It looked stupid and got hung up on everything on the trail, so we'd fashioned adapters to fit over the muzzle that were much less noticeable. They worked like a champ but still allowed the weapon to look like a weapon and not like some kid's toy.

I led the squad down the mountain and we took up a position we believed the girls would use. Sure enough, a group made their presence known with loud, cheery voices and lots of trail noise as they wound their way toward us. When they were well within our "kill zone," the warrant officer simply spit his chewing tobacco out and ordered us to let 'em have it. Talk about pandemonium. Screaming girls and crying camp counselors were racing all around us as we fired blanks on full automatic. The terror for our enemy was real, and the lesson we learned from watching their panic play out was equally as plain. This was my first exposure to that type of urban terror, and I've never forgotten it. I had mixed feelings about it, but I kept them to myself because, at the time, they weren't really important and I was the new guy on the block. I think the conflict inside stemmed from the fact that the girls were innocent. One side of me knew we were training for war, while the other tugged at my conscience as if we were participating in the mass murder of total innocents. The value of this experience, however, was retained in my consciousness. The terror experienced by the girls was real. On the other side of that coin, my respect for the warrant officer began to grow. He wanted us to experience everything we could before we deployed. I found myself doing everything I could to please him. Today, if something like this were to take place, the resulting media exposure and public outcry would make Tail Hook look like kid's play.

The days after the ambush were tough but fun. We were pursued through the mountains by the PRU advisers-in-training and hunted like animals. Everything was as real as possible because Phoenix training was dead-bang serious. I slipped easily into my role as point man. It was clear I was contributing to the platoon effort, and everyone was encouraging me as we ran, slithered, and slid through the mountains. Suddenly, one day, we were given a class about critical intelligence gathering and we were cautioned to take this one more seriously than perhaps others. They briefed us on how to act and react should we be captured. Afterward, the platoon returned to the base camp and began preparing for the upcoming training exercise.

Along the way we spotted Leaping Larry La Page, an adviser-in-training, emerging from a nearby tree line. The warrant officer waved to him and quietly ordered the truck carrying us to stop. When La Page wandered over to say hi we captured him, tied his hands, and then drove to a nearby commercial business with a private latrine. Using what had just been taught us we looped a line around Larry's throat and turned him upside down, his head inside the toilet bowl. The crown of his skull was actually touching the bottom of the bowl, the water line just a hair above his nostrils. If he even flared his nose, the water poured in and our "prisoner" would get all excited about drowning. We braced his legs against the wall, so his weight was centered fully on his head.

If Larry failed to answer our questions we'd flush the toilet. After a while he became delirious. At this point we took our canteens and began pouring their contents on his belly and chest, the sound of pants zippers being pulled up and down adding to the ruse. La Page believed we were urinating on him, and between the water torture and this apparent humiliation, he got even weirder as the interrogation went on. After three hours he was as close to becoming a veggie as a man can get. We let him down, cut him loose, and let him go. None of us gave the experience another thought until the next morning.

We were eating breakfast when Bob Sell came in. He approached our table and told the warrant and me, "Larry is really mad, and you guys are dead. We ain't gonna be responsible." Despite our laughter at hearing this from Sell, we went on guard. SEALs take each other seriously, and we were as close to the combat environment as one could get without having sappers blowing our bunks out from under us.

That afternoon we had a training exercise coming up and had to prepare for it. The operations plan was for us to play the VC in a local hamlet. The in-training advisers would take on the role of both PRU agents and advisers, entering the village to question those present and root out suspected VC or Viet Cong Infrastructure. We'd be using as our training area a local restaurant that had a bunch of log cabins out back. Once there, and with the permission of the owners, we took up our roles and waited for the action to begin.

When the door came crashing down, it was Larry La Page who had us dead to rights. The warrant aimed his M-16 at La Page, saying, "You're dead, Larry." La Page turned and slipped a S&W Model 39 automatic pistol right between Wayne's running lights and told him to move over against the wall. The tension in the room was electric. We suddenly knew Larry had a loaded magazine in his weapon, and indeed he had popped his cork over the episode in the latrine.

A woman who'd wandered in and was signing out one of the rental cabins witnessed Larry's act and ran screaming for the managers. The owners were trying to calm her down when everyone heard Larry say "Get that bimbo outta here before I start killin' everybody!" Two of the instructors present reached for their loaded weapons. La Page was a man possessed. His pistol *was* loaded, and he had the edge and the intention for just those few minutes of hair-raising hell. After kicking me in the face he came to his senses, and Wayne wandered out of the building in a daze at how close he'd come to buying the farm. The woman, who'd thought she was involved in a robbery, was dumping her belongings on the table, and her husband, who'd locked himself in their car when he saw Larry enter the joint with weapon in hand, began going nuts, too.

When it was all over the navy found itself being sued for $150,000, and in 1968 that was big bucks. The woman claimed the incident had made her frigid and had somehow estranged her from her husband. The warrant officer and I found ourselves in front of the CO back at Coronado being warned that we'd be severely reprimanded if anyone found out about the incident. I spent the next year avoiding Larry, and spent a great deal of time keeping close tabs on his movements. After all, one never could be sure . . .

With SBI completed, I was finally a fully qualified Navy SEAL.

6

The Fourth Commandment

I began my odyssey in the Dorchester section of Boston, the city I love to hate. I joined the navy to get as far away from there as possible, and when the plane lifted off from Logan to take me to boot camp I vowed never to return.

As the oldest of seven children I remember having responsibility since my first words were spoken. That was the way it had to be, growing up in a three-story brownstone. My father was a mailman and my mother was a homemaker. During the 1950s, mailmen were on the bottom of the economic food chain. Today they make good wages and they earn them. Both my parents had served in World War II, Dad with the Americal Division in the Pacific Theater and Mom in the navy as a pharmacist at Quonset Point, Rhode Island.

Being the eldest son of a staunch Irish Catholic made life very difficult for me. I remember not so much being taught about religion as being browbeaten by it. There was always that pervasive guilt and fear. The Sisters of Notre Dame held the power of life and death over me at Saint Mark's Parochial School. They knew they only had to tell Mr. Walsh that his little boy, Michael, wasn't cutting it and I'd be in deep *kimche*. My father had his own version of Catholic dogma. If you didn't see it his way, he'd beat you until you'd seen the light. I did what I had to in order to survive.

My animosity toward the nuns at grammar school was one outlet. I made life difficult for them and became known as a street kid. This was true. I never liked going to confession and always asked why priests were called Father. Often as a youth I asked myself, "Why should I tell this man my sins?" No one could give me a good answer to these questions, and even asking them was considered near blasphemy. I began to think of the Roman Catholic religion as a form of mind control, which continued at home after I left school. The nuns were Nazi drill instructors. They forced me into confession, forced me to march from place to place like some prisoner of war. I had to fight back, but how?

My solution was to confess outrageous sins to the priest, receive absolution, then ignore my penance. I believed I was accountable only to God. No mere man could forgive me anything. In my teen years I began to equate Catholicism with socialism. Then as I grew older I saw it as more Marxist but always equated it with guilt, guilt and more guilt. Finally, during my last year of high school, my father and I clashed over our religious beliefs. I'd elected to attend a public high school so as to avoid further religious indoctrination. I was smug about this decision and reacted very badly when my father insisted that I attend the religious instruction in the same classrooms I'd suffered in during grammar school! I was furious. It was the old formula: "If you live in my house, you play by my rules." My only other option was to leave home. Religion classes would be held every Monday night, and none could be skipped. So I bent to my father's will and attended.

I did not say one word in class during the entire four years I endured those classes. Every teacher knew I was there against my will. When I graduated—at the same time I completed high school—I sat in the back of the church, and when my name was called I refused to accept my diploma. The only diploma that meant anything to me was my high school diploma, already hanging in my room. Pop was present, and he was furious with me. We faced off in a quiet corner of the church, and he ordered me to get my certificate. I refused. He threatened to kill me right there in the church, and I could see the look of violence in his eyes about to overflow.

He punched me square in the face for the first time in my life. I'd been slapped before, beaten with a belt and a stick, but never punched. Even though I knew what was coming I couldn't bring myself to strike him back. The blow picked me off my feet and I went sailing. People near us scattered to get out of the way. The service itself stopped for a few moments as I lay on the floor, barely conscious. No one dared come near us. The fear in the eyes of the others looking at us told me everything I needed to know about my father at that point. The look in Pop's eyes, the veins popping out on his neck, and his blood red face left no doubt in my young mind that reason had just gone out the church window.

"Go ahead, you son of a bitch, kill me, 'cause I'm not going up there for that diploma. If it means that much to you, *you* go up and get it!" I screamed at him. The very next day I joined the navy.

Truthfully, the majority of my civilian education experience was negative. Even in kindergarten I was made to feel powerless and foolish. My very first educational experience was entirely negative. When asked along with the other children in my class to print our names, in nice big letters, on the paper, I was horrified. I didn't have a clue. So I sat there while all around me the other children were carrying out their mission. Miss Murphy, my first teacher, made her way to me and asked if I knew how to print. "No," I stuttered. "My mother never showed me."

"Why, are you stupid or something?" she asked. Everyone in the class, including some parents, were watching me. My parents were not there. I was so frightened I couldn't answer. She then condescendingly printed my name, all the while confirming for the others how stupid I was. I remember squirming in my tiny seat, feeling embarrassed, and deciding right there and then I didn't like school at all. I learned how to get on her good side by bringing her an apple every day, however, and soon I was sitting on Miss Murphy's lap while she played the piano for the class, and every day I would smooth-dog her by telling her how beautifully she played. Looking back, I guess she was my warm-up for the nuns who were coming later. At age five I only knew I had to survive, so I learned how. Then I learned to print my name.

On reflection, I've concluded my dad had severe emotional problems going back to his time in the war. I remember as a small child watching him as he pulled bits of shrapnel from his hands and forearms. He had fragments in his face, too, and when he died it was with two old bullets still in his body. I was fascinated with war, and played soldier every time I could. I even thought battle wounds were "neat," but now that I have war wounds myself, his pain is quite clear to me. For example, a piece of steel that lodged in the back of my head in 1971, courtesy of Vietnam, came out the top of my head while I was serving in Panama years later. Strangely enough, my headaches ended for a while after that self-healing.

Dad was given to sudden and violent rages. The veins in his neck looked like one-inch copper tubes, and his eyes scared me when I was under the glare of their blue flames. It was during all of this that the "grinch" was born within me, the little tough guy who would never give in, never give up, and never tell you what he was really thinking. He was my internal defense mechanism. He would later get me through BUD/S and then through a whole series of wars and conflicts. He was—and is today—a good friend and ally.

Growing up, I never enjoyed the closeness a boy needs to feel for his father. I loved him, but I feared him. Always there was fear. We had very few discussions, and he was never comfortable embracing his sons or telling us he loved us. This experience, this lack of warmth between father and son, instilled in me the resolve that if I ever had children of my own I would often tell them I loved them. Kids need to hear this. They need discipline, too, but not the kind I was raised on.

Often I think that my drive to survive and to succeed is but compensation for this often traumatic childhood. My dad's punishment was not meant just to teach a lesson but to humiliate as well. The grinch taught me never to allow anyone to control my thoughts, ever. You might own my body, but never my soul. My spirit was my own, never to be dominated. Only one naval officer during my career would try to equal my father in this realm, and he would fail miserably, outdone years earlier by a war-wounded mailman.

There were some good times with my father, though. He did do quite a bit with us when we were young, such as taking the family to the blue hills woodland on the outskirts of Boston. He taught us how to find things to eat, and the basics of surviving in the wild. He was absolutely at home in the woods or in any natural environment, for that matter. I, too, felt at one with nature. We joined the Boy Scouts, and Dad spent a great deal of time taking scouts on camping trips to New Hampshire. During these times he was calm and relaxed, and I enjoyed his company. He was a good father, with high standards—but only when we were away from the city and life's pressures.

Another thing I feared was the dark. In my eleventh year of life my father cured me of this fear in a unique way. To earn extra money Dad took a part-time job as a janitor at a local bank. In the basement they had a document vault that was pitch dark when the door was closed. Dad would often send me to the very end of this large vault to get something for him. Just as I would reach the end, where the hydraulic trash compactor was located, I would hear the door thump shut. Then the lights would go out. And then there would be total silence and complete darkness. Only my breathing indicated that anything was alive inside this basement tomb.

The first few times this happened I went into a complete panic, but that did no good, as the door remained shut. I began thinking about my situation. Dad wasn't trying to kill me; he was only trying to help me overcome my fear in his own way. I began learning my way around the vault by feel, like a blind person, and I soon became more comfortable in the dark. I knew I was over my fear when I made a game of hiding from him when he turned on the lights and opened the vault door. He stopped the "lessons" when he saw that my fear was gone. It was one of the few times he put his arm around me and told me I'd make a fine man someday. I wish he could see me now.

It may seem somewhat cruel that this was how he dealt with my fear, but I don't believe so. He had his own way of doing things, and what he did made me stronger. Ever since the classes in the bank vault I've viewed the night as my ally—an attitude that helped me when I joined the Teams. Dad's lessons also bore fruit in Vietnam. He died October 25, 1971, just before my first marriage in late December 1971. By then I was twenty-four years old, and I found myself wishing he'd lived long enough to see just how far his little boy had come. Perhaps he wouldn't have been as surprised as I might think!

In his last years Dad had mellowed quite a bit, and his spirit was calmer around me. When I visited home for the last time before his death he told me he loved and was proud of me. We both knew then he was dying. Every bit of animosity left me. I didn't need to tell him what was in my heart. He could see the message loud and clear through the teary glaze of my eyes as I watched him slipping away. He told me he'd been rough on me to make me strong. "You're still not there yet, but you're on your way," he said quietly. Those were among his last words to me. He died soon after of heart failure, but I finally knew how much he truly did love me. He had his faults, sure, but he was still my father.

My mother, Margaret, is like all good mothers. She was, and remains to this day, the heart of the Walsh family. It wasn't until a few years ago I fully realized just how intuitive she is. I never lie to my mother. If I did, she would know immediately; the woman has kept more family secrets in her heart than I care to ponder. Growing up, I was closer to my father, but I have come to realize with time that I am truly my mother's son. She is the true warrior and survivor. Those traits have been passed to me through her.

I do not remember ever hearing my mother raise her voice, curse, or even gossip about someone. She brought seven children into the world. In our family, blood is the thickest thing there is.

I know Mom regrets having given up her career to raise a large family, but wanting a career in the 1940s and 1950s was not the norm for women. They stayed at home, accepted their role as wives and mothers, and did what they were told . . . well, sort of. As a youth I didn't appreciate the fine qualities my mother possessed. She was patient and steadfast, and always thinking. There's an intense look in her eyes, even when she's relaxing. Mom is a keen observer of human nature and nothing gets by her. You don't lie to a woman like this, and I never have.

Mother didn't just survive, she prevailed. Resoluteness and determination are at the core of her being. I inherited these traits from her, and they took me through twenty-six years on the Teams. It must have been hard on her when I was living at home. She lived with a man who exhibited self-destructive tendencies and was borderline suicidal. Yet, she never broke faith. No doubt this faith was buoyed with hope for her oldest son, Michael.

Much later on, I was assigned to Panama from 1984 to 1987. While I was speaking to her on the phone from Panama, she reminded me how strong a mother's love is. I mentioned to her, with gentle exasperation in my voice, that

I was tired of hearing how much she worried about me. I told her I had survived various small wars, injuries, wounds, parachute and diving accidents, and all the other mishaps that come with life as a Navy SEAL. In short, I didn't need any mothering. She heard me out, then casually responded. "True," she said, "but no matter how old you are, you're still my baby." What can a man say to that? My only answer was the most obvious one, a very respectful "Yes, ma'am."

We can sit around the living room all day and discuss our parents' good and bad aspects, their successes and failures. My deep belief is that God Almighty himself chooses our parents for us. I don't try to figure out God or His reasoning. I'm grateful to have had parents whom I knew and experienced as so many in today's world don't. In this regard, I count myself fortunate. No matter what went on during my childhood one rule still applies for me: Honor thy father and thy mother.

As I approach the middle years of my life I'm spending every minute possible with Mom. She has a place of honor in my heart and in my home. She gave me the best of everything a mother has to offer her son, and for that I am truly grateful. Her reward will come from one far mightier than any on earth.

Thank you, Margaret.

7

Vietnam: First Combat

I couldn't help but think of my first tour in Vietnam as the iron bird lifted off like the legendary Phoenix, which rises from its own ashes and we began the journey back to the world. It hadn't been easy getting my shot at UDT training, especially given my original assignment was at Cam Ranh Bay.

My first trip to Southeast Asia was as a newly graduated 3-M data analyst assigned to monitor the aviation maintenance program as a quality control specialist. The unit was a maritime surveillance and antisubmarine warfare outfit known as Patrol Squadron ONE. The patrol's primary duties in Vietnam at the time were long-range surveillance of enemy shipping and checking out the coastline for stuff that shouldn't be there. To say I was bored would be an understatement.

I'd been in Vietnam for about a month or so when word came down that the swift boat unit at Nha Trang was looking for a few good men. The U.S. naval facility, Nha Trang, was part of the overall Cam Rahn Bay port complex, and we might as well have been neighbors where units were concerned. The swift boats intrigued me, or rather their mission did. Those guys were really doing something! Plus they had machine guns, and I love machine guns. But as soon as I voiced my interest in transferring over to the swifts, my boss said, "No way, Walsh, you E-2 puke. You ain't no SEAL and your butt is mine!" He was backed up by the warrant officer, Earl Payton, who gave me the evil eye meant to discourage any further conversation on the matter. Payton wanted me to crawl out of the office, but I didn't. He must have picked up on my silent challenge because he began ranting and raving about my being too short, too scrawny, and not SEAL material. Funny, I remember thinking to myself, no one's said anything about SEALs. I was just trying to get to a swift boat crew.

My determination to become a Navy SEAL was no secret in the squadron, though, and that's a fact. I was running every day, doing push-ups until my arms gave out, and using a stretching program that allowed me to touch my forehead to my knees. I took ice-cold showers to toughen my body as well as my spirit. Oh, they knew I was headed for the Teams, all right. I suppose that irked them, as quality control pukes were mighty important folks to have around during wartime. I wanted combat, and I was in a combat zone. The grinch inside told me to go around the chain of command so I called the swift boat guys on my own. The chief who answered was about as friendly as my own. He confirmed he was looking for men but not "an Airdale E-2 puke" like me. The name-calling was beginning to rankle me some, so I said I'd heard he needed someone who could work a .50 cal or M-60 machine gun, and I was his man. Now I hadn't yet actually fired these weapons, but I'd spent a great deal of time reading the manuals and memorizing all the data as part of my own pre-SEAL training program. I rattled off facts and figures until the chief caved in and told me to come on down and visit. First foot in the door.

So far, so good. But I had to let him know how my own boss felt about me leaving. Sit tight for a few days, he told me. That meant the problem would be worked out between the two chiefs, probably at the club where the really important navy business was conducted. While bridges were being built that would allow me to cross over to the swifts I began pulling any duties that would put me behind a machine gun. Night watch was a good place for this kind of on-the-job training and more than one aviation type was surprised to see me show up as a volunteer for duty most men avoided like the plague. But I needed the experience if I was going to convince my new chief that I was worth having on board. With the grinch guiding me I began racking up time near, if not on, the guns.

The chiefs worked it out, and soon enough I was standing on the pier checking out the patrol boats and feeling good. My first patrol was an eventful one that demonstrated just how important it was always to be in a training mode. The skipper was a young JG whose crew was right out of

Apocalypse Now. The second class petty officer was the oldest man on the boat, and it fell to him to brief me on the night vision scopes I'd later use frequently and to great effect as a SEAL. He saw right through me and just winked. "Don't worry, Walsh," he told me in private. "Let's just sit down and learn about these guns proper, okay?" My relief was obvious. I told him how I'd wormed my way over to the boats from a dead-end job checking nuts and bolts for wear and tear, and he got a chuckle out of the whole thing. After that he was patient enough to answer all my questions. I don't remember his name, but I remember the man. He certainly left his mark on me as I learned about a lot more than machine guns at his side.

As we moved across the waters of the Cam Rahn Bay region of Vietnam I began to encounter, for the first time since arriving in-country, the people who worked the land and fished the waters. Every eye on the water was aware of our presence as the swift boat passed by. The Vietnamese missed nothing, especially those things that brought death their way on a daily basis. Our primary mission was to stop boats and to inspect them for anything illegal, like armed VC. It was scary work, and every Viet boat seemed to have a hidden compartment under the false deck. Most of the time these were used to store the family's possessions, a simple arrangement that made sense and worked. At the same time, the bad guys usually used these hidey-holes to store weapons and other contraband. Again, it made sense and it often worked.

No one could explain to me exactly what constituted "contraband," nor could anyone come up with precise criteria as to the rules of engagement that we were to follow. Those rules seemed pretty important to me, as I wanted to know who I could shoot at, and when it was appropriate. Everything became quite clear, though, when we selected a boat to search and began to draw close to it. We could see that a Vietnamese man was at the tiller, his wife was in the day cabin, and a bunch of kids were scrambling around the deck. We'd just about reached the boat when a much smaller sampan about 500 yards behind us began sending small arms fire our way. I looked back and saw three men on the sampan, obviously VC, happily hosing down the swift. The range between us made their fire pretty ineffective, but it struck me I'd gotten my wish: at age nineteen I was finally under fire and in combat.

One of the swift boat's crewmen had just boarded the sampan we'd wanted to check out, and now he was leaping over to the swift's deck. In a flash he was moving to the twin .50 caliber gun mount, our most powerful weapon and one guaranteed to turn sampans into kindling wood in a few short bursts. I wasn't sure what to do, so I sat tight and watched the war unfold around me. The swift began to give chase as our port side machine gun, an M-60, let loose with long bursts of wild fire at the now fleeing VC sampan. I don't know if the gunner hit any of the three enemy troops on board but I do remember seeing his rounds splintering their craft as we took a wide port turn and began our attack run. I yelled over to the second class and asked why we were chasing them. It seemed odd to me they would risk their lives for a few potshots from half a kilometer's distance. "It's a trap!" I said. Another man standing next to me sneered and said I sure knew a lot for a new guy on board. I looked him dead in the eyes but was unsure of myself. After all, I *was* the new guy. What did I know? No one said anything to the JG who was plotting our intercept course, and I assumed he knew what was going on.

The swift quickly caught up with the much slower sampan just as we were approaching a small inlet. That's when the world caved in around us as the shoreline erupted with gunfire. Green tracers came crashing into us even as the patrol officer threw the boat in to a high-speed turn and made for open water. The VC had indeed set us up, and we were alive only because they'd gotten trigger-happy and set the ambush off before we'd gotten deep into the kill zone. Once out of small arms range we slowed down and gathered our wits. I mentioned that VC fire might have hit the sampan we'd been checking, and we decided to double back and see if anyone in the family had been hurt. But which sampan was it? There were hundreds on the water and ours was lost among them. We couldn't linger around very long, so without much fanfare we moved out smartly and continued our patrol.

After two more days of rather tedious patrolling we returned to Nha Trang and I headed back to the boredom of Patrol Squadron ONE. But now I was blooded and very much different from the administrative personnel who days before were my buddies and co-workers. I'd been bitten by the combat bug and was terminally infected. Counting airplane parts was no longer my mission in life; the swift boats had captured my warrior's heart. Before long I showed up on the pier again, my plotting having proved successful. We pulled out of Nha Trang as the sun was just coming up, the water as smooth as glass just before the ocean breeze began to ruffle its surface with powerful, rippling waves. The day's patrol was uneventful although very scenic.

I spent my time studying the faces of the people we stopped to search. The very old men showed no expression whatsoever; they'd seen too much and were war-wise in that respect. We were a necessary evil, an inconvenience in everyday life. They indulged our petty curiosity out of resignation and tightly controlled fear. After all, we held the power of life or death over their heads. The children, however, were just the opposite. Their eyes filled with a mixture of hate and fear whenever we passed close by. It was the rage of innocence, for the children had listened to their parents bemoan our presence when it was safe to speak, and the children witnessed their parents' humiliation as we stomped through their waterborne homes, sticking our noses and our fingers into what little they owned, always with a loaded weapon standing ready to cut them down at the slightest hint of noncompliance. At this point in my young life I wasn't at all used to anyone being afraid of me, least of all little children, and I found the feeling strange and very uncomfortable.

At the same time I noted that some men on our boat enjoyed having absolute power over the helpless. The darker side of human nature was beginning to make itself known to me, and as always I listened and learned, even though I didn't like it. I had always been a survivor, and to survive you have to pay attention to the bad things in life as well as the good. Some men relished imposing their will upon the Vietnamese, perhaps out of frustration at having the military impose its will upon them, a will under which they felt equally helpless. At times the end result was that the people we were supposed to be fighting for ended up hating us more than they did the Vietcong.

As we were patrolling we accidentally ran over one

Vietnamese fisherman's anchor line, cutting it in two. The skipper came about after being informed of the incident and pulled alongside the man's sampan, leaning over and giving him our own line while apologizing for his error. I registered this act of professional kindness immediately. Once back on patrol the skipper casually told us that what he'd done was simply right and proper and that ethics don't change just because of war. It's very easy, almost natural, to become totally uncaring and even inhuman during armed conflict. Vietnam was about as inhuman as anything that has taken place during this century, and after five tours of combat in Southeast Asia I would learn one thing about war that no armchair college professor could possibly appreciate: War brings out the very worst in men and women, and it also brings out the very best in human beings. At times these two extremes occur within moments of each other, and this is what causes such introspection within the souls of those who fight our country's battles. I was pleased at our officer's gesture with the anchor line—at least one Vietnamese wouldn't be bad-mouthing us over the evening meal.

That night we continued our mission. The patrol was becoming more boring by the minute when suddenly the skipper picked up an object on the water moving very quickly. It was well after midnight, and no small craft were supposed to be moving at all. We plotted a course to intercept the sampan, and that was when the fun began.

The sampan hadn't been there when we first passed through the area, and by the time we caught up with it, it was no longer moving. No women or kids on deck, no sounds coming from below. The sampan's skipper claimed that everyone was asleep. We've walked into another ambush, I thought to myself just as a hoard of fiery green tracers came racing toward our starboard side, lacing into the swift boat like angry termites and rocking us with solid hits. If this wasn't bad enough we started taking fire from the port side as well. No trigger-happy VC here, just cool, calm professionals going about their business. I let loose with a long burst from the twin .50 mount, aimed right over the water toward our attackers. All that accomplished was to make a lot of racket and to waste some good brass. The VC were too close to us and I couldn't traverse or depress the weapon to the necessary angle. Realizing this, I grabbed an

M-79 grenade launcher just as total chaos erupted aboard our boat.

Everyone was yelling, screaming, crawling to and fro, and firing. Battle plan? We didn't have a battle plan. My heart was pounding so violently I thought it might erupt from my chest. I was delighted to be in battle but deathly afraid of being shot. I watched a long, steady stream of green tracer fire come directly at me, falling just short of my position and skipping across the water's surface or smashing into the hull. Then another flight of tracers came speeding over my head, missing the boat and winging off into the distance until they burned themselves out. Two M-16s began firing from our starboard side, but we still weren't moving. The term "sitting duck" took on a new meaning to me. The gunner's mate who normally manned the .50 came scrambling up the ladder and ordered me off the gun. "I'm doing fine," I told him while firing a 40mm grenade toward an object about 300 meters off the port side. Being atop the swift boat gave me a great vantage point from which to use the M-79, if only the gunner's mate would shut up and let me do my job. He began screaming at me, using those old-time profanities only true sailors are aware of, ordering me out of the gun mount. I decided to evacuate, gripping the grenade launcher in my left hand as I made my way down the ladder, guiding myself by hanging on to the rail with my right.

We met at the halfway mark, and I smacked him with the butt of the M-79 right atop his head. Down the ladder he went, landing on the hard deck with a solid kersplat! The coxswain thought the gunner had been hit by enemy fire and began screaming "Wounded," as if anyone could or would do anything about it at that point. I was already back up the ladder and in the .50 mount, trying to get the gun lined up so we could do some serious damage. The boat was still sitting dead in the water. So much confusion reigned among all hands that it's a wonder the VC didn't stop firing and just sit back to watch the show.

The skipper finally grabbed the wheel, spun it all the way over to the left and honked down on the throttles so we could break free of the fire coming from our starboard side. Now I had some running room for the .50! I wasn't very accurate at first. I emptied the entire box of ammo in one long burst, which didn't make me any friends among those below. After all, we were supposed to be breaking contact and trying to do some damage at the same time. Someone managed to radio back to the rear that we were in deep doo-doo, and so was another swift boat, as several gunships had been dispatched to help us out. We told them to stand by while we put flares up using our on-board 81mm mortar.

The mortar was a great indirect fire weapon, and a good gunner could turn valuable real estate into a toxic dump in short order using one. As the flares burst high above us we spotted one set of bad guys heading for the beach. Not a good move, Charlie. We sent streams of red tracer fire at them, which the helicopter gunships used as an aiming line for their own high-explosive ordnance. The VC craft simply evaporated under our false sun, the helo's hellfire turning the fragile sampan into toothpick-sized wood scraps. Enemy bodies were floating on the surface, the remains unrecognizable due to the ferocity of the explosions and machine-gun fire we'd sent their way. Payback, as they say, is a mother!

The larger enemy barge was trying to chug its way up river. It was making about eight knots of speed and going nowhere fast. Even in the escape mode the VC were determined to put up a fight, and we watched as the entire crew made their way to the barge's stern, loaded for bear. As our swift closed in, the barge made a hard right, forcing us to maneuver opposite so as to avoid hitting them broadside. Smart move, as now our entire flank was exposed to their firepower. No one on our boat had been injured yet, except for the gunner's mate whom I'd knocked out during our fight over the .50. Even as we were trying desperately to avoid being raked from stem to stern with small arms fire he was ranting and raving to anyone who would listen about how I wasn't ever going to be on swift boat again.

His one-sided conversation ended as we closed in on the barge. The gunner's mate, whose headache must have been impressive, manned the .50, and I was impressed with what followed. I toted ammo for the big gun up the ladder but was advised as I handed it to my injured shipmate that I'd better not come up the ladder again if I knew what was good for me. Point well taken, and I hit the deck. When the .50 opened up, the VC barge came to a shuddering stop as if someone had pulled the reins in . . . hard. Its tinderlike upper decking and cabin structure were set afire by the .50's tracer rounds as they chewed their way inside the now pilotless boat. Dead enemy soldiers littered the deck and were hanging from the stern. Wounded VC were crawling around searching for safety as those still whole jumped overboard. A secondary explosion aboard the barge blew it out of the water, and the tortured hull slipped beneath the dark water so quickly I was left dumbstruck.

Now we had to search for bodies or, more accurately, for someone left alive who would make a good prisoner. This was a dangerous time because we were preoccupied with scanning the surface for corpses, and that made us extremely vulnerable to those enemy troops who simply didn't know when to quit. It was a perfect time for a swimmer to come up on our blind side, board the craft, and wreak havoc among the crew with either an AK-47 or bag of grenades. I didn't know anything about this, though, since I was the new guy and still climbing that ever-increasing learning curve.

I was leaning on the aft-located 81mm mortar mount when I decided to move around toward the stern for a better vantage point from which to look for dead VC. There was no sound as the enemy swimmer approached our boat and none when he scaled the side opposite me. The second class had spotted him, though. He let the VC get up as far as the rails and begin worming his way toward my exposed back. Then the second class let loose with a 12-gauge shotgun, and the blast blew the man clean off the boat and back into the oil-stained waters.

"You okay, kid?" my savior asked.

My eyes were as big as saucers, and I wanted to urinate so badly I nearly couldn't make the side before doing so. I shook for quite a while afterward, as the gunner's mate made it clear that he wished the "gook better luck next time." I held my tongue, figuring that enough was enough. We'd both gotten our licks in on each other, and the important thing was no one on the crew had been wounded or killed. The boat was sporting some new, unissued holes, so we decided to head for the pier at dawn. Sounded good to me. I needed the downtime to think about how close I'd come to dying and why. I've never forgotten my tour of duty with the swift boats. They did a wonderful job in Vietnam. I learned about war firsthand aboard one, and I took those experiences with me to BUD/S and to the Teams after I'd earned the right to be called a frogman.

Hey, anything was better than being a quality control specialist!

8

Vinh Long: Point Man

It was September, 1968. SEAL Team ONE's predeployment training cycle was over and Charlie platoon was certified ready in every respect for Vietnam. The day we departed brought out the wives and children of those SEALs who were married. That "will I ever see you again?" look in their eyes said it all. I specifically remember Warrant Officer Wayne Boles's wife as she saw her husband off. For me, the war was a challenge faced by myself and my teammates, but for the families it was as close to a living nightmare as one could imagine. We left the SEAL Team ONE compound amid the jeers and cheers of our fellow warriors, many of whom we'd spent our last night in the U.S.A. with partying in the San Diego area.

The Tradewinds bar was the official watering hole for the Teams on the West Coast, and the party that went on the night before we left makes the Tailhook scandal pale in comparison. I remember at one point being given a small plastic bag with a chip of sponge and some red-colored water inside. Gary Gallagher was the master of ceremonies that evening, and no more notorious SEAL could have conceived of such a prank. The chiefs and officers at ST-1 gave Gary wide berth out of both fear and respect. Many a SEAL commanding officer owes his career to Gallagher, who handled all the paperwork that allowed us to pass our annual man-packed nuclear weapons inspections. These systems have been taken away from the SEALs since then, but we had them and for a very good reason.

Gary was and remains a master of deception. He delighted in starting rumors and could wreak havoc within the command by lunchtime of any given day. As a SEAL instructor he possessed the ability to train his people without wanting to own their souls at the same time.

Gallagher became my mentor, unwittingly at first, and I watched and listened to everything he did. SEALs are too often seen as purely physical animals, but this is really only 10 percent of the total product. A good operator uses his mental capacities and instinct 90 percent of the time, which is what Gary always managed to get across to his people. Much of what I learned about intelligence, operations planning, and other special forms of warfare I owe to this remarkable man.

Gary was standing at the bar when he handed me the ominous plastic bag. "This is for you, ya little turd," he growled. "It's all the body bag you're gonna need!" I was delighted and kept the soggy little baggie in my uniform pocket throughout the flight from California to Saigon. The man had a style all his own.

Later on that same evening I wandered back to the house several of us were sharing with roughly twenty-three hippies from up around Monterey. Four SEALs and two UDT guys from Team ELEVEN were living with the landlady, her four children, and the hippies in what can only be described as an interesting arrangement. The hippies were all hair, beads, crazy clothes, and drugs. The SEALs and UDT frogs were stone-cold killers who preferred alcohol. Whenever we were together the freaks were careful, as they didn't want to screw up our security clearance, mostly because we were the only ones paying the rent. While living there I was exposed to a world I'd never heard about in Boston. The learning curve was steep, as by day I was a good navy man but at night I behaved like a creature of my surroundings.

At age twenty I found myself buried in a lifestyle centered on pure lust. The landlady had her choice of men any night of the week, and we had our choice of the women present.

While I was going over my personal gear one more time before hitting the sack a woman came to my door. She was just under six feet tall in her bare feet and possessed large luminous eyes, long dark hair, and a fine figure. She pulled me to her breast, wrapped her arms around my head and neck, and began talking to me about how terrible the war in Vietnam was and asking me why I had to go there to fight! I didn't have a clue as to what I should say. After a long silence I responded that it was my job and that I'd been waiting a long time to prove my mettle as a Navy SEAL. As she began crying I simply held her close, no longer sure of what else to say.

After a few moments she said, "Grab a blanket. We're going down to the beach." It was now after one o'clock in the morning, but I grabbed two camouflage military poncho liners, and we headed toward the shore. As we walked along the street she popped what looked like a sugar cube into her mouth while I took a solid hit of wine from the bota bag slung over my shoulder. In those days I toted a wine bag with me during long bike rides alone, wearing a Mexican serape to hide the bag from prying eyes. A long length of clear surgical tubing ran from the sack up to my mouth so I could take hits while in flight. Today I shake my head in amazement when I recall such things.

I asked my date for the evening what she'd just swallowed. "Acid," she replied, looking me dead in the eye. Suddenly I was nervous. I wasn't at all familiar with LSD, and as we neared the beach she seemed to slip into another world. Even so, we made love on the beach and fell asleep afterward. In the morning before I left for the compound she told me she'd seen the devil during our lovemaking. I was at a loss for words. In retrospect, I wonder if I didn't sleep with the devil that night. As for LSD, the experience my lady friend described convinced me it was bad news. I'll stick to wine, thank you.

As the door of the C-118 slammed shut, I watched as wedding rings were slipped off fingers, carefully tucked away, and big smiles come over the faces of the married men on board. I knew I was looking forward to battle, but so were the guys with wives and families! Dave Wilson, sitting nearby, made what would be a fateful statement while looking out the window at his beautiful wife who'd come to see him off. "Either I come home with the Big Blue, or I don't come home at all!" He was referring to the Congressional Medal of Honor, which most SEALs call the Medal of Horror. I learned to be wary of those who seek this award—they are the guys who get either themselves or others killed. When I heard Dave's comment I got real uptight. Wilson was already difficult to control in the field, and he was the rear security man for my squad. I decided right then and there to watch him, and if he appeared to be putting us in jeopardy I'd go right to Wayne Boles for guidance. If Wayne got killed or wounded, I'd take care of Wilson myself if he endangered the rest of the platoon. Dave had already told me my life meant nothing to him, so my decision was all the easier to arrive at. Civilians and les military men and women might be shocked to hear of such a thought process, given its implications. But in our line of work the team is what counts, and it is the team that must survive. Glory boys endanger the mission and the men carrying it out. Our missions as SEALs were the toughest, the worst, and the most likely to see body bags filled before they were over, if we weren't careful. We took care of our own in every respect, including guys like Wilson if they put a medal before their teammates' safety.

It took four long days to fly from the States to Vietnam. Upon our arrival we suffered through the typical brain-dead in-country briefings that were always given by either army or navy headquarters pukes who'd never seen the war outside of the streets and back alleys of Saigon. I had to pinch myself when the army sergeant who met us felt it necessary to remind everyone we were "guests of the Republic of Vietnam" and should behave ourselves! I couldn't help saying out loud, "If we're guests, then why are the bastards trying to kill us?"

Our radio man, Lee, slammed me in the ribs with his elbow. "Shut up, you little clown," he whispered, "Just humor this turd and let's get this over with." Lee wasn't someone you messed with for fun. His eyes were like a cobra's just before it strikes to kill. As an operator he was deadly, very steady on the march, and he missed nothing. I respected him, even liked him a bit, and never ignored his advice.

"Okay," I whispered back while rubbing my sore ribs. Sometimes being humble is the smartest way to go.

Our first night operation at Vinh Long included three operators from the Sadec Province SEAL platoon, Warrant Officer Scott Lyon, Barry "The Bear" Enoch, and Harlen Funkhouser. Harlen Funkhouser holds the distinction of going through hell week twice after breaking his leg the first time. Barry Enoch was a SEAL Team ONE plank owner, or original member. Each was already a living legend in the Teams, with Barry a chief petty officer and Harlen a senior petty officer. You couldn't ask for a better wrecking crew than these guys. Enoch, who today is a retired fire chief living in Sisters, Oregon, left his mark on many a SEAL walking around alive today, including me. He is one of the few original West Coast SEALs, and no one to take lightly. I still get regular "rudder guidance" from him.

As we prepared for the mission, Harlen personally checked my gear. My excitement was obvious, and he told me not to worry about anything. Scott Lyon was scanning the platoon one man at a time. "Who's your point man?" he asked Mr. Boles. Wayne looked over at me, and Lyon checked me out real good as he nodded in my direction. Harlen nodded back at Scott, and some unspoken message passed between them. I later learned they'd decided right then and there that I would cut it as a point man. When the words "Let's Go!" rang out, I grabbed my weapon and hoisted my gear. I'd waited for years to hear that command. We were going into battle at last, and I was the forward element of a SEAL squad. It was a dream come true. I didn't know how to pray very well back then, so I just trusted to my own abilities, my instincts, and my boss, Mr. Boles. Nothing and no one else mattered. My world was complete.

Our evening's target was a Vietcong tax collection station on Five Mile Island, a bit of beach and jungle in the middle of the Co Chen River just south of the provincial capital of Vinh Long. This was an area rich in farming, and the VC made good money from its people. Our job was to eliminate the tax station and its staff using good solid SEAL tactics and firepower.

As our boat approached the insertion point I began getting apprehensive. The muddy river water was slapping loudly up against the boat's hull, and its bottom crunched over heavy growth as we came ashore. Everything was too loud, each noise bouncing off the small tidal flat like gunfire. On top of our own sounds were those made by the animals as they scurried across the jungle floor, climbed trees, or dived into the river to escape us. The acrid smell of men's sweat hung in the still, humid air like a dirty cloak. Suddenly everything went silent. Dead silent. The sound of the boat's engines faded into the distance, leaving us alone in enemy territory. It would return either to extract us under fire or to take us aboard in the aftermath of a successful mission. Only those who have conducted a combat infiltration can truly understand how alone you feel when your only means of getting out leaves you. It is a weird, crazy realization of one's mortality, and I never got used to it no matter how many times we got off a boat or helicopter.

Our seven-man squad and the three "straphangers" began the slow movement required to reach the target undetected. Mr. Boles and I had a good system worked out where he'd give me a point to work toward by whispering in my ear as we huddled face to face on the jungle floor. I was so high on natural "speed" that every emotion, instinct, reaction was 100 percent functional and vibrating. My training took over and I took a reality check, reminding myself we were not playing a game. This was war and men would probably die tonight. Better the VC than my teammates, who were counting on me as the point man to get them to the target undetected.

As we negotiated a high dike line I lost my footing in the soft mud every ten feet or so. I'd roll off the dike and make a beautiful splash as I hit the soggy rice paddy below. No one said anything, except Lee, and I never quite caught his comments, which must have been good. It was my job to break trail, alerting the others to booby traps or enemy personnel before either could go off on us. Each time I pulled myself up out of the foul-smelling mud I'd hear someone spitting tobacco juice onto the ground. Many SEALs chewed in those days as a means of passing the time and keeping a good buzz going. I tried it once and got sick enough never to do so again.

We reached the ambush site without fanfare and spent the next two days waiting in chest-deep paddy water. Our targets were a high-level VCI political cadre who would be coming in by boat, according to our intelligence sources. We wanted the tax collector himself, who always had a wad of money on his person. In those days we never turned in any money taken; it went into our party fund. The rules said otherwise, but we didn't care; we had our own rules. After all, we'd earned the money by risking our lives, and there was always a need for a black fund way out in the jungles that were our camps. The navy paid us, but the VC gave us our bonuses for a job well done.

Finally the VCI advance party showed up. The security

force moved past our position and nearly stepped on us as they conducted their reconnaissance of the area. They never had a clue that we were there. Some VC moved so close to us that we would have been compromised if a man had breathed too loud. Our SEAL training paid off, as we already knew that just because a man is pointing a gun at you doesn't mean he's seen you. More than once I would run into the enemy face to face, a weapon inches from me, but the man would glide by or pull back into the jungle. I'd learned from my father how to walk in the woods, and this experience was reinforced on the Teams. When someone looked right at me I'd simply look away, my own focus becoming larger than simply eye-to-eye contact. But instincts in combat are double-edged swords and warfare is a two-way street. Even as your own instincts are greatly enhanced by the moment, so are those of your enemy.

At those times when you and your foe make eye contact it is body language that signals a reaction. If he's seen you, his whole body will change; if not, he'll simply move on. If he stands straighter, flattens out, or begins shooting, you're compromised. You have to sense this one split second before it happens, and shoot first. It is the gunslinger mentality that only those who have been there can relate to. Civilians freeze under such conditions; combat veterans react. It is the difference between life and death.

To their grim disadvantage the VC scouts didn't spot us. I was well camouflaged with plenty of jungle masking my form. I was to alert Mr. Boles when I saw the sampans coming. He in turn would alert the rest of the squad. Our weapons were resting atop our UDT life jackets in front of our positions. We'd been in position for two days by now, with my greatest challenge the vomiting fit I'd gone into from the smell of tobacco juice. During this horrible event Mr. Boles had simply observed me puking on myself. Lee whispered just loud enough for me to hear how he was going to gut me, skin me, and hang me out to dry if I even looked like my discomfort was going to get us killed. We'd been urinating and having bowel movements while standing chest high in the slow-moving water, which was why no SEALs ever wore underwear. You just slid your cammie trousers down and went into a half squat without rippling the water. The current would move the waste away from you and within minutes it'd be business as usual again. Ambushes are tedious events during which the slightest error will get you killed. Thankfully, I got my stuff together and cheated our radio man out of his mumbled threats.

Putt, putt, putt . . . I didn't have to say a thing to Mr. Boles. We could all hear the sampan's little engine as it moved the boat toward our position. Wayne could read me like a book. He once informed me that when we were in danger the hair on the back of my neck stood out so straight it looked as if it had been spray-starched! This wasn't the Chocolate Mountains or the Silver Strand at Coronado or Cuyamaca. For the first time we were looking down our gun barrels at the enemy and preparing to kill them at point-blank range. They were alert, ready, on edge. I forced myself to control the rising anxiety that comes with one's first kill. I heard every sound around me no matter how slight, yet my ears were buzzing as if they were infested with millions of wasps. My pulse was slamming against every vein and artery in my body. The blood was flooding my skull in a torrent. It was all I could do to make myself stay dead still as the boat slipped closer.

Mr. Boles always initiated fire. My eyes slid his way, and his expression told me everything I needed to know. He was absolutely calm, with no hint of distress staining his camouflaged features. That's what you need to look like, Mike, I told myself. Message received, sir. Slowly I lined up the sights of my AK-47 on the enemy, my breathing suddenly much slower and my heartbeat dropping back to near normal. We let the first sampan go by, knowing it was a decoy filled with bit players. The smell of death suddenly flooded my nostrils. Their death or ours? A brief but sobering thought.

In twelve seconds it was all over. Using three Stoner light machine guns, two M-60 light machine guns, several rifles, and one M-79 grenade launcher, we delivered such a vicious stream of high-velocity steel that the sampans seemed to melt away. The current pushed bits of wood and fabric along the river's bloodstained surface, the equally destroyed bodies of the enemy dipping and bobbing past us like burned corks. There was no time to lollygag around to review our work. With contact initiated we needed to get clear of the kill zone ASAP.

I climbed back up the dike, moving slowly and cautiously, my eyes roving back to Mr. Boles as he, too, scanned the area around us. Everyone went down on one knee, weapons ready, trigger fingers resting loosely near the most important part of the weapon when it's time to rock and roll. Wayne pointed to the tree line. Was I seeing everything he was? It became our immediate objective and I was to decide if and when we would enter its relative safety. Boy, does Boles have confidence in me, I thought to myself as I approached the wall of inviting foliage.

At its edge I stopped, lowering myself to one knee to wait, learn, and listen. Something crawled up the back of my leg. It felt big, really big. I don't dare look at it, much less take a swipe at it. I was so alive right then that I couldn't believe it. A slight breeze came up to wipe away the hot, humid air for just a moment or two. Every branch and leaf reacted to it, parting so I could see a tiny muddy trail just meters away. I could get the entire squad on it, checking for booby traps and taking a compass reading once we were hidden away. Maybe we could take a break from all the action for a minute or two.

The entire squad was exposed on top of the dike, but it was now so dark I couldn't even see them. To bring us back together I gave off a series of clicking-sucking noises we'd put together in the States. Within minutes Boles moved up with the rest of the men, everyone disappearing into the tree line with hardly a sound. Wayne and Scott Lyon conferred in an inaudible whisper just feet from me.

The signal to move was given, and our break was over. I took the squad deeper into the island's guts, crossing several streams along the way. Streams were considered danger areas and we always transitted them at a 90-degree angle or at a bend, which offered a clean field of fire in case of a chance contact or ambush. It was my job to swim across to check the opposite shore, and to see if it was safe. I signalled the others, who followed, one man at a time. I remember Mike Crisp, one of our Stoner gunners, crossing in full field gear but wearing no UDT life vest! The 60 gunner, Al Whistler, did the same. Tough guys in every respect.

SEAL squads often crossed up to fifteen streams a night during operations, so that it became no more difficult for us than crossing a city street. We also became proficient at crossing "monkey bridges"—one or two bamboo poles lashed together across a river or stream. Most of the time our boots were caked with mud, which made using such a bridge difficult.

Some time after the first of several stream crossings I found a monkey bridge and scurried across it. Mike Crisp fell off about halfway across, but the only sound was his body hitting the water's surface. I ran down the bank to where I figured he would come up, and when he did, he handed me his Stoner. "Don't hurt my weapon" was all he said to me as he slithered out of the stream like a snake.

We moved on. The jungle's sights and smells were running through my brain as I registered each, always wary for one that was out of place. A hootch popped into view and I saw someone moving around inside. Everyone was VC until we knew better. I picked a spot to stop, and the patrol leaders moved up to where I was resting. As I leaned forward to tie my jungle boot, one of the men pointed to a tiny pulley nailed to a tree—the exact spot the VC tax collector used to set up his station when preying on the island's populace. We mark the spot on our map for intelligence purposes. This is now our second ambush point.

First, though, we have to check out the hootch and its occupants. I was so focused on the tiny dwelling that I'd missed the pulley. Lyon turned his head, and Boles gave me an encouraging look. He signaled with his hands that I should slow down a bit, and I nodded in acknowledgment. Inside I was cursing myself for missing the pulley. It was my job to discover that, not Scott Lyon's. Perfection was my goal, and I hadn't delivered. To be the perfect point man you had to bring your people home alive. I couldn't miss something so important again.

Wayne brought everyone up off the trail and we settled into a defensive perimeter. Boles and I moved forward to reconnoiter the immediate area. As we came close to the hootch I saw an old Vietnamese man with a cradle in his hands, but I didn't know what he was doing. It was so dark that I couldn't see clearly. Then the rain started, slow and hesitant at first, then building to the kind of shower only the tropics are capable of. We figured the old man was alone, and Wayne gave me the nod to rush the hootch.

I leaped up and hit the doorway at a full run, my attention totally focused on the Vietnamese as I raced toward him like a vision out of hell itself. When I hit the inside of the hootch I slipped and went ass-over-teakettle, rolling across the floor, my weapon flying from my hands. A frantic screeching enveloped me, along with the horrible odor of filth as I rolled to my feet. The biggest pig I'd ever seen came running across the hootch at me, furious at the intrusion. The old man was seated now, just watching the show. Both Lyon and Wayne Boles were in the doorway, Scott covering the Viet with his weapon as I searched for mine.

"On your feet, point man," said Mr. Boles. "Thank God Pittman didn't see this," he continued with a smile.

I was angry and embarrassed. "Don't get emotional," cautioned Wayne, "this is just the first day." It was good advice. Besides, the pig had calmed down, I'd found the AK, and I'd put on quite a show for the lonely old man.

We questioned the man and were told the VC tax collector ate with him whenever he was in the area. I noted the Viet was not one bit afraid of us. The pig, I wasn't sure of. Lyon informed the man he would travel with us until we left the island. The old guy just nodded and pulled on his black shirt. He was a security risk we couldn't trust to leave behind. We left the hootch and our new "friend" guided us right back to where we'd left the squad. The trail running parallel to a small river was a good spot for an ambush. The foliage was heavy on one side of the trail. There were only two avenues of escape from our fire, either across the flat ground or across the river. We rigged the site as a killing zone.

The old Viet took up a position with Wayne Boles. He agreed to point out the tax collector for us. Who were the VC on the sampans we hit? We didn't know. Maybe our original target was already fish food and this would be an empty hole. On the other hand, perhaps we'd luck out and bag someone new. It was after 0300 hours and we were exhausted. As morning rolled around I heard the small hamlet coming alive. Every sound seemed directed at me. I closed my eyes and just listened. Mr. Lyon whispered in my ear as he pointed to another village across the river. He told me what was going on, what the early morning routine was. I needed to know this, to remember it. As a point man it was my job to note things that were out of place, like how folks got up in the morning. Those details could mean the difference between life and death for my squad and for me.

Lyon nodded as I took it all in. He turned to Boles and said, "The kid learns fast, Wayne." Mr. Boles spit out a gob of tobacco juice from his mouth and nodded proudly. Inside I was beaming, the incident with the missed pulley and angry pig forgotten. I also noted Mr. Boles was completely at ease despite our dangerous position. I took that as a good sign.

The tax collector never showed. At 0800 the officers decided we'd patrol back to the main river. This would allow us to see the terrain during daylight for intelligence purposes. We tracked parallel to the trail we had come in on, avoiding booby traps and overnight ambushes that might have been set up by any VC who were trailing us. I checked to see if our new trail had been used by the locals. If they walked it, so would we. I didn't want to miss a thing.

The squad reached the river without incident. The boat came right up to us, and we were out of the water in less than a minute. "We need to do that one better next time," Boles told me. "If they were shooting at us, we'd be in deep doo-doo." Everyone nodded. On the ride back to Vinh Long I discovered that my legs had become a leech farm. I burned off a total of twenty-nine of the creatures, then pulled off my boots and dropped my trousers for a better look. Stuck to one side of my penis was yet another blood-sucking leech! Yucko. "Great," I said, "another leech right where I don't need it most." One of the guys with the boat detachment saw my predicament and within seconds the whole crew was looking, including my now curious squad.

Everyone wanted a look at the offending leech. Without thinking I grabbed the military-issue mosquito repellent we used, knowing it was death on these slimy thugs. I squirted the monster with repellent as my teammates urged me on. Big mistake, grasshopper. The stuff works great on every part of the human body except the genital area. My poor abused penis exploded in pain as the liquid hit it. I grabbed a canteen and began pouring water over myself even as I jumped and leaped around the boat. What happened to the leech I'll never know, but everyone on board was hysterical with laughter as their ultra high stress levels were suddenly given a vent. We had a great ride home.

Our first operation as a platoon was over. We were alive, with no wounded. I liked my job as point man and had the approval of my peers to continue. Vietnam, to me, had become home.

9

First Kill

Two weeks after executing our version of tax relief on behalf of the Vietnamese people we hooked up with fellow SEAL, Gary Shadduck, whom I liked tremendously. He was an accomplished skydiver who loved free-fall parachuting with a passion. Shadduck was a PRU adviser with Phoenix in Vinh Long Province. His reputation as an operator was as solid as New Hampshire granite. We took the opportunity to link up with him to see what we could do with each other. He knew this was my first deployment with the Teams, but as far as Gary was concerned we were all on the same team, period.

Our meeting took place at the embassy house, a CIA station in the provincial capital. We were seated around a table in the courtyard when a loud explosion rocked the neighborhood. The detonation took place right outside the embassy house and was totally unexpected. I watched a human head come flying over the wall toward me. It landed with a soggy thump and rolled to a stop at the base of a nearby tree. Gary immediately ran to the front gate to observe the street. People were either standing stock still or dashing around as in a Chinese fire drill. A Nung mercenary reported to Gary that two VC had passed by on bicycles, one of them carrying a satchel charge. As the younger of the two would-be sappers lit the fuse and prepared to toss the explosive over the wall, it went off in his hands. His head was the makeshift Frisbee I'd noted sailing into the compound.

I wandered over to the head. The eyes were open, and the face was black. The sweet, stomach-turning stench of burning flesh rose like steam from the battered head. The man's body, as well as his destroyed bicycle, had been thrown clear across the street by the force of the explosion. The damage done to both told us how powerful the bomb had been. We figured it must have weighed close to thirty pounds! Had it hit its intended mark—us—it would have been quite a coup for Mr. Charles.

Again I elected to examine the VC's twisted corpse. Everything had its learning points in Vietnam, and I wasn't about to overlook anything that might improve my own chances of survival. The separation of his head from his body was not clean. This was no ritual beheading conducted with a razor-sharp sword. The blast had torn the man's skull from his neck, popping it like a cork under pressure. The rest of the body was grotesque. There is no glory in violent death, no matter how hard the movies try to depict such nonsense. Shadduck suggested we bury the head at the base of the tree, and we did. Then we sat down and enjoyed a nice meal. After all, this was supposed to be a working supper, and we all wanted to know how we could help Gary with his more difficult targets in the Vinh Long area.

For several weeks after this meeting the platoon conducted a series of "Welcome to Vietnam" operations. We didn't encounter much opposition, which allowed us to really get settled into the combat environment. Several bad guys got themselves captured by our squads, though. Most of them were sleeping soundly when we tiptoed into their hamlets and villages, taking them by surprise and rushing them off into the darkness. All the stuff we'd learned on the Mexican border with respect to POW handling came in quite handy, but once again I got a bit cocky and learned another lesson the hard way.

The word came down about a district VCI headquarters located on the outermost fringe of Vinh Long province. The enemy considered themselves so secure they were said to walk around the area at night unarmed. Now, this got me excited. I'd stopped wearing issue cammies and was now dressed exactly like a VC foot soldier. At five feet four inches and 125 pounds soaking wet I could pass in the night for one of the bad guys, especially armed with an AK-47 assault rifle.

I loved the AK because it was absolutely reliable under the worst field conditions. I could swim with it, crawl through mud, bang it against rocks, and the weapon would always function perfectly. The knockdown power of the Soviet round was tremendous, as anyone hit by one will attest to. I leaned toward the AK because its bullets would not deflect off foliage as easily as did the much lighter M-16 round, and again the knockdown power was better. When I hit something in a firefight I wanted it to go down, not get up and fire back at me.

We prepped the mission, and the word came back that it was a go. My big smile turned to letdown, though, when I discovered Mr. Boles wouldn't be leading us on this one. The number one position went to the platoon commander. Our other point man, Ron Pace, was out of the program for a few days, which added to my insecurity. The CO, whom I'll call "Peaches," was a very young junior grade officer in whom I had little confidence. Generally, officers handled administrative concerns while the warrants and enlisted folks ran the actual operations. This is not to imply there weren't more than enough superb officers who were on-the-ground combat leaders. There were. But Peaches wasn't one of 'em.

We elected to infil our seven-man SEAL squad plus Sam, the interpreter, by PBR. Taking the boat from Vinh Long to the objective area during one of its routine patrols was the cover for our insertion. The boat crew dropped us off the main river, then continued with their established track as if nothing unusual had just taken place. Standing by to provide gunship support were our own navy Seawolf gunships, a helicopter unit that literally ruled the air during SEAL ops. The patrol boat's secondary mission that day was to monitor our frequency should we need assistance. The unique thing about our helicopter support was that the Seawolf helicopters were cast-off army Hueys. Many a Vietnam SEAL owes his life to these guys. I certainly haven't forgotten them. Thank you, gentlemen.

The first part of the patrol was uneventful. The terrain was the usual assortment of tree lines surrounding rice paddies and inland marshes. If you're caught in an open rice paddy, you're an easy target, so we look for commonly used trails, which are the easiest way to navigate. If trails are booby trapped, signs are posted on trees to warn the VC and the local populace of that fact. I quickly learned how to read the Tudia signs. At night the trails were slippery, but I didn't fall off them anymore. I later understood why we had the balancing poles at the O-course in BUD/S. I hadn't worked much with the other squad, so I had to learn another whole set of hand signals and such.

Peaches was noisy—too noisy, I thought as we worked our way through the jungle. If I had my way I'd never work an operation with this guy again. I punched out through a tree line and found myself staring across a huge expanse of open field. The objective was to our front, a large hootch all lit up with lanterns that glared back at me from some distance off. It had a real door, actually two, and I wanted to fire a Light Antitank Weapon (LAAW) rocket right through the sucker just to let the VC know we were in town. The LAAW rocket is a 66mm warhead and is man portable. It has been replaced in the modern era with the AT-4. Totally awesome! However, reality won me over, and we began crawling across the field.

Suddenly I noticed that the closer I got to the hootch, the farther behind the rest of the squad seemed to get behind me. Looking back, I couldn't see our rear security. Matter of fact, I couldn't even see past the radio man. Something was very, very wrong. Moving back to Peaches, I asked what was up and got a ration of crap in return. Peaches was upset because he thought I was telling him how to run his patrol. Rather than argue, I took point again. We reached a massive dike and Peaches said this was where we were to hold up—everyone but me.

Peaches felt that a one-man reconnoiter of the hootch was in order, so I was off and running. Despite our detailed planning we knew we had to be flexible in the field; adapting to circumstance was no surprise to anyone. I moved carefully to the hootch, weapon at ready and praying there were no pigs hanging around. The moon was at my back, making it fairly easy for me to see but also making my form visible to the enemy. Sam, our Vietnamese SEAL, moved forward to accompany me. Two heads are better than one, and I was happy to have Sam backing me up.

We creepy-crawled up to the hootch, the Viet SEAL staying to my left and slightly behind me. The house was well constructed and solid, very odd for a structure nearly four kilometers from the river. Behind the hootch on the edge of a tertiary river I saw a small finger of land about a hundred yards further on. Several barge-sized sampans were loading supplies aboard. VC were everywhere, all of them armed. So much for our intelligence source. I motioned to Sam that it was time to fall back, and as we did so we searched for booby traps and noise makers. Once we were clear of the hootch we linked up with the squad and I briefed Peaches as to what was up ahead. What we were doing here was observing the target from more than one perspective. This was especially important at night. Modern night optics have made this job easier today. However, the fact remained that the more perspectives we could gain on any target, the better.

The word was given to move out, and we began circling around the right side of the oversize jungle hut. I picked out radio antennas, and my excitement level started climbing. This was it—the command and control site we were intent upon destroying! No one was moving around this area; all the activity was apparently centered around the sampans. The squad was waiting somewhere behind me as I conducted this second reconnoiter of the objective. I began moving back to fill them in. Looking up, I saw a tall, lanky man walking directly toward us. He was too far away for me to accurately gauge his height, but he was definitely a tall man. He held a cigarette in his right hand; the left one was stuffed casually in the pocket of his black pajamas. I knew he hadn't seen me yet, but Sam became so unglued that he lost control of his bowels. The smell was overpowering and I could only hope whoever was striding toward us didn't catch a whiff.

No such luck. The man stopped and looked directly at where we were crouched. Time to do something, so I stood up and began walking toward the guy, who was now very tense. My short size became a powerful ally, along with my black VC duds and the AK, so it was possible for me to pass for VC in the darkness. As I got closer I lowered the rifle and offered a greeting in Vietnamese. I saw him relaxing, going for the bait. I realized I was going to have to kill him very quickly, very quietly if we were to remain undiscovered. The thought didn't surprise me; it was just part of the job.

From five feet away I leaped at the tall VC and watched as his eyes opened wide in the moonlight. Grabbing him by the shirt collar with my left hand, I prepared to drop him to the ground. I helped him along with a vicious blow from the AK's barrel as I jammed it hard into his exposed gut, but still he remained upright. As we collided, I twisted the shirt around his throat to try to gain more control, but his size was surprising and he was strong! Without warning, he broke free and dropped into a fighting stance, right hand back, left one clenched. I sensed a blow heading for my temple and ducked it, taking the solid punch on the left jawbone. The inside of my head exploded in a bright flash of light. This guy could hit!

Stunned, I felt the left side of my head begin to go numb, but I got ready to duke it out. Sam was worthless, still standing where he crapped his pants, his mouth wide open, his eyes glued to us. The VC went for my rifle, which was now lying between us, and the fight was really on. We couldn't see where the weapon actually was, so it was a grappling fest as we scrambled around, punching and slugging each other on the ground. There was no sound other than our breathing. I couldn't believe he hadn't yelled for help, but for some reason my enemy was content to go one-on-one. My visibility sucked, and the blow had screwed up my balance. I saw the AK and crawled toward it, but the VC caught sight of it at the same time and made it his objective as well. He landed a well-placed kick to my ribs that nearly doubled me up. He knew how to hurt people, and I was finding out the hard way. I couldn't get my wind, but I was able to roll atop the weapon, grab it, and come up with the gold. He was screwed now and knew it. I watched him turn to flee, knowing if he got away we were all dead. Given the circumstances, we were all gonna die anyhow, I figured as I squeezed the trigger. We'd never make it to the river with all these gooks around.

I sent seven rounds his direction, two of them hitting him square in the upper back. He went flying, arms out to his sides. Four more rounds smashed into the man's lower back, breaking his spine and shutting down any coherent movement. I was already moving toward him when his shirt burst open and a mass of wet entrails spilled out onto the ground as he impacted. The VC raised his right hand toward the sky as if either pleading with or praying to the gods. It was spooky, really weird. An M-16 went off behind me, and a single round snatched the wounded man's life away for good. It was Peaches. Moving quietly—for once—he'd come up to support me, although I could tell he was super nervous.

The acrid stench of burned gunpowder combined with the sweet smell of fresh blood and human entrails, filling my nostrils and almost gagging me. I'd just killed my first man, up close and personal. A whole range of emotions and thoughts washed over me, drowning me with their intensity. It was a short-lived moment, though, as there was no time to stand around and have a group hug. VC rifle fire was coming at us with deadly accuracy and I yelled for a rocket to be fired into the hootch. "No way!" screamed Peaches. "They're for emergencies only!"

"What the hell do you think this is?" I screamed back at him.

"Walsh, get us outta here *now!*" ordered the officer.

"Rats," I muttered to myself even as I was moving. "I really wanted to fire that rocket!" The shoulder-fired rockets were great for breaking contact while on the run, as we now were, almost as good as the claymore mine with a thirty- or ninety-second delayed fuse screwed into it. Peaches didn't think about that stuff, though. He was on his first honest-to-Buddha combat nightmare and only wanted to get back on the boat as soon as possible. Where was Mr. Boles when we needed him? I wondered. I gave the young officer credit, though. He did put the gook out of his misery, which was more than I could say for Sam.

Naturally it had to get worse. The rear security had come up missing, and I thought back to the point where I couldn't see him while we were crawling up to the objective. It turned out that our machine gunner hadn't signaled the man that we were moving out and had left him over a kilometer behind! Frank had realized something was amiss, however, and had been working overtime to pick up our trail. When he heard the shooting he understood how badly split up we really were. Peaches was beside himself at hearing Frank was missing and went into a state of total confusion. With no time to lose, I popped a red star cluster into the sky, aiming it back toward the hootch. Frank spotted it and was not so far away that he couldn't pick up our silhouettes in the flare's dying glow. Like a snake in high gear he crawled up to our position, giving the machine gunner a look that told me we were going to see even more action once we got back to the base.

The VC were now on line and advancing toward us. They knew we were a small force because we didn't take them on. If they could get around us we would be done for, so Peaches ordered me to head straight for the river. I took off at a fast trot, using the trails, since the VC hadn't bothered to booby-trap them—at least we hadn't seen indications that they had. As we raced past one tiny hamlet a man stepped into an open doorway with an old bolt-action rifle in hand. I swung toward him, AK ready to let loose, but he was gone. Smart cookie, that one. Our radio man had already alerted the patrol boat, and it was en route to extract us. Seawolves were in the air, too, but we couldn't talk to them yet, although the coordinates for the command hootch would be sent up as soon as contact was made. The helos were armed with brand new mini-guns, however, so the boys needed some range time. It would be very bad for the VC when the Seawolves arrived on station, very bad indeed. But until then we had to survive. Peaches told us that the Seawolves were forty minutes away and had fuel for one pass only. At least we now knew that gunships were on the way.

Upon reaching the river, we slid down the steep, muddy bank and sat in the water. One man stayed on top of the bank watching our rear. We wouldn't forget him this time. I was dirty—soaked in sweat, blood, human grease, camouflage paint, and Lord knows what else. I could only enjoy the cool feel of the water and wish I could dive underneath it and clean myself completely. We were the same color as the earth around us and we could easily have faded into the environment even as the sun was coming up. But we could endure the situation because hell week and every day of BUD/S had conditioned us to accept being dirty as a normal state of existence.

The boat passed us twice before we got their attention. On the first pass I waved to the coxswain. We were sitting half in and half out of the water, completely camouflaged by the mud of the bank, all of us within arm's reach of each other. The coxswain could not see us and passed us by. The radio man started talking to the boat, which executed a turn and passed closer to the bank while the radioman talked the pilot to our position. Someone sent a flashlight signal, and the boat headed straight for us. They looked amazed when they finally spotted us moments before the boat touched the muddy riverbank, and we climbed aboard. After that, the extraction went off without a hitch, and we headed home. Another day, another dime. I wanted a cold Miller, a shower, and some time alone. It had been one heck of a mission, any way you cut it.

I later found out that the man I had fought in the dark was a Vietcong general. Sam, our foul-smelling Viet SEAL, explained that he'd heard the other Vietcong yelling for the "general" and calling his name as they ran toward our position. When we returned to base we sifted through the materials we'd taken from the dead man's pockets. I'd pulled 10,000 Piastres in South Vietnamese currency off him, including a 100-piastre note which was covered with precise little stamps. The piastre was the currency of South Vietnam at the time, and was then worth 118 to the dollar. When this bill was examined it turned out to be his safe conduct pass all the way from Hanoi to Vinh Long! Our intelligence folks confirmed the man was indeed a flag officer. Further, that he'd been sent to the South to personally plan and organize a second Tet offensive to follow on the heels of the 1968 nightmare. Mr. Boles told me later, after we'd gotten the final rundown on our operation, "You're going to be a great point man, maggot." As always, Lee Pittman had the final word.

"Sure he will . . . as long as I'm there to keep him straight!" Lee was never one to let me get a big head. He was a great operator. As for the dead general . . . better him than me, I figured. But, oh, how that man could punch!

10

Chau Doc

After three months at Vinh Long it was time for Charlie platoon to find new hunting grounds. Operating too long in any one area tends to create patterns, and patterns get you killed. There are only so many places to infiltrate and so many others to get out of. The VC and VCI weren't stupid, and they badly wanted to bloody the SEALs for all the grief we were causing them. So we packed our bags and found new digs.

Chau Doc was a hot province situated adjacent to Cambodia at the northern edge of the IV Corps tactical zone. This province, was home to a multitude of ethnic groups including Chams, Hao Hao, Chinese, and Vietnamese-Cambodians. The Three Sisters and Seven Sisters mountain ranges were impressive obstacles as well as hideaways for the VC. Outside Chau Doc itself was the mountain of Nui Sam. The Viets considered this small mountain a holy shrine complete with its own goddess. We would use Nui Sam as an observation point, watching the comings and goings of the infamous black marketeers who traded between both countries. Goods included huge herds of cattle that were smuggled to and fro; from atop the peak we sometimes watched them coming or going from as far as twenty miles away inside Cambodia.

Cambodia offered miles of flat land from the base of the Seven Sisters onward. There was thick jungle at the base of the ranges, which tended to move southward. The Vinh Te canal runs parallel to the border and many consider it the actual border between Vietnam and Cambodia. The French had dug the canal, and it runs as straight as an arrow for miles. Chau Doc would prove to be a difficult area for us to operate in, and a prophetic killing ground.

We'd brought our floating home with us from Vinh Long

to Chau Doc, the navy barge being as secure a place as we could devise given the VC's excellent intelligence network. Also on board were the River Division guys who operated our PBRs. These patrol boats were thirty-one feet long and could crunch their way into the heart of Vietnam's river systems. The River Division crews were top notch and always there when we needed them most. Of course we kept two gunships from the Seawolves on rotation from Can Tho, for obvious reasons. When we needed close air support we needed it immediately. Nothing brought more pain to the VC than the Seawolves, unless it was us on the ground and in their face, that is.

With the barge anchored in and all the political handshaking taken care of in town, we got started with our visual reconnaissance of the province. Mr. Boles and I wanted a good feel for the terrain we'd be operating in. Since Wayne was the officer in charge and I was the platoon's point man, the task fell to us. Visual reconnaissance gives the officer a better idea of the tactical situation he might end up facing, and it helps the point man get a handle on the kind of ground he's going to have to cover. We were preparing to begin long patrols and wanted all the intelligence we could gather about the area of operations.

SEAL Team ONE tended to specialize in short patrols, raids, and ambushes. But with the top-quality warrant officers we got from SEAL Team TWO this changed—in my opinion for the better. These warrant officers were long-range fanatics. They respected the unconventional warfare doctrine being developed at the time and dived into it with their flippers on. The new warrants brought this new manner of operating with them. Bear in mind that they were all former enlisted SEALs who had elected to go for a commission. Mr. Boles, for example, was cut from this mold. Pat Patterson, Malcolm Campbell, Jes Tolison, and Ed Jones are but the few who helped set the trend at SEAL Team ONE where evolutionary tactics were concerned. Once they arrived on the West Coast their input went right to BUD/S and it was then that we really began taking long-range patrolling seriously. And when you worked for Warrant Officer Boles, every patrol was long range. He taught me a lot.

The concept of raids gained increasing attention as the

war dragged on. Our inventory of nasty little tricks grew larger as well. All of this demanded we learn how the intelligence wheel operated because you can't go long-range or run successful raids without excellent intelligence beforehand. Each provincial capital had its own tactical operations center (TOC), normally managed by the U.S. Army. It was here we soon began to hang out. I had learned very quickly while at Vinh Long not to trust the U.S. side any more than the Vietnamese, as most every TOC was a combined operation between the two. Security at these centers was poor in many respects, especially where SEALs were concerned.

For example, during one visit we'd entered the TOC and found to our grim surprise a blacked-out grid square marked on the provincial map. Inside the square was one word: "SEALs"! Talk about being compromised from the get-go. Earlier we'd chatted with a U.S. soldier who'd defected to the VC. We later learned that he was calling in artillery fire on us while we talked to him. He had dialed in our radio frequency and was happily exchanging insults with the squad even as rounds were landing all around us! Where he'd gotten his intel was of concern, and we surmised that it probably came out of some screwup at the TOC level.

After the map incident we devised a method of safely clearing an area we would be operating in. We'd give the TOC a sealed envelope prior to going out, instructing them to open the document only upon radio authorization from us. This way neither the U.S. side nor the Vietnamese would have prior knowledge of what we were up to. It was fairly well accepted that every TOC in Vietnam was infiltrated by the VC or NVA and that ongoing enemy intelligence operations were gobbling up information from a hundred different sources a day. The bottom line was that we had to take care of ourselves, especially when operating in an area like Chau Doc.

The Paris peace talks were just getting under way as we settled in Chau Doc and began running operations. First we ran a series of night patrols up and down the Vinh Te canal. We wanted to ascertain whether or not the VC or NVA were actually crossing from Cambodia into Vietnam, which was a big no-no. One evening we crept up onto the bank on the Cambodian side of the canal and set up a portable radar unit. It began registering contacts immediately. On the other side of the canal was an enemy column, which our radar team tracked as it moved quickly back into Cambodia. Our confirmation of the illegal infiltration route excited me. It meant we'd have some good hunting back in Vietnam, and that prospect made Chau Doc a great place to be.

Several days later the U.S. outpost at Tinh Binh called to tell us they had a defector who could pinpoint on the map where a suspected NVA base camp was located. As intelligence poured in, we began planning. A base camp was a major score, and we wanted one badly.

On the night of the operation we set out from the outpost prepared for a hard evening's work. I'd brought the squad roughly two kilometers when I heard a strange noise just ahead of me. We'd just exited a tree line and were preparing to cross an open area before regaining the cover of another forest when I spotted a dike. These made great barriers against being spotted and against being struck by small arms fire, so I headed toward it, intending to move parallel to it until we were safely inside the next tree line. As I moved farther down the track, the noise got louder. And suddenly, I realized what it was.

Right in front of me were five local Vietnamese militiamen known as Ruff Puffs, our name for the Regional Force/Popular Force troops developed under several U.S. programs, including CORDS or Civil Operations Revolutionary Development Support. They were sound asleep and snoring. We crept up on them, took their weapons, and sent them back down the trail. I didn't want to get shot in the back, and we wanted to teach these clowns a lesson. I hope it worked.

By the early hours of the morning we were all feeling the effects of the march. Breaks were few and far between as the warrant was so totally focused on the mission. We had to remind him about taking a breather now and then, and I figure it was the Red Man chewing tobacco that kept him so wired up. We hit a well-used trail and decided to set up an ambush position just to see if any main force NVA units were using it. Along for the ride were three U.S. Army types from the district headquarters. They were so noisy that we began to worry about being compromised. The warrant had a little heart-to-heart talk with them, and all of a sudden they got real quiet. I also noted Lee Pittman in conference with one of the men, that kill-ya cobra look in his eyes.

Shortly thereafter I heard voices. Our Vietnamese SEAL went rigid like a pointer. I swear if he'd had a tail it would have been straight out. "NVA!" he whispered to me.

"How do you know?" I responded.

"They speak North Vietnamese," he offered.

Wayne put everyone on alert and grabbed me and the Viet SEAL. We moved forward to gather more poop and discovered that the trail we were on ran right into a large bivouac area where troops could rest and relax while on the march. Boles urged us on, and we crept closer and closer until the insects stopped singing. Then we stopped moving, an old Indian trick from our own Wild West. I checked my watch and saw it was just after 0200 hours. There was a dike ahead about three feet high. At its base was a barrier of twisted jungle vines. On top of the dike walked an NVA guard. I told Sam to stay put as I didn't want him freaking out again and ruining another perfectly good uniform. Boles and I continued on, weaving our way toward the camp.

As I hit the edge of the vine barrier I realized what it was. The NVA used the vines much like we used concertina wire. It's thick, hard to cross, and certain to create noise so as to alert the roving sentry. It also had the advantage of channeling the unwise or unskilled into an area where a booby trap or machine gun awaited. As I was lying on the ground face down trying to figure out my next move, the guard slipped right up on my position and was standing over me. I couldn't move, and I was holding my breath. As I started getting light-headed I began letting the stale air out of my lungs slowly. I must have sounded like a water buffalo, but the guard didn't seem to notice. I was not a happy camper.

Turning my head, I was disappointed not to find Wayne anywhere near me. The insects were dead silent. The guard dropped into a squat and lit a cigarette. The light of his match played over my black pajamas and sandals, but he'd blinded himself by staring into the tiny flame and didn't spot my outline on the ground. The waiting game began. I prayed Sam didn't go off half-cocked. We were at the edge of a major NVA base camp, and there was no place to run where they wouldn't find us. Now the guard was humming a little ditty, his cigarette smoking away. I couldn't—

wouldn't—move. I focused my attention elsewhere so as not to give off bad vibes that the guard might have picked up. It was quiet inside the camp. Instincts work both ways—it didn't matter who you were, friend or enemy; the combat environment brought out the primitive in all of us. We had practiced not focusing our attention on someone, looking at him with our peripheral vision instead. With this in mind, I checked to see if my sleeve was covering the luminous dial of my watch. Normally the face was hidden by a snap-on leather sleeve. Mine was in place.

I needed a plan in case I was discovered. Would I shoot or go for a hands-on approach, as I done with the general? My body was stiff from tension and cold, so moving quickly was going to be quite interesting. My ribs ached from lying on something sharp and there was nothing I could do to ease the growing discomfort. Thankfully, my wide-brimmed jungle hat looked exactly like the ground I was cemented to. Just needed to be patient and hope for the best.

The guard finishes his smoke and flicked the butt into the jungle. As he got to his feet I tensed, expecting to be discovered. Instead, I heard water flowing and realized he was peeing all over me! If it wasn't Sam the SEAL crapping his drawers it was the NVA whizzing on mine. Nothing to do but wait it out. The guard finished up and moved off. Crawling slowly backward, I moved to where I thought Mr. Boles might be. But he wasn't there. Two clicking sounds reached my ears and I moved to my right. It was Wayne, and he wanted to know what had happened.

"You wouldn't believe it," I told him.

After picking up Sam, we linked up with the patrol. The Viet SEAL explained that he'd overhead an entire NVA company was sleeping in the bivouac site. Boles huddled us up and told us we would wait until the company moved off before checking out the area. A security watch was set up, and I grabbed about an hour's sleep. I was beat, but then, so was everyone else.

At first light we began slowly to enter the NVA camp. The barrier was obvious, but I couldn't locate the entrance. Wayne ordered me to find a hole, and I began feeling my way along the leafy structure, hoping to trigger a hidden doorway. Instead, I triggered a booby trap, and as the *ting* of the grenade's spoon reached my ears a second too late, I took the full blast in my face. Thrown back, I hit the ground hard. My eyes were open, but I couldn't see anything out of the left one. The right was blurry, and everything was numb. I asked myself why I was lying on my back, which seemed stupid.

The squad was already braced for an attack. But it didn't come, and Mr. Boles was checking me out. "Ya gotta quit taking these unauthorized breaks, Mike," he told me as he wiped my face clean. "They're slowing us down." I was a bit shaken, to say the least, and Wayne knew this. His attempt at humor was meant to calm me down, loosen me up. The grenade had gone off on a low plane; had it been set higher I'd have been a dead SEAL. The corpsman moved up to bandage the left side of my head, and Boles asked me if I still wanted the point.

"Yep," I answered.

"See if you can't find us a way in there," he ordered me with a smile on his face. Right, boss, anything you want. Mr. Boles's belief in me did wonders, and I grabbed my weapon and got with the program.

As we slipped into the camp, we were stunned by its intricate trench network. The army personnel were put on security and the rest of us began searching for anything of interest. Someone uncovered a cache of documents meant for whoever occupied the camp next. Sam translated each one for us, and we copied down radio codes and other vital information. Some papers we took, others we left behind. The frequencies were important, as we could monitor them without the NVA knowing. Moving to the command-control portion of the camp I uncovered a Chinese antipersonnel mine mounted on a tripod and ready to blow. I stared it right in the kisser and felt very insignificant. Talk about having all the luck in the world! First I got pissed on, then blinded, and now I was looking to become a hamburger patty courtesy of the People's Republic of China. Mr. Boles padded up behind me. "Ah-so, nice claymore eh, G.I.?"

I checked it out and found it had been disarmed by the previous night's campers. Each group of NVA that passed through put their own fuse in the bomb and then removed it for the next unit. Made sense to me. The mine was large, very heavy, and would only slow down a group wanting to make time on the trail. We decided to booby trap the booby trap, just for grins. In addition, we threw in a rigged

Instamatic camera, two GI canteens, and one U.S. issue claymore of our own. Push the button on the camera and it would all be over. Twist the tops off the canteens and same ending. The claymore was set up with a trembler switch. Any movement of the mine whatsoever would set it off. Payback is a mutha!

I loved these devices and used them every chance I had when operating in Vietnam. It got to the point I would carry gasoline in my canteens. I got my water from the jars at virtually every hootch we passed by during patrols. I used the gas to burn down every hootch I came across that had either bad guys or their propaganda present. Another method of harassment was to urinate on VC rice caches, leaving a note for the owners saying we'd done so. The big outfits liked to mount major recovery operations for just such food stocks. They'd put up security, call in helicopters to load the rice or whatever out, and then use it as a propaganda tool elsewhere. Small, unconventional forces like our own didn't have the time, manpower, or interest. We moved light and fast. In special warfare, you do things differently. Once we found a hog farm in the middle of the U Minh Forest and destroyed every creature alive. I didn't like this kind of thing, but I did a lot of things I didn't like or approve of personally. Food kept the enemy going, and if he was going, he was going after us. Deny him food and some slack entered the play of the game. That's what we did, period.

Once the booby traps were set, we headed back to the district headquarters. Army medics patched me up proper and pulled the grenade's shrapnel from my neck. In a week I was as good as new. Mr. Boles was busy planning our next operation, and we used the downtime to relax, clean equipment, and chill out. We were gearing up to do a reconnoiter of the entire trail system around the base of the Seven Sisters mountains. We'd be out for some time, walking our buns off and facing untold numbers of hostiles. I began mentally preparing myself for what I knew would be a killer patrol.

We launched from the Army Special Forces camp at Ba Xuy. It was a great camp, well laid out, as most SF compounds were. The Green Berets put a lot of detail into their camps, making them hard to attack successfully and harder yet to overrun. If a Special Forces camp was overrun, it meant they'd been hit by everything but the kitchen sink. Much of the SEALs' doctrine comes from Special Forces. We figured that if it worked for the Berets, we could use it, with some minor modification, to meet our needs. As most of the time our missions were special reconnaissance, direct action, counterterrorism, or limited civic action, the material we obtained from the Special Forces was of great help.

The platoon left Ba Xuy around mid-evening. We figured the less the Vietnamese present knew about what we were up to, the better. I was carrying my AK-47 with six magazines, one claymore mine, five M-26 frag grenades, one LAAW rocket, two canteens of high-octane gas, one smoke grenade, and one morphine syringe hung around my neck. I led my equally burdened squad of SEALs north toward the Vinh Te canal. Anyone working against us and watching would report our direction of travel to the VC, so we gave them some bad information right off the bat. About three kilometers out we turned abruptly west and ran along a tree line. For a while we stopped and pulled a security halt just to see if anyone was dogging us. The trail was clear. Moving onward I pulled an azimuth south toward the base of the Seven Sisters. We moved all night without making contact.

When the sun came up, we were still on the trail. I saw a sign stuck to a tree and moved forward to investigate. It read Tudia—danger. My adrenaline began to pump. We were about to enter—or were already inside—an area that was booby-trapped big-time. Mr. Boles would want to check out the area, so I pretended not to see the sign and began taking us away from the spot. Wayne caught up with me and motioned toward the written warning. "Well, whaddaya know?" I offered. "Must not have seen it, boss."

Boles looked me dead in the eye. "Get me in there, midget."

"Are you sure we want to do this?" I asked.

A thick gob of chew landed on the ground by my feet. "Look," he says, "that sign means there's something hidden away that the VC want to protect. I want to know what that is . . . I mean, when's the last time the VC warned us about booby traps?"

Good point, and I knew it. I shrugged my rucksack a little

tighter and began heading back toward the danger zone. My concentration was trashed by this time from working point all night and I barely noticed the nasty little things scattered all about the trail we were now creeping down. Mortar shells were rigged from trees so they'd explode when they fell down on us—an old Belgian gate booby trap no longer functional but no less scary to look at. We were moving deeper into the jungle when I stepped on a Bouncing Betty. *Ting!* No, not that sound again. A Bouncing Betty is an explosive device placed in a pipe, tin can, or a thick piece of bamboo off to one side of a trail. As you step on the mine's activator the charge is propelled straight up in the air about four to six feet before it explodes, usually killing everyone nearby. It was bad news for me, and I knew it.

My eyes swiveled toward the mine as it left its deadly nest. It flew up into the air over my head, and I just reached up and grabbed it. Then I held on and waited for the explosion to send me to SEAL heaven. Nothing. It didn't go off. I was standing there on the trail with a Bouncing Betty in my right hand, looking back at the rest of the squad, which was moving very quickly back down the trail away from me. Nowhere to go and not a lot I could do except hold what I'd caught and keep praying for rain.

"I told you the little dummy was denser than a box full of rocks!" Pittman said to no one in particular. In response, I threw the mine as far as I could into the jungle. Nothing. No explosion. A dud. I looked back at Mr. Boles, and he spit a wad onto the jungle floor. I got the message: time to quit screwing around and get back to work.

Not more than twenty feet later I stepped into a perfectly camouflaged hole. The reed mat went flying and I could now see a trip wire tied around a small stick running the length of the square hole. I followed the wire to a shrub and peered around the back of it. A U.S. fragmentation grenade was strapped to the stump, its safety spoon removed. Only a common safety pin was holding the detonator in place . . . and just barely.

I gulped down deep drafts of oxygen and turned to brief Wayne, who'd come up behind me. He got down on one knee, and I was grateful for his presence. We elected to secure the booby trap and I reached around and pushed the pin back in so it fully secured the firing device in place. Mr. Boles was staring at me with a curious gleam in his eyes. "There has to be someone around to maintain all these things, right?" he said. I nodded in agreement. Too many traps and most in semi-working order. We'd just been lucky, dirt lucky, that none of them had blown. "Then let's find out where he lives," said Wayne.

Before moving out I was ordered to blow the grenade in place. I pulled the fifty-foot rope out of my ruck and carefully hooked it up to the booby trap. After moving down the trail a safe distance I stopped and gave the line a tug and *boom!* the grenade detonated. When the VC came to investigate they would find nothing, which would freak them out. It would add to the growing SEAL legend, which made the enemy fear us even more.

On the way back out of this nightmare killing ground Lee stumbled across a trail I'd missed coming in. Thirty meters down it we found a large earthen bunker which had been heavily reinforced with logs. Sam entered first, then emerged and told us the booby trap squad lived there. I pulled my gear off and squeezed into the bunker. Tit for tat, Mr. Charles. Digging a hole under where one of the VC had placed his makeshift pillow, I neatly laid in my Claymore rigged to go off when disturbed. Once I'd set the screw, I filled in the hole and neatly cleaned the place up. I laid the VC's reed mat and little pillow back out, all nice and neat like we'd found it.

As we were leaving a tree line on our way back to safety, a sniper opened up on the squad. The rounds came closer and closer to us, but we simply taunted the unseen gunman. Finally, rounds started smacking into the ground about three feet from our positions. Mr. Boles pointed out that snipers liked to kill radiomen and everyone pulled away from where Pittman was holed up. He didn't find our clowning around at his expense funny. On Wayne's signal we let loose with a wall of lead toward the sniper's position and hit the trail at a trot. Enough goofing around for the day. It was time to go home.

Back at district headquarters we relayed the booby-trapped area's coordinates to the gunships, and they headed inland to wreak havoc. A bomb damage assessment conducted by the army later revealed that eight VC had crowded into the bunker to escape the Seawolf gunships' wrath. Someone apparently decided to take a little nap during all the shooting, and the claymore accomplished its mission.

Not a bad day's work.

11

The Phoenix Program

Over the years since the Vietnam War ended I've seen a great deal of bad press and misinformation about Phoenix. Not only have the American media distorted, and in fact fabricated, a false history of what the program was all about, but sad little men claiming wartime honor and affiliation as SEALs have wrapped themselves in Phoenix pins and badges, claiming to have been card-carrying assassins on the payroll of Uncle Sam's naval elite. Until now most of us who actually participated in the program have kept to ourselves. The fantasy-ridden opinions and observations of the media are not really our concern. But since I left the navy it has become important to me that Phoenix be put in perspective, from an operator's point of view. Why? Because it worked!

The Phoenix program had one main purpose: to identify, locate, and neutralize the Vietcong Infrastructure (VCI), that invisible enemy government that patterned and paralleled the legitimate Government of South Vietnam (GVN). Phoenix remained focused and ready to simply move in at every level and take control. The Phoenix program existed in virtually every province of South Vietnam.

SEAL training never stops. Never. Not for a moment. This is something every operator understands. If you want it done right, you must train for it. It was our unique training for Phoenix that set us apart from the other services. And until now no one's ever spoken about this specific and dynamic program conducted in the arid mountains of southern California.

Pre-Phoenix indoctrination was conducted at Camp Machen in the Cuymaca Mountains east of San Diego. That camp, named for the first SEAL killed in Vietnam, was nothing more than a clearing in the woods that offered a reinforced bunker for ammo storage. Pretty simple, pretty sparse. That's the way we did it in the old days. The program was six weeks in duration, and every minute was dead serious. We studied combat tactics, intelligence gathering, land navigation, communications, combat medicine, reconnaissance organization, more weapons, and most important, how to use one's head as a Phoenix adviser.

Of specific interest to me were the classes on intelligence, as this is what Phoenix was all about. We delved into basic agent handling, recruiting, record keeping, how to set up an intelligence network, and how to maintain it. We learned how to read photographs correctly, which was easy for me, because photographic intelligence was my naval specialty. It was during this period that I discovered my love for and ability in the field of planning and executing solid intelligence operations. In retrospect, Jane's a lucky girl.

The Provincial Reconnaissance Unit, or PRU, was our primary means of carrying out Phoenix ops. At Machen, we were introduced to PRU camp organization and management, a new concept to almost all who'd been selected for future Phoenix assignments. We worked off the army's Special Forces doctrine, which was going great guns in Vietnam at the time. The methods of the Green Berets are tried and true, and you can't go wrong relying on their doctrine as a basic tool in special warfare. For the rest of my career I'd run into guys from the Special Forces who were plying their unique trade the world over. They got the job done in El Salvador using many of the concepts developed during Vietnam. Hats off to you, gentlemen.

At age twenty-two, I was the youngest guy in our Phoenix training class. I was also the least experienced, so I took a number of direct hits during the first tactical problems given us. After one exercise, which I had totally bungled, our group was standing around in a semicircle while the instructor, Frank Flynn, issued his critique of the operation. "Better to start off with a bloody nose, Mike," he told me. "This way you'll remember how *not* to do it when the real thing comes along." He was right. I swallowed my pride and never forgot the lesson. The object of the exercise was to teach us how to communicate with foreign senior officers, namely Vietnamese province chiefs. The province chief, usually an army colonel, was the senior military Vietnamese officer in the province. We were taught from day one that all of them were corrupt. The lesson was to get a PRU mission order signed. Dick Pierson, an instructor, played the role of province chief. When I failed to realize that I wouldn't get the mission order signed until I had "imaginatively appropriated" a new air conditioner for the colonel, the exercise ended.

The six weeks I spent in the mountains offered one challenge after another, and because I was so high of spirit I was a bit difficult to manage. Nonetheless, Frank Flynn handled me like the professional he was, though not without a bit of help.

As serious as we were during this period, there were the usual SEAL high jinks. Dick Pierson, then known as "Atomic Jaws," was a Phoenix instructor—very tough, an excellent SEAL operator, and remarkably knowledgeable about medicine. He also possessed a loud mouth, no question about that. Dick had been one of my diving instructors during UDT training, and now we were together again. This time I was much cockier, thanks to being fully qualified as a SEAL rather than miserable as a tadpole.

We'd heard that two movie actresses had shown up at a small resort near where we were training. The instructors, whose intelligence net had somehow brought them this information, were already visiting the resort and flexing their macho SEAL muscles while spinning war stories to the impressionable young ladies. Invited to go along for a look, I shaved, threw some money in my pockets, and joined Atomic Jaws for the date. One of the actresses was short and very petite. Her companion was the exact opposite—tall and built like an Amazon warrior. Dick and I zeroed in on her upon our arrival at the pool. Both women were blondes and very well put together.

Pierson and I poured down far too many glasses of beer and began arguing about who was going home with whom. Dick had the high card, though: he was an instructor and I was a mere mortal, so the outcome was preordained. One thing led to another, and I was ordered back to camp . . . alone. I've never liked losing, so on my way home I stopped in the parking lot and let the air out of all four of Dick's car tires. In true SEAL fashion I didn't stop there, knowing he'd have a backup plan for just such a move on my part. So out went the air from the actresses' Jaguar, too. Big mistake on my part.

Much later that night a band of instructors kicked in our hootch door with guns blazing. They grabbed my naked butt and dragged me to another building where they hog-tied me and then wrapped me in a wool military blanket. Then they put me on ice . . . literally. They stuffed me into an old Coca-Cola ice chest atop a mass of Coke bottles, all nicely iced and most uncomfortable. My kidnappers poured water all over the blanket I was wrapped in, just to add to my discomfort, then slammed the ice chest shut and locked it. I figured Dick didn't have too great a sense of humor over my little stunt with his tires.

It turned out one of the women had given Pierson the nod to take her to a nice quiet spot for some heavy R&R, but the flattened tires on both cars killed the mood—and Dick's chances. He insisted that I beg for mercy before he'd let me out of the chill box, but I refused to. "I'll die first, Pierson!" I yelled back at him. I wouldn't give in, but neither would Dick. I decided I'd just go to sleep; after all, I'd been plenty more uncomfortable than this. Frank Flynn finally persuaded everyone to let me out, as he knew if I died in a Coca-Cola chest there'd be some serious flak headed his way. I had to keep a sharp eye out for Dick for some time afterward, but in the end we grew to like each other, sort of.

In Phoenix training we spent a great deal of time learning how to make things work and figuring out why they didn't work. The major challenges revolved around getting the mission accomplished when others were either not working, unresponsive, or uncaring. Today our young SEALs are much better prepared after their initial training. In the old days, we were still formulating what a Navy SEAL and a SEAL Team should be. The only thing I see lacking in the new kids is the blood-and-guts mental steel, mixed with a bit of outlaw mentality that makes men win when bad has gone to worse. A SEAL needs to be a tough, honest man with mettle, not a criminal with a chip on his shoulder and a complete disregard for anyone or anything other than himself. We're seeing some of the best kids our society has to offer coming into the Teams today, but I wish they had a more solid base of core values to fall back on during the tough times.

I learned to think on my feet during this period. Really think, questioning everything and ticking off the options and alternatives. I learned to lock my file cabinet when leaving the embassy house, to watch my back, never to trust the obvious. We were expected to survive, prevail, and conquer as lone wolves in the Phoenix environment. After all, we were being licensed to hunt the most dangerous prey in the war, the VC infrastructure.

There was quite a bit of note taking, all of it practical. We enjoyed a close working relationship with Special Forces, and one young SF captain, himself a former PRU adviser, taught our group his intelligence methodology. Enter Captain Geoff Barker, U.S. Army, who I truly believe must have been a navy man in a former life. Barker could travel light, his entire intelligence system fitting into a single briefcase. He told us he could go anywhere in his province and be immediately in the know. I was curious, and decided Captain Barker was someone I had to get to know much, much better.

Geoff's whole intelligence system was predicated on the military grid reference system, or how we are taught to read maps and navigate. Geoff developed his system so he could better track the infamous figure eight movements of high-level, or priority target, VCI. Barker broke his area of operations into 10,000 meter squares. He then added a color-code system to plot his intelligence information using six-figure universal transverse Mercator coordinates, the standard format for military map reading. Barker plotted the known or suspected locations of both friendly and enemy agents on his intel map, not caring if he knew specific names or agencies, only that he knew someone was operating there. He then developed a source control chart to help him keep track of the information routinely provided by intelligence agencies.

The source control chart allowed the Phoenix adviser to levy the necessary requirements in terms of material support and manpower to either confirm or deny the raw information coming in from various collection methods. It also allowed us, as Phoenix advisers, to plant bad information in the system without tipping our hand to other Vietnamese intelligence agencies we were unfriendly with, or suspect of. Many times we'd discover agents working for other projects. When this happened we'd drop them like a hot rock. You couldn't serve two masters in this game.

We used several different colors in plotting. Green, for example, stood for VCI. After implementing my own system I soon had a small map of my province in Vietnam filled with colored dots. By careful tracking and management I was able to discern the pattern of movement the bad guys were following. This took about a month of careful study and hard work. I combined our order-of-battle map with a captured VCI chart and was therefore able to track their military support units in conjunction with those of the VCI. With time, I was able to trace the movements of individual VCI figures, ultimately resolving the problem of where to intercept the individual with a Phoenix snatch operation.

Using Captain Barker's blueprint for success, we could locate and fix a VCI target, then simply stake out his house. I paid informants to keep the place under surveillance twenty-four hours a day until the target showed up. Anyone with a family was vulnerable, and sooner or later everyone came home. In Phoenix operations we exploited this truism to its fullest potential.

I had to teach my reconnaissence unit that counter-terrorist tactics were unacceptable. We wanted—needed —the VCI alive so that we could learn more about their activities and possibly turn them into an intelligence asset for ourselves. Dead men tell no tales, and in intelligence work you need people talking. It's pretty tough to inter-rogate a corpse, so I concentrated on getting my boys to give up the counterterrorist dead-bang mode and start making arrests. People sometimes died during a snatch, but after a while we sorted out the attitude problems and our record improved.

Today I can't help but equate our Phoenix experience with the international drug war. We enjoyed a large war chest during Phoenix, and I could draw up to $10,000 from the program without having to answer serious questions about its intended use. Just sign the receipt and hit the trail. We began searching for VCI within business and religious institutions, making contacts and connections, finding out who the players were. We then expanded our intelligence-gathering network by finding out who could be bought, bribed, controlled, intimidated, or all of the above. Money talks. In Phoenix we played as hard as the bad guys—who apparently had a better public affairs staff than we could muster—and I could back up any threat I needed to make. After all, 105 PRU operators was a fairly sizable force in addition to the seventeen Chinese Nung mercenaries. We first learned all of this during training at Machen. But in the field the challenge was to make it work. Geoff used to say, "Agents in place, and separate the wheat from the chaff." In intelligence work there's lots—no, tons—of chaff. The beauty in Barker's system was that it left you with only wheat germ in your briefcase if you maintained it correctly. Today our special forces operators are learning to rely more and more on high-tech wiz-bang devices to get the job done. We're bringing in so many administrative support pukes to assist the field operators that the community is losing its Special Operations Forces attitude in favor of the restrictive conventional mind-set. Only simplicity succeeds in combat. Just look at Haiti and Somalia for a point of reference.

At Phoenix training and later in the field in Vietnam, we relied on warriors, not clones or office pogues. In the system I've described I've been careful to leave out plotting and systemic details for reasons of security. The program of instruction has evolved since Vietnam and has been used in Latin America and the Gulf with great success. Although I can no longer go to war, others can and have to. The critical aspect of Phoenix was our decision to take away the enemies' command-control-communications network, or to cut the head off the snake. To do this we needed solid information, which meant live bodies. Yes, people died under various circumstances and conditions. This was war at its most brutal level. But as a SEAL adviser I did my best to fight as honorably and fairly as possible against an enemy that did not practice similar restrictions. To win we had to destroy the snake's head . . . or as many as we could find.

12

Operation Phoenix:
Uncovering the VCI

From day one at SEAL Team One we studied the Vietcong infrastructure, discussed it, then studied it some more. Our training operations kept pace with the latest developments reported to us as SEAL platoons came back from Vietnam. I studied and memorized my little yellow manual entitled "The Viet Cong Infrastructure, Modus Operandi of Selected Political Cadre" until I was almost VCI myself. It was the bible of Phoenix operations, and I've maintained my records of such material all these years.

Our basic Phoenix operation was the snatch, or kidnapping, of VCI personnel. It became an art form for the SEALs, and I conducted over fifty such ops during my tour as a Phoenix adviser. No one could snatch like the Teams, and for very good reasons. My first practice exercise took place in the mountains east of San Diego. There was a retired gunnery sergeant named Bill Rogers who, along with his wife Doris, took care of the local Boy Scout camp. Bill, who liked to tip the bottle—who didn't back then?—agreed to support our training program any way he could. Doris was our point of contact, or friendly agent, and it was she who would set Bill up for the snatch.

On my watch we set Bill up and made ready until he and Doris were in bed. On a signal we came through the doors, grabbed and subdued Bill, then carried him away to the lake for some humility training. About the fourth time we did this, Bill began to get a bit sore at being woken up so dramatically. We hit the door and this time he really fought us, but to no avail. After hog-tying him, we moved his unconscious body to the lake where we stripped him naked, then tied him face-up between two canoes which we then set adrift on the lake. When Bill woke up early in the morning only to discover his predicament, well, some awful things were bellowed out concerning our combined family trees! Frank Flynn ordered us to retrieve Bill "before he starts attracting tourists."

We practiced on other folks as well.

Another favorite target was the Camp Fire Girls. One night we raided their camp and tried making off with one of the older, more mature beauties and ran into the battle-ax who was responsible for their safety. She told us in no uncertain terms that we would face kidnapping charges if we came back one more time. Remembering our encounter with Larry La Page—as well as with the old man afterward —we elected to leave the young women alone . . . at least for a while.

Prisoner handling was conducted along the San Diego–Mexican border. We went out as squads and intercepted illegals as they scurried across the border. I learned to search both men and women thoroughly, as we later would in Vietnam. We took the men's clothes as the VC were reported to be experts at hiding documents and weapons in these. We were careful with female prisoners, though. We conducted a pat-down for hidden weapons and whatever was in pockets. Later they would be searched at the provincial interrogation center.

Once prisoners were turned over to the Vietnamese it was anyone's guess as to what really happened. The My Lai trials were on everyone's mind and no one wanted to go home to a court-martial. Searches had to be done quickly, as once a capture was made and shooting had started, the wisest course of action was to get out of there. People, being ingenious creatures, will find clever places to hide things. I once discovered NVA top secret documents wrapped around the batteries of a flashlight during just such a search. Training pays off.

Once on a training exercise we ran into the wrong bunch of illegals and were taken under fire from automatic weapons right there on the U.S./Mexican border. There we were, big bad SEALs with nothing more than a magazine full of blanks. After this incident we never conducted these exercises without half the team being fully armed, and I have never gone anywhere without a firearm since. In those days you could check your issue handgun out on a near-permanent basis, and even M16s found their way out to the desert over those long weekends.

When the French made their way to Vietnam in the 18th century they brought with them the Jesuit priests whose mission it was to save pagan souls in Southeast Asia. The Jesuits became embroiled in Vietnamese politics, which is something they specialize in, as their involvement in Latin America during recent times demonstrates. It is, in my professional opinion, a track record written in the blood of innocents. This immersion and rapidly growing intervention into all facets of Vietnamese society soon spawned a violent response, and the doors were opened for French military intervention. Battle between these two national forces erupted and led to open warfare. It came to an end when the French were defeated at Dien Bien Phu in 1954.

This entire chain of events, along with over two thousand years of fighting between the Vietnamese and the powers that attempted to dominate them, led to the birth of the original Vietcong Infrastructure in the Ca Mau province of South Vietnam. There is no more horrible piece of dirt to fight a war in than this province, save for the Rung Sat Special Zone. Ca Mau is home to the U Minh (Forest of Assassins) and Nam Cahn forests, and I never ran more difficult operations as a SEAL than here. The triple-canopy jungle blocks out the sunlight so totally that you operate in darkness even at noon. At night the jungle is so eerily black it becomes difficult to describe. I can only thank my dad for his unique approach to curing my fear of the dark. You could step one foot off the trail and completely disappear from view, so thick and dark was this hell on earth.

The VCI organization was composed of the People's Revolutionary Party (PRP) whose existence was officially acknowledged in 1962, the year I started high school. The PRP was the southern branch of North Vietnam's formal Communist Party, and it was ruled with an iron hand by the Central Office of South Vietnam or COSVN.

This is where we came into the picture at Phoenix. It was my job as an adviser to target the VCI from the COSVN level downward, to include the hamlet and individual sublevels so important to their control. The lowest common denominator in Vietnam was the hamlet, the most basic community unit of the society. A hamlet was part of a village; a village was part of a district or county. Districts made up a province, which we would consider a state. We split the country into four corps-level tactical zones as a war fighting command, and I worked in IV Corps, which was basically the delta region of South Vietnam.

COSVN was staffed by approximately 8,100 people who ran the VCI. Originally located in remote portions of III Corps, which included the capital, Saigon, this important command was moved into Cambodia when the heat became too great due to effective operations being conducted against them. Like my comrades, I was always looking for every bit of information I could use on COSVN.

Hamlet- and village-level VCI sought to gain control over their areas of responsibility by any means possible, including terror and murder. They would monitor each inhabitant's movements, often confiscating and then destroying government-issue ID papers necessary for these poor simple folks to conduct their daily lives. U.S. and South Vietnamese forces often arrested innocent citizens because they didn't have proper documentation. Figure it out, guys. The VC knew this would happen and exploited the situation ruthlessly. Hassled by the government and our own forces, we no doubt saw many a Vietnamese become a VC asset due to this stupidity.

Government administrators in the villages and hamlets were often targeted by VC military units and death squads, then neutralized by execution or assassination. They would be replaced by VCI cadre, who then ruled by edict backed up with the barrel of a gun. Heavy taxation followed, and each hamlet was turned into a combat village to bolster and support VC actions in the province. Young people were encouraged to join the People's Revolutionary Youth Association, and peasants were forced to house and feed VC troops.

The people were forced to act as messengers and mules for the VCI upon pain of death. They had to feed to the VCI intelligence information about their sons who were serving in the South Vietnamese Army. That information was then forwarded up the chain. VCI propaganda was so intense that eventually schoolchildren had neither free thought nor

123

free movement in their own province. Control was total, and fear was the weapon which ensured it.

I am reminded of one counteraction we undertook to rattle the VCI on behalf of the people they were enslaving in this manner. An air force buddy and I got together and worked up an idea involving hundreds of little yellow balls with three red stripes running lengthwise around each one. These were the colors of the South Vietnamese flag. This done, we dropped the balls in on contested or unfriendly villages under the influence of the VCI. The kids would recover the balls and begin playing games with them, delighted to have a new toy. In would come the local VCI. They'd take one look at the GVN colors and confiscate the children's toys. Now who was mad at who?

Another countermeasure we devised was to get photos of every dead VC possible and figure out which hamlet he came from. We'd then reproduce his photo and drop hundreds of copies over his village—airmail notification that all was not well with the so-called freedom fighters known as the Vietcong. The Australian SAS, or Special Air Service, operated in III Corps, and they had the best version of this effort I ever saw. The Aussies would leave two blank death certificates on every VC they killed. They would also leave a note that said, "Please be sure to put this man's correct name on his death certificate. The other one is for you. Be sure your name is filled out properly when we come back." These were men who knew how to wage war against the VC, and I am proud to have worked with them.

We realized early on at Phoenix that the key to the whole infrastructure question was to neutralize the VCI district chief. We made their lives hell on earth. There was nothing worse for a man than to come home, step through the door, and find a SEAL squad waiting with open arms. Every once in a while a chief would attempt to escape and evade, but he seldom outran the backup team hidden outside with their 5.56 bullet launchers.

13

The Phoenix Blacklist

The ardent VCI wanted nothing to do with the blacklist prepared and distributed within Phoenix for our use in operations. If your name came up on this list, it was only a matter of time before we came knocking at your door . . . or put you in the sights of our weapons. We compiled the blacklist from source intelligence and from programs that gathered intelligence on a daily basis in support of the war effort. Once I had a name on the list I began the targeting process. It was during this period that targeting became a fever with me, and I became more than good at it. Once I targeted someone, that person was as good as dead, or at least captured. I clearly remember one such target, a VCI district chief named Nuguyen van Truhn, who was the head schmuck in An Phu Province.

This blacklist was not only a tool to facilitate targeting. I also used it to cover my backside, as we were all under the legal gun by the time I got to Phoenix in Vietnam. Everything had to be documented, and to this day I have all my paperwork stored safely away, and I would bet most of the other players do, too. So, in a very real sense, the list was a legal tool where we as PRU advisers were concerned. On the other hand, it was a two-edged sword that corrupt Vietnamese officials and military officers used to their own benefit.

It didn't take me long to figure out that any Vietnamese I encountered in any position of power was more than likely on the take. The ultimate power was the province chief. He signed each mission order that employed troops, and my learning curve went up dramatically when I saw you had to give something to get something. My failure in the mountains of San Diego had now come full circle. The province chief would tell me he needed an air conditioner for the office. I'd find one on the U.S. Army compound and deliver it, and suddenly my mission order would be signed, sealed, and delivered! (Scotch was also a biggie.) The VCI blacklist eventually became corrupted. It became a place to put the names of these corrupt senior officers' enemies, to avoid repayment of debt or to even a score. Elimination of the VCI operating in the province often fell by the wayside. Got someone you don't like? See to it the word came in through channels they were VCI and, *boom!* your enemy's on the blacklist and headed for elimination. It took some real work on our part to ferret out such misuse, and in the end I think we were wrongly blamed for much of the damage done to the Phoenix program by those corrupt Vietnamese senior officials we thought were our allies.

Over half of the VCI I was targeting lived in Cambodia. A very smart move on their part. Chau Doc was adjacent to Cambodia and an easy commute for the bad guys, coming or going. Still, I was so successful at rooting these folks out with my PRUs that the VCI put a one-million-piastre bounty on my head. In that period there were about 118 piastres to one U.S. dollar. I became somewhat concerned, as I knew that even some of my own PRU might be tempted to collect that bounty and then head for the border. But in true SEAL fashion, I elected to up the ante and really put the pressure on the VCI who wanted me dead.

I took my cue from the Israeli approach to terrorism, which was to keep the pressure on and let your enemies know their lives were in danger every day, every minute, everywhere they went. Before going to sleep at night I'd review the gains and mistakes of the day. I divided the list up into those who lived in Vietnam and those in Cambodia. Then I divided up the intelligence organization to match the demographics of the province. Each of the five districts in a province was given a code letter, and each agent we'd developed in that district was assigned a code number—An Phu district was A, for example. I kept my agents' real names separate from their code numbers even in my office. I wanted one coded agent for each village and one for each hamlet, although I knew this would be tough, if not impossible. Why? Because an adviser could not spend more than six months on the job at Phoenix before being rotated back to the States; this was navy policy governing SEAL tours in Vietnam.

Looking back, I believe that the hardest part of being a PRU adviser in the Phoenix program was the administrative mountain one had to climb just to get to the field. I absolutely hated dealing with corrupt Vietnamese senior officers, but learned to simply cope as best I could. To this day I disdain bureaucrats. Moving a contingent of PRU, which could number as high as forty men, always offered me a chance to excel as a logistician. We'd go either by boat or by vehicle; rarely were we able to obtain helicopter transport. Obtaining gunships was often much easier. If the mission was to be an overnighter, food and water had to be arranged, as well as Medevac should we incur wounded. The list went on and on, and I found going to the field great, once we got there. That was when I seemed to relax the most. Patrolling along a stretch of ground with the PRU was a whole lot different than being with a Navy SEAL squad. These men knew their territory intimately. When we left our insertion craft and began a combat patrol, all our training and discipline came into play. No talking, no noise, constant stealth. The PRU on the other hand would walk along a dike line smoking, their rifles on their shoulders. Then as we approached a certain tree line cigarettes were thrown, rifles came to the ready, and everyone paid attention. We as advisers came to rely on their knowledge of who lived where and what their loyalties were.

We became pretty successful. My predecessor had done a superb job of training the PRU to pay close attention to intelligence and surveillance, and his work paid off for me. We began to target and capture district-level VCI. The amount of information these individuals gave up during interrogation was of enormous value. Our success rate began to speak for itself.

A tremendous asset in the early stages of our campaign at Phoenix was the census grievance program. This project was run by CORDS—Civil Operations and Revolutionary Development Support, a slick cover name for a very slick intelligence operation with all sorts of aspects which have to this day never been addressed. CORDS was supposed to bring all the military and civilian pacification efforts together to make better use of our overall resources at Military Assistance Command, Vietnam—MACV. Here's how it worked and how we made it work for us at Phoenix.

In 1965, William Colby, who was the CIA Far Eastern division chief at the time, oversaw the operation of the counterterrorist teams. The term "counterterror" had a bad connotation in Mr. Colby's mind, so he ordered the name changed to Provisional Reconnaissance Unit, or PRU. Still, there were three drawbacks. First, no matter how well the agency camouflaged its involvement in the financing, re-cruiting, and training of the PRU, the Saigon rumor mill abounded with stories of direct CIA association with Phoe-nix. Second, the South Vietnamese government was reluc-tant to attack the VCI. They either could not see the advantages of the program or chose to ignore the obvious rationale of cutting off the snake's head in order to kill the body. In my view, their gutlessness in accepting their own corruption cost them their government, their country, and the war to a superior enemy: at least the NVA had guts and standards. I believed then and I still believe that the NVA at the national level knew they could win in the end. Our national failure on many fronts cost us dearly in lives and global prestige. At the tactical level, the NVA had dedicated soldiers with a higher moral code than many of their South Vietnamese counterparts. Our former South Vietnamese allies had become enamored of our material wealth, and that had a devastating effect on such a poor nation.

The GVN preferred to use bombs and artillery against the masses instead of concentrating on the brains of their enemy. This attitude led to my third point, which has to do with how the CIA's actions were regarded as merely an extension of the Diem regime's policies, which were mostly either totally corrupt or fatally flawed. The agency wanted to be selective in ferreting out and dismantling the VCI with as little damage being done to the people as possible. But the GVN screwed this up with their "more bombs and bullets" attitude and devious ways of making negative use of such potentially positive programs as Phoenix. The result? Today the world thinks of the CIA as black-hearted devils and regards those who supported "their" efforts as assassins.

By 1966, PRUs were active in every province of South Vietnam. A new touch was the census grievance and aspira-tion program, or CGAP. Quite a few SEALs from this time period believe this new effort was a waste of time. I disagree. For me it was another valuable intelligence tool—but only if you took the time to use it. It was a CIA brainstorm that worked. I had begun researching CGAP documents long before I went to Vietnam with Phoenix. The program, I discovered, was designed to give the GVN province chief an accurate count of all the people in his province and to ascertain who didn't belong there. It was also meant to keep tabs on the corruption level and to track the personal aspirations of each individual villager. In other words, what did he or she want from the government? The census and grievance program also provided a way in which each villager could be interviewed, making it very difficult for the VCI to tell who might be fingering them for us.

After I came on board with the program, I'd send a small recon team into a contested village with a sanitized copy of the census and grievance report for that particular village. The team would not be wearing military uniform, as we did all such ops in civilian or indigenous clothing. Weapons were always kept low profile. Once the recon team spent some time in the ville they would target a particular individual who we thought we might be able to recruit as an agent. Recruiting an agent in a contested village was done by the PRU intelligence cadre, not by advisers. It had to be done carefully and without compromising the potential agent. If the conversation went well the prospective agent was told to just sit tight until contacted further. This done, we advanced to the next stage, which was to conduct a medical civic action program—nothing more than a good-will traveling medical clinic. Great intelligence can be generated when you're handing out doses of Christian goodwill.

On one such medical mission we left the capital city of Chau Doc in the early morning hours, essentially sneaking out of the city when most people were still asleep. I was taking fully half of the 105 members of the Chau Doc PRU with us, a sizable force indeed. With this many gunslingers our confidence level was very high should we have to duke it out with the local VC.

With me, one other American, and forty PRU aboard our flat-bottom barges, we made good time to a point adjacent to Cambodia. Once we reached the outskirts of An Phu village we beached the boats, leaving a security crew behind to watch over them. As we began moving toward the ville our point element came nearly nose to nose with the point element of a VC battle group. Somehow we were able to fall back without being compromised, and I decided we'd hunker down and wait until dark before making our next move.

We overnighted and when the sun began coming up the next morning we assembled and moved toward the ville. When a machine gun opened up ahead we froze in place, the point man holding up his hand to indicate we should not return fire. He pointed in several directions at once, and not one man moved or gave us away. The VC were conducting a recon by fire, meaning they were teasing us, hoping we'd open up in response and give away our position. I wanted an agent in this village, so going in with guns blazing would do us more harm than good, as many innocent folks would be wounded or killed in the exchange.

We moved forward and secured the village. This is a methodical effort when done with a small, lightly armed force. The point element crept up to a hidden vantage point on the edge of the village and took up position. From here they could observe any activity going on. Are the people nervous? Are they looking around for hidden VC in their midst? The main body moved toward the village on signal from the point element. The VC had detected our presence earlier and melted away. The main body element leaders fanned out and deployed the security teams to further discourage the bad guys from firing on us once we were inside the village. Using an old census report I found the names of several potential agents. The medics were set up by this time, and the village chief was told we'd treat his people as best we could. In no time a long line had formed and all matter of ailments were being treated. In a number of cases we could only inject sterile water and tell folks they'd be fine. We gave away all the cough medicine we had, as well as aspirin and other minor supplies of this nature. The bottom line was the bottom line . . . get an agent into the ville.

Eventually an old man came forward, and my interpreter, Fuzzy, whispered to me that this man was our potential agent. Fuzzy told me the old man would report to the capital in a few days where we could safely debrief him and issue further instructions on how to report to us. This man turned out to be a valuable agent. Through him we were able to target all the district-level VCI cadre in the area with no suspicion ever falling on the old man. I do not recall his name, but I can still see his tired and withered face. There was despair in those features, but a ray of hope as well. Who knows what motivated him to take such a risk for us? Perhaps an atrocity was committed against him or a loved one by the VC? In any event, he was my agent and our conduct of the war in his ville went very well after our medical visit under the guise of the census program.

The information provided by the old man enabled me to update my blacklist. We used his information to drop propaganda leaflets on the areas known VCI lived in, and to conduct snatch operations. I made sure the old man was well taken care of, and he lived well and in relative security while I was the Phoenix player in his neck of the woods.

As my tour went on, I became more and more comfortable as a PRU adviser. Things were never dull, and my experiences at fighting the VC at their own level and by their own rules was proving fruitful.

14

Adviser or Assassin?

Getting myself assigned to Phoenix wasn't easy, especially as I was so new to the Teams. Competition for the very few advisory jobs available was intense, because almost everyone wanted to work with this highly classified project.

In our operations office we maintained a status board that listed the entire Team's manning roster and each man's assignment. The board was broken down by platoons and departments, as that was how we were assigned. Our operations boss was Lieutenant (j.g.) Dick Flanagan. Today Dick is addressed as Captain Flanagan, a very bright guy who speaks directly and has one of the most winning smiles in the Teams. Dick oversaw the continuity of all our operations and insisted the manning board be kept 100 percent accurate at all times.

The year was 1969. My commanding officer at that period of time was Lieutenant Commander Dave Schaible, one of the true legends in our small community. He was a big man, well over six feet tall with huge, powerful hands. Dave was both respected and feared by everyone, and I mean everyone. He passed on some time ago, a true leader who said what he meant and meant what he said. I suppose Dave was feared because the men didn't want to get called in for a "private chat" with him. More than one officer had felt his wrath, and we enlisted men didn't escape it either. Schaible sometimes used the beach for his chats, or he'd catch up with us at the Tradewinds bar.

That was where he caught up with me one evening. We sat at the bar discussing the merits of the SEAL Basic Indoctrination training. Of course, there are always differences of opinion on how to do things. Schaible had his ideas, and I had a few of my own. He had already had a few drinks somewhere else before entering the Tradewinds. One thing led to another, and I unwisely told him he was screwed up. Then he made a remark I just didn't like. Wish I could remember what it was. After a heated exchange of words I elected to take a swing at him. Wrong move. The captain lowered one massive fist against the top of my head, pounding me into near senselessness. It was like getting hit with a Virginia ham lined with a lead diving weight. I went near unconscious. Captain Schaible then grabbed me by my pectorals and lifted me, dazed and unsteady, off my feet, squeezing my chest as hard as he could. The pain was unreal! Then Mrs. Schaible, who had accompanied her husband that evening, ordered Dave to "leave the poor boy alone." He did, and I have never forgotten that good woman's kindness. No matter what, he was still my commanding officer the next day. The incident was never discussed between us. I did hear from one or two of the chiefs however.

Our status board, as I said before, was updated on a daily basis, and one evening while standing duty I made my move. Swapping my name from its berth in the intelligence department, I slipped it over to the list of men awaiting province assignments with Phoenix. That's what you really wanted as a PRU adviser, an entire province of your own. Dick Flanagan was at a loss as to why and how my name kept appearing on this list until he caught me one night in a classic Flanagan ambush. I didn't catch any real flak about messing with the board, though. Dick was pretty good-natured about the whole thing. We discussed my desires, and he decided that if I wanted it that bad, he'd see to it my wish was granted. He was true to his word, and I ended up on my way to Vietnam as a player in the Phoenix program.

When I arrived in Saigon I was told to change into civilian clothes. This was a new twist to me, but if I could go to war wearing Levi's and jungle boots, great! The SEAL platoon I'd flown over with from the states went their separate way, wishes of good luck passed around before our group split up and headed off to our assigned combat zones. Those with Phoenix stamped on their foreheads went looking for the project's offices, which were located in one of the MACV buildings in Saigon.

A lot of people confuse MACV Studies and Observation

133

Group (SOG) with Phoenix, believing SEALs operated with SOG's war effort in Laos. Not so. The navy kept tight control over its people during the Vietnam War, ensuring we served under temporary duty orders that kept us well beneath the navy's parochial umbrella. Laos, a highland country, was doctrinally outside SEAL mission parameters. As SEALs we could operate from the mountains to the deserts, and from the deserts to an arctic environment, but the rule of thumb in Vietnam was that coastal and riverine operations were our bread and butter.

Our first briefing in Saigon was with a marine bird colonel named Allen. He immediately told the three of us present how much he hated SEALs. Any time a man has to tell me right off the bat how much he hates me, I begin to question his ability to lead. Good leaders, people with internal strength and ability, don't need to browbeat those who have to serve under them. Strong men follow strong leaders. Weak men look for leaders like Colonel Allen. I simply tuned him out, nodding my head politely and murmuring a mandatory "Yes, sir," whenever appropriate.

We'd jacked up the colonel's all-powerful rating pretty high by the time he dismissed us, but we dumped all the phone numbers he'd given us in the wastebasket outside his office, and I figured I'd never have to deal with him again. Unfortunately, I was wrong.

We then moved on to Can Tho, the regional capital, where Lieutenant Mike Collins was our military boss. His deputy turned out to be Ed Jones, an old friend. I felt like I'd made contact with the outside world upon meeting these two; Vietnam not so strange and exotic any more. It was at Can Tho that I first met William Buckley, who was working in the regional office and claimed he "was going crazy" shuttling between it and the offices in Saigon. Buckley made us feel that he would support our efforts to the max. Few people knew he was a Special Forces officer prior to linking up with the CIA. This was to his benefit, as most Agency guys I was to meet during my career were of the opinion that "why tell the truth when a lie will do just as well?" Buckley was a cut above the issue CIA operator, and I grew to respect and like him a great deal.

Throughout our train-up for Phoenix we'd been told that we'd be serving in a good program and that Agency money and supply systems were the best in the world. I do remember Frank Flynn's admonition about the CIA, though. "They'll shake your hand and pee in your boots at the same time," he told me. As usual, Frank was right.

After Buckley left the room both Mike and Ed told us he was the best guy in the office. "If we need anything, Bill's the guy we call," said Mike. That was good enough for me. At this point I really began to understand that Phoenix was a CIA operation, with all that this entailed. We'd known that from our first day of training in secret at our mountain lair in California, but the reality of what I was now a part of truly hit home for the first time.

One of the reasons the Phoenix program was so resilient as far as SEALs were concerned was the fact that returning platoons updated both the cadre and soon-to-deploy SEAL platoons.

As SEALs were rotated back to the States, they'd be brought out to us in order to update both the cadre and ourselves as to the latest changes in how Phoenix was being run. This covered both the regional and province levels, and our people were pretty candid in their observations. Our time with the old hands was short, and the usual military BS wasn't entertained by those soon to head off to the war. Mistakes were brought up and discussed. Possible solutions were offered and filed away. We covered everything from how to deal with corrupt Vietnamese province chiefs to making the Agency guys happy. Primarily we learned how to stay alive and happy, in the administrative sense as well as in the combat sense. Of the two, the former was the most difficult. Admin pukes run the world, it seems, and they are the death of warriors, sometimes literally.

I'd asked for a mission, and they gave me one. My assignment was in Chau Doc province, located in the northern region of IV Corps. Chau Doc butted up against Cambodia, another fun spot in the Southeast Asian war games. I'd be the junior adviser assigned to a highly experienced senior petty officer whom I'll call Jerry. It appeared I'd finally found a home.

Arriving at the provincial capital I took my first look at the PRU camp, which was located at the airfield. This was something I'd see time and time again as the years went by: special units tasked to do special things in special wars are always teamed up with special air assets. I was apprehensive at the responsibility now resting somewhat uncomfortably on my shoulders, but I was determined not to fail. Though not as mature as I would later become, I was sincere, although still much too wild. Only time and experience would carve away the drawbacks to my professional status as a savvy SEAL operator, and it was good that those above me took the time to link me up with seasoned veterans.

Whenever a PRU adviser needed to get somewhere in Vietnam he took the local Air America flight. The Agency owned and operated this airline throughout Southeast Asia, and I liked it because there were no questions asked once you were on board and headed wherever you needed to go. We flew military aircraft as well, but Air America was a special perk that came with the job. Once we left the region headquarters we'd have with us a special pass. It made us bulletproof where the military police were concerned, and was signed by the regional provost marshal. It stated that you were not to be detained or delayed, that you were authorized to carry exotic weaponry and demolitions, and that every courtesy was to be extended to you so that your mission might be accomplished.

I've heard this card referred to as a "get out of jail free" pass, but with it we never went to jail in the first place. It got me lots of salutes, and more than a few stares and winks. Later on as the Phoenix program began to fall apart at the seams, all of our special ID cards were confiscated. That was a meaningless gesture, as we simply duplicated the document thanks to the air force psychological operations guys who worked with us. Just because some admin clown now had cause to screw with us didn't mean our manner of fighting the war had gotten any easier, cleaner, or less dangerous. Part of the Phoenix program was working under a cover identity. One of our senior petty officers went over as an army captain, and he pulled it off with no problem. My cover was that of a former SEAL now working on a contract basis. At twenty-two, I couldn't have passed for much else, as I was barely shaving and actually looked more like eighteen! Cover identities would become second nature to me as time went on, my work as a SEAL demanding them.

Phoenix gave me a responsibility I couldn't have gotten anywhere else in the Teams, and certainly not in the Navy. I was the commanding officer for a group of men hired by the government of Vietnam to fight for the country . . . or stay in prison and rot. My PRUs were an early version of today's Crips or Bloods gang members—first-class dirt bags in every respect. The Provincial Reconnaissance Unit was composed primarily of mercenaries, most of them criminals, all of them outcasts from their own societies. And here I was their adviser. I didn't know whether to laugh or cry, so I just got on with the mission.

As a PRU adviser I did all the operational planning along with my counterpart, the PRU chief, Nguyen Van Bao. Bao was a real piece of work whose functional intelligence was far greater than his years of formal education. He was essentially illiterate, although he could write his own name quite well. But Nuguyen had a Ph.D. in human nature, politics, and even polygamy. He was a first class Phoenix PRU chief, and he was all mine.

Jerry, the senior PRU adviser, had a high school education, knew SEAL business inside and out, and was hip to Bao's head games. Games were the rule of thumb in Phoenix, all of them bought and paid for by Agency money. As SEAL advisers we truly tried to keep the system honest, but men like Bao worked overtime to corrupt it, gleaning enormous amounts of intelligence funding for his own misuse.

My first day in the PRU camp brought me into contact with Chau Soc Bey, a PRU mercenary. It was a one-sided meeting as Bey was lying dead as a doornail in the duty shack. Examining the corpse, I noted there were no marks on him, and we later confirmed that no morphine was missing. Why he died and how I remember his name God only knows. Welcome to the PRU! Jerry and I toured the camp together. He was over six feet tall, and I was just five-four in jungle boots. The PRU began to gather around us, measuring my height against their own. I believe they liked having a short American in camp whom they could look square in the eye—or even down upon in some cases. I made every attempt to blow off the physical comparisons taking place. Bottom line? I was their boss and wouldn't take any crap. They got the message soon enough.

Like all real special operations guys, I wanted to get to the field as soon as possible. As our first mission came together I insisted on carrying the M-60 machine gun, thinking it was necessary for me to demonstrate that I could hack it as a player. This was a reaction to my training in California, and an error in judgment. The true military adviser both commands and leads; he does not take on the role of grunt. An enlightened adviser will be lightly armed with a submachine gun or carbine-type weapon. His real firepower comes in the form of a radio, a compass, a map, and intellect. His job is to accomplish the mission while keeping himself and as many of his people alive as possible. Civilians, especially those in the media, haven't to this day figured out the reality behind military advisers. When you send them in, you are in fact declaring war on the enemy. Advisers are not benign; they are lethal.

We hit the bush and were soon spotted by a U.S. Navy hunter-killer group as we were making our way through the jungle and paddies. Such groups were made up of two helicopter gunships and two "slicks," which flew all over the countryside looking for something—or somebody—to kill. These folks fired at anything that was moving, and we were moving. As the birds began to circle above us, Jerry informed me that although we had cleared the area of operation no one at higher-higher really knew we were here. Here we were at the foot of the Seven Sisters mountain area, just a hop, skip, and a jump from Cambodia. I'd worked as a point man for Wayne Boles during an earlier tour of Vietnam with a SEAL platoon, and thought I knew my stuff. How wrong I was!

The gunships lined up on our small group and began their run. We scattered, racing for a nearby graveyard that offered huge burial stones as cover from the machine-gun fire. These huge square blocks of rock stopped rockets pretty nicely, but my left eardrum was destroyed and I soaked up some nasty scrapes on my face while dodging bullets aimed my way by the "good guys." But there's a big difference between wounds and injuries during wartime. I'd been injured, not wounded. No big deal.

The thirty of us regrouped after the helos got tired of searching for us and went looking for other targets. Jerry and I ordered the PRU to move out smartly, as night was coming on and we had only binoculars to assist us during the hours of darkness. Today you can just strap on a pair of night vision goggles and never stop operating. Not so in Vietnam.

After I'd survived my first operation with the PRU, Jerry carefully went over everything—both good and bad—about my performance. He was good, and I learned a great deal from working alongside him. The first thing he told me was to stop trying so hard to prove myself. Every day in the program would be a learning experience. Jerry was very good at reading people. He understood human nature, and cultural differences did not confuse him. At that point in time, I was easily confused. Those who know me well still tell me that nothing has changed. He also told me never to carry a machine gun in the field. That was the troops' job. Mine was to lead, think, and get them out of trouble.

We relied heavily on our interpreters, and my best one was a PRU called Fuzzy. He weighed ninety pounds soaking wet and was exceptionally courageous under fire. He saved my bacon more than once. It was Fuzzy who alerted me to a VC bomb that had been set in a shopping district where we were wandering around one day. He got me out of there just before it went off, doing incredible damage. Battle is one thing; terrorism is another. I remember seeing a little girl who'd been blown in half, her legs on the ground with the rest of her hanging from a tree. Her dead eyes were upon me as we recovered the bits and pieces of her. I still feel her silent stare even to this day. Some things just stay with you regardless of time or distance. Those of us in the Phoenix program were sometimes called assassins, but the real assassins were the scum who planted bombs that blew little Vietnamese girls in half. It was my job to hunt such terrorists down and take them alive, if possible. I have no problem taking down a terrorist, anywhere, anytime, anyplace. They deserve neither remorse or mercy. They deserve only an express elevator to hell.

By the end of my first month with Phoenix I was becoming comfortable in my role as a PRU adviser. I was sorting out the players, getting the routine down. I'd stopped carrying the M-60. Jerry and I shared a room at the embassy house, as our quarters were known in-country. We were the only two military personnel on the premises, the rest of the occupants being Agency. For the most part, our roommates were a good crowd. Jerry and I watched their antics the way some people watched soap operas. The backstabbing was incredible, and routine to their world. In this, at least, the CIA is consistent.

The man in charge of an embassy house was known as the provincial officer in charge, or POIC. At Chau Doc our POIC was the civilian equivalent of a two-star general. Some heavy clout here. One night I asked, in total ignorance, why he was in the province if he outranked the senior Agency man at regional level. A frosty silence swept through the dining room. The POIC, who just happened to hate military people to begin with, gave me a condescending lecture in response.

According to His Majesty he'd somehow committed a mortal sin in the Agency's eyes—as if there was such a thing—and he'd been banished to the outer limits of Vietnam as punishment. He was a real blue blood, highly educated and well connected. My Boston background did not impress him in the least, and we waged a real class war between us during my tour. If I was blue-collar scum to him, I couldn't imagine what he thought of the PRU who did his bidding . . . or of the Vietnamese alongside whom we were supposed to be fighting.

All this aside, I did learn quite a bit from him. He taught me the importance of writing correctly and of taking and maintaining notes. I was trying to do everything in my head once Jerry was rotated out of the program and I became the senior adviser. With guidance, this haphazard practice came to a stop and I became more organized and more efficient at my job. I even learned about fine wines from the Agency man, although I never did grow to like him. He was a brilliant man, though, and I respected him for that. I've always been able to learn from belligerents and from enemies. Both can teach you a lot, if you can put aside your personal hostility and get on with the job.

Cameron J. LaClair, Jr., the POIC, was also a diplomat; in fact, that was what he did when not being punished for whatever sins he committed while on the job. He was a career spy for his country, and I became his bodyguard while he worked his magic. As a PRU adviser I suddenly found myself in a world most SEALs in the program never experienced. The fine art of diplomatic intrigue was introduced to me and I absorbed all I could. It would not be my forte, as time would later tell, but I learned to recognize superior ass-kissers for what they were and what they wanted. One thing LaClair taught me was not to hate my enemies. Such an emotion clouds your judgment. I learned from my enemies and allowed them to enrich my professional life.

Your foes cannot betray you . . . only your friends can.

I also owe Cameron LaClair a personal debt of gratitude. Halfway through my tour with Phoenix my mother broke her back. Upon hearing the news I stopped operating for a few days, my mind totally focused on her health. Communications were scanty, at best, and information hard to come by. No matter how tough you think you might be, when your mom is hurting and you can't be there, you cry. I did my share of crying when I heard the news. LaClair finally got word from my mother that she was okay and that I should not come home. "Stay on the job, son," was the message. It was at this point that my relationship with LaClair began to improve and we got back to the business of hunting VCI.

I soon became well versed in the fine art of interrogation. Each provincial capital had a provincial interrogation center (PIC) manned by CIA operators. Our guy was a real pro, and he invited me to watch him work. We both knew I could use the training for field application. During this entire time I never witnessed any of the media horror stories that abound to this day about Phoenix interrogations at the PICs. The men I worked with were experts in their field, and they used their minds to conquer the spirit of those they were questioning. Women were the hardest to break down, knowing if they could hold out for just twenty-four hours whatever information they had would have been made invalid by the hardworking VCI we were still after. I was only twenty-two years old when I was introduced to the inner strength of women POWs. The females we captured and brought in to the PIC were hard-core VC and VCI, no doubt about it.

There was a great difference between VCI prisoners and those from the hamlets, who were normally simple Vietcong soldiers. Female VCI were not likely to talk, due their higher level of training and commitment to the revolution. Very political, these women. A woman from the hamlet or village, on the other hand, would talk your ear off. As I became more adept at interrogation and witnessed more and more at the PIC, I observed that female VCI seemed to travel from one point of internal refuge to another, going deeper and deeper in their efforts to stave off cracking. José, the Agency interrogator, knew this very well and possessed an ability to get down real deep, real fast. He was invaluable to us.

Male VCI and VC were just the opposite. Most tried as quickly as possible to make whatever deal they could with us to avoid being uncomfortable. They opted for the Chieu Hoi program we offered, which meant that if they cooperated in locating and capturing VCI, they would avoid becoming POWs at places like Phu Quoc Island. I'd visited this quaint little Vietnamese-run "summer camp" for Vietcong prisoners, and I'd take the Chieu Hoi deal any day of the week, too. So, in return for weapons caches or high-level VCI names and locations, the local Vietcong male would cut a deal and end up working for Phoenix as an intelligence asset. Not pretty, perhaps, but just another aspect in the daily life of a PRU adviser.

One significant benefit from my closer-than-normal association with the PIC was the insider's perception I gained in my dealings with the PRU and army intelligence officers at the district level. Bear in mind that each province was divided into districts. At each district was a District Intelligence Operations Coordination Center, or DIOCC. The U.S. staff for these offices was, by and large, army second lieutenants with little or no experience as anything but boot-grade officers. The PRUs were deployed by districts. They reported to the DIOCC, as the PRU adviser couldn't be everywhere doing everything at once. The reporting process, I was to learn, was abysmal.

What little intelligence we got from the DIOCC was virtually useless. I went to my boss about coming up with an intelligence debriefing format of our own after my sessions with José at PIC. He agreed it was necessary, given the garbage the DIOCC shoved our way. Together we worked through the rough spots and I took the finished product up to Can Tho for review by Mike and Ed. They, in turn, took it to William Buckley.

"You did this?" Bill asked me after reading it.

"Yes, sir," I responded.

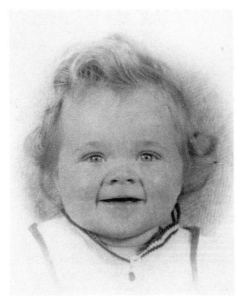

Mike Walsh at nine months, May 15, 1948. Proof that SEALs are made, not born.

The author, thirty-four years later, while on a SEAL training mission in Puerto Rico, 1982.

My first combat experience was aboard this Swift boat, Cam Rahn Bay, Vietnam, 1967.

Land warfare training on San Clemente Island, California, with the M-1 Garand rifle. Couldn't touch an M-16 until I made the Teams!

Graduation day from BUD/S, May 1968, with Frank Sparks—the other shortest guy in the Teams.

This is how we lived in Vinh Long in 1968—home sweet home.

Chief Warrant Officer Boles (far right) briefing our platoon on the river.

During a Phoenix Operation in 1969. Gotta keep the backtrail safe.

In my Viet Cong uniform with my Phoenix Operation interpreter, Fuzzy.

Dung Island, Vietnam, 1970. This is how we usually looked after a day at the office.

SEAL Team One Blues Brothers prepared for a daylight mission. Dong Tam, Vietnam, 1971.

SEAL Team One, Victor Platoon, Dong Tam,
Vietnam, 1971. We don' need no stinkin' badges!

The USS *Ft. Snelling* just off St. George's, Grenada,
during Operation Urgent Fury, October 1983.
(Official U.S. Navy Photograph)

This is Melanie Kazan, who we rescued in Lebanon during the evacuation. The daughter I never had. Juniah, Lebanon, February 9, 1984.

The MK-8 SEAL delivery vehicle. We call it the bus. At times, this can be the coldest, darkest and longest ride of your life. (Official U.S. Navy Photograph)

My mother, Margaret, just after she joined the Navy in 1941. These are my true beginnings.
(Margaret M. Walsh Collection)

Lt. Cmdr. Mike Walsh, USN (Ret.), 1991.

He went over the debriefing format with me and offered some suggestions for making it even more effective. I told him that I was spending time in the PIC with José and that Jerry had added more than his two cents' worth—always give credit where credit is due. Buckley gave me one of his rare smiles and told me to get back to Chau Doc and rework it. So we added more biographical questions along with some family history. Then we tested it at the local DIOCC. Within two weeks the quality of intelligence improved dramatically! My format was distributed nationwide within the month and became the standard questioning tack taken with VC and VCI prisoners throughout the Phoenix program. It was a solid victory for me as an adviser, which was encouraging, as we faced so many defeats on a daily basis.

After this I began to hit my stride in Phoenix. Intelligence gathering was always a challenge, and since money was no object, anything and anybody was fair game. Jerry came up with the bright idea of using the Medical Civil Action Program as a cover for intelligence gathering operations, and we implemented it immediately in a string of contested villages along the Cambodian border.

Under the cover of providing medical relief we would move between fifty and sixty PRU into a village, the recon teams going in first to check out the local VC environment. Any doubts on their part would result in a recon by fire, meaning they'd engage all four points of the compass with weapons fire to see who shot back. No shoot-back, no bad guys . . . maybe. After this took place we'd come in behind the recon teams and set up shop. Our training in the mountains of California stressed medicine, including shots. Jerry and I would play doctor and give injections, mostly of sterile water, which wouldn't hurt anyone. We'd hand out aspirin and generally practice basic field medicine. In the meantime, our PRU would comb the village for possible agents willing to work for us.

This intelligence gathering practice continues today; the army's Special Forces people are some of the best in the business. The SF medics truly are some of the finest field physicians in the military, and they certainly do care a great deal about their patients. (These medical programs are now known as Medrettes, which is merely a different name for the same game.) In the Phoenix program, however, we were not interested in setting up baby clinics; we were interested in setting up VC. In this case there is a great difference between our medical programs and today's Medrettes. No one today will admit that we conduct intelligence gathering operations via this program for fear that some admin puke might be looking for a sacrificial lamb to appease the media and the rabid left-wing activists so alive and well in America today. As I said, same game, new name.

Our medical programs were great successes. Agent recruitment went up and we targeted more VC and VCI than ever before. Because our interrogation process was now more effective, we learned more from our POWs at a faster rate. Hence, the circle completed itself as more successful operations were mounted and run. Being VCI in Chau Doc was no longer a breeze, and we ensured they had to work to stay out of our reach. I've often wondered whatever happened to all those whose aid we enlisted as agents after the United States pulled out of Vietnam. A lot of records were compromised, having never been destroyed because of our fast "honorable" departure. More blood on the heads of those who executed policy at the highest levels, in my professional opinion.

The VCI were smart, real smart. They operated with the same compartmentalization today's terrorists and narco-terrorists utilize. No one knows more than necessary, and there's a heavy emphasis on security layers. Your reward for becoming untrustworthy? A public beating, torture, or a bullet in the head. Simple, direct, effective management. These three aspects of the VCI formed the bedrock of their activities.

As it got closer to the time when Jerry would have to leave Chau Doc, the Phoenix program came under increasing fire from the antiwar activists in the United States. Everyone involved with or even remotely linked to the program scurried for cover. The word came down from Can Tho about four months into my tour that the advisers were no longer allowed to go on operations with the PRU. I was incredulous! It was absurd, asking us to lead from the rear. It was also stupid, as without American advisers present, the PRU could do whatever they pleased with no restraint or witnesses. This same insanity was played out during El

Salvador's civil war when U.S. advisers were hobbled from overseeing various military units during operations. Then they were painted as the trainers of death squads when the results of this inane policy—meant primarily to appease an American public kept deliberately ignorant and misinformed, as well as to appease leftist-leaning politicians and activists—became public.

PRU advisers began privately to discuss strategy. How about going forward to the point where we actually launched the troops? This idea was snapped up like a tuna hitting the line on the Outer Banks. The forward area was fluid. It could change in an instant. So the trick was to keep getting the forward area of the battle zone declared as being farther and farther away. We saw this technique repeated in El Salvador, so someone somewhere learned the lesson well from our experience at Phoenix.

The intelligence boys at Can Tho finally caught on when the reports of PRU advisers being ambushed became overwhelming. Hey, it worked for a while, okay? Plan B was even better. I would operate while visiting my PRU at the district headquarters. As soon as I got there, we'd go to the field so I could conduct a working "inspection." In addition, I'd check records, check the morphine stock (these guys loved ripping us off for morphine), issue my complaints to the district chief about poor performance, poor records, missing dope, then get on my merry way. As time went on we eventually angered the bureaucrats in both Can Tho and Saigon to the point where the program was squeezed to death on an administrative basis, day by day.

The last few months were the worst. Field time was no longer something to be played with, and the POIC was everywhere except in my back pocket. The most effective program in Vietnam, which dealt directly in breaking the enemy's stranglehold on the populace was being dismantled by idiots.

There were day-to-day activities I had to accomplish as a PRU adviser. One was keeping tabs on a huge supply system. Ours at Chau Doc was run by Chinese, and their business ethic was to steal ten percent off the top. In return they made sure the system ran effectively and the books always looked great. Those Chinese living in Vietnam were feared by many Vietnamese. Our embassy house guards in

Chau Doc were Chinese Nungs, true warriors for hire and the fiercest men I've ever met. I had seventeen Nungs with me, and they were top-notch professional fighting men. Their families were always close by, because the Nungs have long roamed Asia as gunslingers whose talents go to the highest bidder. It was the Nungs who had saved the entire city of Chau Doc eighteen months earlier during the Tet offensive, with a PRU adviser earning the Medal of Honor. A Navy SEAL platoon was also involved during this fight, but not to the degree or depth reported in another recent book. It was the Nungs, not the SEALs, who saved Chau Doc during Tet.

No matter where I went in Chau Doc, I always had a Nung with me. At night, when I was fast asleep, a Nung stood guard outside my bedroom door. They didn't do this for the Agency guys, which gives one an insight as to how valued a CIA agent was to these folks. I began spending more and more of my time with the Nungs, even taking my meals with them. The talk at the embassy house was boring anyhow. Too much intrigue. It was from the Nungs that I learned to appreciate the ancient Chinese culture. The Nung were simple warrior people, intensely loyal to the point of dying for you, if necessary. A far different caliber of man than my PRU.

One incident that stands out in my mind took place during a reporter's visit to Chau Doc. He was sniffing around for a story about Phoenix, and he discovered who I was while I was on the U.S. Army compound looking for equipment. As he walked up to me he began taking pictures. I politely asked him to stop, which he just as politely refused to do. I did the honorable thing under such wartime circumstances and proceeded to knock him on his butt. Picking up his rather expensive camera, I unloaded the film and then stomped the camera into the compound's hard earth with my battered jungle boots. A bad career move on my part.

To make matters worse, I politely asked Nago, the head Nung who happened to be with me that day, to remove his pistol and press it ever so gently against the reporter's skull, allowing me at least a ten-minute head start back to the PRU camp before letting the man go. Before bidding him farewell I impressed upon the now totally frightened news hound that if I ever saw his face anywhere near my camp I'd open fire. No discussion, no argument, just hot flying lead.

He got the message. Nago was somewhat uncomfortable in his role, but he carried out my orders because it was a matter of honor. The reporter was lucky. If it had been one of my PRU, he would have seen his brains blown out five minutes after I left the scene.

That afternoon it hit the fan. The reporter, after pitching his bitch to anyone with authority who would listen, grabbed the first thing smoking back to Can Tho. I was summoned to chat with POIC, who was furious with me. Poor Nago was almost fired, but I immediately cleared up his part in what had taken place. After all, it was a matter of honor for me as well. "What could have possessed you to do such a stupid thing, Michael?" The POIC was playing with me now, pulling his holier-than-thou act as Rome was burning down all around the embassy house. I told him this jerk had been pestering me and that he'd been warned before to leave me alone. I believed he would compromise my operations, my men. There was an impressive reward on my head, put there by the VCI. I didn't need to have my picture appear in some Stateside magazine so that an antiwar lunatic could cut it out and send it on to the "Support Your Local Vietcong" clubhouse. That had actually happened. That's how one of Jane Fonda's close friends identified Green Beret officer Nick Rowe to his VC captors after he'd spent several years convincing them he was just a run-of-the-mill army guy.

The POIC told me my men were "just PRU," and that their lives meant nothing to him. I was ordered aboard a special Air America flight headed for Can Tho. The plane was a two-engine job, which meant my butt was dearly wanted by someone higher than the local headhunter. Upon my arrival at Can Tho I was driven to headquarters, where everyone took a shot at the brash young third class petty officer who'd knocked a reporter up alongside the head, taken his film, destroyed his camera, and then ordered a Nung mercenary to introduce him to the business end of a rather impressive handgun. But the worst was yet to come.

After being passed around from office to office, I finally ended up in front of Colonel "I Hate Navy SEALs" Allen, my old buddy from day one at Phoenix. There was nothing I could say at this point. The only thing I could do was stand at attention and take his admin guff, and I hated every second of it. From the clean marine's office I was told to report to MACV where they got their licks in, and then it was off to NAVFORV (Naval Forces, Vietnam) headquarters where one of my own, a SEAL commander, quietly read me his version of the riot act. Oh, the power of the press.

By the time it was over, I knew the war was over for me. Visions of leg irons and handcuffs swam before my eyes, all because of some stupid reporter who shouldn't have been where he was in the first place. That night I was back in Can Tho, a swift round trip from Chau Doc to Saigon under my belt. Ed Jones and I got together for a drink, and Ed—God bless him—filled me in about reporters. The next day Ed took me to the plane, which would off-load me back at Chau Doc. "Back to work, Mikey . . . go get 'em. All your sins have been forgiven," he told me in a fatherly tone of voice. I'd learned my lesson.

"It'll never happen again, Ed," I told him. "Next time he comes out I'll invite him out to the camp for a helo ride with me and the PRU." Just as Ed's face began to get red at my implication, I smiled at him. "Just kidding, Ed," I said, and was airborne. Seems like every time I made an error in judgment there were guys like Ed Jones around. As I said, you learn from everyone smarter and more experienced than yourself.

The last days of my tour with Phoenix were marked by three events I'll never forget. The first took place in the mountains of Tri Ton, near the Seven Sisters region. The PRU there lived in a small walled compound and were due for a visit from their adviser—me. They were having a class on perimeter defense before I got there, and live booby traps had been set up all around the base. There were M-60s in position, as well as the deadly claymore mines we used to decimate the enemy's ranks when they assaulted our position. One of the PRU disconnected a claymore and was busy showing a new man how to test the firing circuit. Hooking the firing handle back up to the electric wire linking the system together, he cautioned the younger PRU, "Never do this," and then cranked down on the handle.

There was a school nearby, and the kids were coming home from classes when the mine went off. They were

148

caught in its sixty-degree arc by over seven hundred .30 caliber steel balls. It was bad, awful bad. Within three hours I arrived there, flying in from Chau Doc. Standing amid the carnage I forgot about being a professional PRU adviser. I was completely unsure of what to do, the ripped and shredded bodies of little children literally at my feet. My men were all hiding; I found only a few. The deputy province senior adviser was breathing fire down my neck, and all hell was breaking loose over the incident. It was not a good day.

I regained my composure only through tremendous effort. Even if I was not in control I had to look as if I was. The army colonel knew who I really was and asked if he could take over the scene. I firmly told him no, that I would handle it. He shook his head and stepped back, waiting. As much as I didn't like this guy, he did spark me back into action. I ordered the PRU out of the area immediately, moving everyone back to Chau Doc. Then we went about making amends as best we could. It was tragic. A stupid mistake over a weapon system we'd trained on day and night. The dead kids now became a part of me, a reminder of how inglorious war is. I remember them every now and again, and I am still sorry.

The second incident took place when the Chau Doc PRU were awarded a huge sum of money from the government of Vietnam for being the most productive unit in IV Corps. It was a great party. We roasted an entire cow, and the men got drunk. During the day a battalion of Vietnamese rangers came to town and Chau Doc became Dodge City in short order.

The town square was not large, and it seemed even smaller to me when my PRU ran headlong into the Viet rangers. Guns came out—every rifle, pistol, and automatic weapon on hand. My Nungs woke me and told me that Fuzzy, my interpreter, needed to talk with me "right now." It was "berry, berry important, Mr. Mike . . . you have to fix." They called me Mr. Mike because my last name was too hard for them to pronounce. The jeep with the .50 caliber machine gun mounted in it was outside my door, six armed-to-the-teeth Nung waiting to kick some butt. I went unarmed, figuring it was time to earn my leadership pay.

I was scared, no doubt about it. I had no idea what I

would do once I got to the town square. I whispered a quick prayer, asking God not to let me die today. As always, God answered my request. I got on the phone to try to learn something of what had brought these two armed forces together for the grand remake of the Gunfight at the O.K. Corral. Both units had been seriously partying at separate locations. Insults were traded, threats were then passed back and forth, and now blood was about to be spilled. Time for the Nungs and me to get on the road.

The Nungs love theatrics. We came barreling into the crowded square with the high beams on, spinning a tight circle and coming to a screeching halt right in the middle of the drunken, howling armed mob. I sent the Nungs to the edge of the square, but ordered them to stay away from either side. The interpreter and I were right in the middle and had to stay there. The last thing I wanted was for one side or the other to think I was playing favorites. Putting all the command presence possible on my twenty-two-year-old face, I placed my hands on my hips and began walking up and down the square, telling both sides how ashamed I was of them and how they'd brought disgrace on all of us.

I told them I was so ashamed I would not look them in the face. Their code of honor became my greatest tool, and the POIC's knack for diplomacy rose to the occasion as I invoked it. It wasn't clear if I was having a positive effect at this point, but I sounded good.

The PRU capitulated first because, as their adviser, I had now lost face in front of the Vietnamese. Both sides gradually realized this despite their drunken state, and slowly weapons began to be lowered as I continued on. At any minute I fully expected the bullets to start flying, with my Nungs having the greatest effect as they were the better warriors and wonderfully sober. Of course, I would die but that was the price for being the man in the middle. My Nungs' presence made me braver than I really had a right to be, and little Fuzzy stayed next to me the entire time, his face as pale as a ghost. When it was all over, the sputtering time bomb had been defused and the men staggered off to their own parties around town. I had the Nungs drop me off at the bar afterward . . . I needed a drink.

Finally the tour was over. It came time for all Navy SEAL Phoenix advisers to leave Vietnam. As I was in the process of turning over my command to an incoming Special Forces captain, we began receiving intelligence about yet another American serviceman who'd defected to the VC and was now fighting alongside them. We were tracking him, preparing to take him down when the time was right. The Green Beret officer assumed responsibility for the chase as I packed my rucksack one final time at the Phoenix embassy house.

I wished him well, said good-bye to my faithful Nungs, and headed for the airfield without looking back.

15

Victor Platoon: The Dung Island Gang

After wrapping up a tour with Phoenix at Chau Doc I was selected as an instructor in the highly advanced SEAL Basic Indoctrination Program, an eight-month tour of duty. It was an interesting period for me, primarily because I met more characters in the business whose impact on the SEAL legend carries over to this day.

Lenny Horst and Terry "Doc" Bryant were two such SEALs. While returning Stateside from a tour in Vietnam, Lenny's platoon found itself delayed in Hawaii for two extra days due to aviation problems. Horst was terribly upset and wanted to get back to the States in the worst way. His attitude made him ripe for a practical joke, and Doc Bryant could never pass on an easy target.

Terry put on an act equal to Horst's. Striding to a pay phone, he announced he was going to complain to his congressman, the Honorable L. Mendel Rivers, who was known to be a friend to the military. Bryant actually got through to the congressman and issued his complaint about being stuck en route home from Vietnam because the air force couldn't do its job properly. Hanging up, with all ears tuned in by now, he faked a call to the White House. When Lenny inched up to eavesdrop, Terry began roaring about being hung up on. Horst, encouraged by his teammate's courage, grabbed the phone. "I'll get through, just watch this!" he exclaimed.

And he did. Right to a presidential aide who took down Lenny's Social Security number, full name, and unit as well as his rather verbose complaint. Not one hour later the squadron's commanding officer roared into the terminal.

Confronting him was a SEAL platoon straight out of the jungles of Vietnam. They were wearing worn Levi's, faded and torn camouflage fatigue shirts, VC sandals, beat-up jungle boots, beards, and long hair. The flier couldn't handle the scene at all and after calling them "pirates" he ordered them airborne immediately. Lenny Horst's call to the president appeared to have turned the trick.

But for every action there is an equal and opposite reaction. The navy bureaucracy was working at full speed and the chain of command was smoking from Washington, D.C., downward. When Horst and company finally landed at North Island in San Diego, California, the commander of SEAL Team ONE—Captain Dave Shaible—had already been beaten up by the group commander at Coronado. As I said earlier, Shaible was loved and feared in equal measure by his SEALs. When you were right he sang your praises, and when you were stupid he would physically beat you up. The captain was so good at this he only needed to land a single blow to get the message across loud, clear, and painfully. This doesn't happen today, simply because we've got too many limp-wristed specwar techno-geeks in and around the Teams.

The newly arrived platoon trooped into the skipper's office and began filling out their deployment leave requests. Doc Bryant was done and out the door before the commander could get organized and dig out the real culprit behind Horst's ill-advised presidential call. Lenny was left holding the bag when Captain Shaible loudly demanded "Horst, in fifty words or less would you please tell me why you called the freaking president?" Lenny survived the encounter, but it became one of those stories that never stops being told by the old hands to the new guys coming on board.

My tour as an instructor allowed me to defuse somewhat and get things back into perspective. My tactical skills got even better as I honed them by putting platoon after platoon through the demanding course we'd laid out. I evaluated my own performance as a combat operator as well as my students'. The key was to always learn, always improve. I didn't want to repeat past mistakes once I was back in Vietnam, nor was I content to rest on my limited laurels like some others I'd met. Without much warning I found myself assigned to the newly formed Victor platoon, a ticket back to the war in my hands and a "job well done" offered for my time teaching school.

The platoon went through the same predeployment training I'd been handing out for nearly a year. Nothing was taken for granted back then; you trained and trained some more regardless of your reputation or degree of proven skill. Halfway through the cycle we learned our destination was a place called Soc Trang, adjacent to an island complex called Dung. Made up of nine small islands, the objective was located in the middle of a major river with its source in China. It emptied into the South China Sea and was a great natural route for moving enemy equipment and troops around. Dung Island, a haven for such troops, was to be the object of Victor platoon's attentions. Former SEAL Darryl Young had spent an intense tour in this area, which he would later describe in his book *Element of Surprise*.

Our new home was a riverbank about 3,000 meters wide. Little more than 1,500 meters away was Dung Island. We used to sit on the shore and pick out the points where we'd be infiltrating during operations, we were that close! With us was a platoon of Vietnamese SEALs advised by Gary Shadduck and Lenny Horst. I arrived at the small Vietnamese naval base as part of the advance party. As the chopper prepared to land I saw Horst acting as our ground guide and knew this would be one heck of a tour. That very evening Gary and Horst took our tiny party on an operation. Shadduck was a cool operator, although I was given the impression he was internally a very nervous man, and if so, he hid it well.

It was time to hit another VC tax collector, an island hopper who made life miserable for the locals. It was a simple plan, normally the best kind. We'd cross the river by light SEAL support craft (LSSC) and there patrol to a trail intersection where the VC were expected to be later on in the evening. The ambush would cancel out some of Uncle Ho's illegal income, and we'd head back to our shoreside retreat. The Chu Hoi center had provided us with a defector who'd worked in the area before, and everything looked and sounded pretty clean. I would stay with Lenny for the evening's fun and games.

We were creeping down the trail when Horst turned, pointed to his right, and loudly whispered, "VC!" Everyone went for cover and for the next ten minutes we waited, trigger fingers ready to unleash everything at our disposal. "What did you see?," I finally asked Horst.

"Nothing, I just wanted to see how good my guys would react."

My BS meter went into overload upon hearing this. It was all I could do to keep from shooting him myself, but I fought the urge and regained control. "Look, you idiot," I snapped. "Don't ever pull anything like that again!"

Lenny's face took on the look of a wounded puppy. In many ways he was just that, and as frustrating as he could be, everyone couldn't help but love the guy. He was impervious to pain. I remember hearing that Horst was having a few beers at the Tradewinds one evening when a fleet sailor stumbled in and began pouring the booze down like no one's business. Somehow the two men got into it and the blackshoe smashed a beer pitcher over Lenny's head, then smacked him alongside the face with the broken glass. Horst didn't flinch. The fleet sailor grabbed a pool cue and prepared to use it as a club. In a show of bravado the sailor began pouring salt on one end of the cue, telling Lenny he wanted to season the club because the SEAL was going to end up eating it. But when he swung the cue at Horst, hitting him in the side, the cue broke in half. No reaction from Lenny. "Look," said Horst, "we could do this all night and get nowhere. How about we go outside 'cause I've got two .38 caliber pistols. We'll finish this once and for all, okay?" The sailor stared hard at his tormentor, then ran for the door and disappeared into the night. Lenny, shrugging, ordered another pitcher and resumed his quiet evening away from home.

With no gooks in sight we resumed our patrol. The sights, sounds, and smells of Vietnam were coming back to me, and I was grateful. It felt good to be back in the jungle. The mud smelled just as I'd remembered it, and it stuck to my jungle boots so that I felt as if I were wearing lead boots. Vietnam's mud was strong, pungent muck. We used to cover our bunkers with it, as it was like concrete when dry. Despite a twisted ankle during the insertion I was moving fairly well, the pain deadened by my steady pace.

For once the Vietnamese SEALs were doing a good job. They stopped at all the danger areas, sending a point man across to check out the other side before moving on. So far so good, I thought, but we hadn't come under fire yet. Then it happened again. "VC!" blurted Horst. He might as well have just cried "Wolf!" I moved quickly off to the side of the dike we were traversing, my ankle giving out and dropping me like a stone right into a military-style latrine. As I sank into the rancid mixture of feces and urine, I could see the back of Lenny's head.

I wanted to kill Lenny so badly now I couldn't contain it. Shadduck was too far away for me to get his attention, so I moved the muzzle of my rifle so it connected with Horst's rib cage. *Click!* The safety came off with an unmistakable sound. Lenny looked back at me, quizzically, almost innocently and wrinkled his brow.

"What's up" he asked with doelike innocence in his eyes.

"Horst," I hissed from between latrine-soaked lips, "You dumb s.o.b., look where I am!"

"What's the problem, Mike?"

I began yelling, all sense of tactical consideration gone. "I'm neck deep in crap, that's the problem! It's a bloody latrine, Horst, and there's not one stinking gook around here for a mile!" So much for self-control at this point. Despite my intense anger and the fierce urge I felt to kill Lenny right there and then, a little part of me was marveling at his ability to miss the whole point under such circumstances. Please, I prayed, let this operation end real soon.

After some fast talking by Shadduck and the others, I was mollified and we began patrolling again. As we neared the extraction point the radioman called for the LSSC to come in and get us. Our usual practice was to pop a smoke grenade. Once the thick, acrid cloud began billowing away we'd radio the boat crew and ask them to identify the color, and if they did so correctly, we had our ticket home.

Lenny, handling the radio and the smoke, said, "We've just thrown yellow smoke. Can you identify?" I turned in a heartbeat and began running for the jungle, the Vietnamese SEALs way ahead of me. This kind of screwup could bring heavy firepower in on us from our own boat crew or from any VC who happened to be watching or listening.

"Way to go, Lenny," was the bored LSSC commander's only response. He aimed his craft at the smoke cloud and came on in.

To the wary Viet SEALs I could only say, "We go home now." They gave me a funny look, and I couldn't tell if it was about Horst's perverse sense of humor or my truly bad smell. At this point, I didn't really care.

The LSSC was a great infiltration craft. Powered by two Ford 427 engines the vessel was armed with two .50 caliber machine guns, a mini-gun capable of firing 3,000 rounds a minute, and a direct-fire 60mm mortar. Then there was the arsenal we SEALs carried, the result being serious firepower if needed. The boat could come to a complete stop and then turn around within its own length and push itself up a mud river bank nearly three-quarters of its length. If the engines hit a log or something in the river they would automatically reposition themselves without any appreciable loss of speed.

Once back on Dung Island the platoon settled in and began cleaning up. The naval intelligence liaison officer arrived from Soc Trang with some good intel for us. Our target would be a district-level VCI meetinghouse with an added bonus—a tax jockey. I have to admit we really got aroused over these guys, as taking one down meant our party fund would increase greatly, plus bagging this form of VC was good karma for all involved. The operation would have to wait a few days, however, as the platoon, sans those of us in the advance party, needed to unpack.

I soon noticed that the little Vietnamese hamlet on the other side of the security fence from us was populated by first-class thieves. Everything that wasn't nailed down seemed to disappear, and soon we tired of our hosts' penchant for highway robbery. Don Barnes, Victor platoon's radio man, and Mike Woods, the point man, decided to build a hangman's platform, which they called Barnwood's Scaffold. The look of horror on the villagers' faces told us we'd scored a point in our favor. Don would stare over the fence at them from the scaffold, with a death's-head leer that would put Freddy Krueger to shame. The two SEALs even conducted a series of mock hangings for effect, the results of which were entertaining to us but a nightmare for the Viets watching. The stealing stopped and

157

we were able to keep Barnwood up for about a month before the commander ordered its destruction. Guess it wasn't politically correct.

Special operations don't just happen; they must be meticulously planned. In addition, you need the best possible intelligence, and good intel has always been the nemesis of this business. During our platoon meetings we agreed early on that we needed more and better intel if the upcoming raid was to be a success. Once again we turned to the Chieu Hoi center for a defector from the area, and they delivered, thanks to our very effective liaison officer.

Our guide was sixteen years old and was none too happy with the VC anymore. As we prepped for the mission his face took on a somber tone, one I'd seen before and would see again. SEALs preparing for war are professionals. Every action, every inspection of uniforms, weapons, equipment and so on is as precise as a surgeon's. When the war paint goes on we become different animals entirely. The overcoat of civilization is dumped on the floor as the perfectly trained combat artist is revealed for what he is. Every man has his own unique twist on what is standard operating procedure. Some prefer a specific camouflage pattern; others wear a drive-on rag rather than a patrol hat. I opted for VC dress, right down to sandals and an AK-47, whereas others wore sturdy Levi's with their fatigue shirts. Watching as an observer, especially one who'd either been attacked by us or heard about such events, must have been disconcerting to the young man.

He knew we were serious players and that we would be bringing death to his former comrades. The evil-looking Stoner light machine guns caught his eye, and I could read his thoughts. The VC were good weapons people who knew a killing machine when they saw it. The Stoner gave a SEAL squad awesome firepower, and skilled operators could play it like a well-tuned instrument. We gave the turncoat our usual soft sell: "You betray us, you get bullet in back of head, see?" Whenever we had a Chieu Hoi with us we'd brief him in this manner. One SEAL would stay with the man or woman until the operation was over and the guide was safely returned to the center. If things went badly and it was the former VC's fault, the baby-sitter was responsible for paying him off with a well-placed round. On this mission we put the teenager behind the point man, where he could do the most good or take the most lead.

It was decided to go with a reinforced squad-size element. Gary Shadduck and two Viet SEALs would beef up our already weapons-heavy team and I was pleased to have Gary, rather than Horst, along for the ride. The weather was poor, which was perfect for us in every respect. The clouds were gray with rain, and the wind was stiff across the water. As we clambered aboard the LSSC, I could see our intended insertion point just across the river. It was weird, because if we could see them they could certainly see us. This time around, penetration would occur in a narrow inlet. Combat senses on full alert, the small craft slipped toward the island complex. Shadduck was leaning into the sway of the LSSC. He wouldn't fold under combat, and having him with us made me feel secure.

Coming in from the north we picked up the inlet on the radar scope. Radar was a mixed blessing. On one hand, its mast could become a rocket catcher during an attack, but on the other, we needed it to navigate in the delta region. Our night vision devices were first generation and not that good for spotting small openings in the jungle. We preferred using tiny inlets like streams and rivers as they formed a natural trail, which most VC wouldn't figure men would travel on. If such watery pathways eluded us it would mean landing on the leading edge of any landfall available, which always meant possible detection and ambush. The jungle was so thick that moving at night was exceptionally difficult. A stream bed made things easier, way easier.

I plunged into the jungle and felt as if I were entering a wormhole on *Star Trek.* It was a new dimension as opposed to the openness and light of the river. There was no wind. There was no light, not even a faint glow. The insects stopped their cheerful singing as they sensed our presence among them. The only noise was the muffled throbbing of the boat's engines as it crept back out to safety. The smell of the tropical forest enveloped us, attacking clean clothes and bodies with a vengeance. I slipped into my environment like a knife into soft tissue. The jungle was talking to me, leading me, taking me with it. I became an animal, a hunter of men. My senses were overloaded, jacked up, roaring. This is what would keep me and my teammates alive.

The clinging odor of combat emanated from everyone around me. A sudden sharp noise from the distant LSSC echoed off us like a gunshot. Had any nearby VC heard it? We were nearly growling, wary and concerned. Dumb little mistakes like that one could compromise us in a heartbeat. With the LSSC gone, we had no support from its weapons systems. We were on our own. If someone began shooting at us it looked like a movie on the VCR on fast forward. Some said time slowed down; others said that it sped up. In the end, how we reacted to our own private movie was what counted.

We moved onward and soon realized the field surrounding us was filled with punji stakes—hand-sharpened bamboo stakes that are sunk into the ground, point up, at a forty- to sixty-degree angle. Falling on one would gut a man like a Christmas goose. When the VC really wanted to get vicious they'd smear the stakes with human excrement, which could kill you with infection if not treated immediately. Certainly this story has been heard by most Americans, but few have ever heard of how we played the same game. When setting out our claymore mines we'd place wood chips and nails in front of the mine. When driven into the human body, the wood chips would fester and become painful; the nails just shredded people. This proved two could play at the same game. I noted for the record that the punji stakes were laid out pointing toward the river in an apparent attempt to discourage infiltrations such as ours.

One by one we took our weapons off safe. There was a bad smell about this operation, but the Chieu Hoi was still calm. He was down on one knee now, pointing to the target hootch, which sat less than sixty meters off the river. We got down on our bellies in the stinking mud and began slithering like eels toward the hootch. The insects paid us no attention, their constant buzz lulling whoever was on guard into believing all was well. Reaching a low dike, we settled into position and observed the objective. There was a trail running past it, and I began registering the night's common noises while scanning the immediate area. Soon I allowed myself to drop into an alert sleep, knowing that any unusual sound would bring me awake. My eyes were tired, and any time one of us could close them for even a few moments, we did. No one with any field savvy stared at anything for very long. It drew the objective's attention (bad vibes) and created a tunnel vision effect for the watcher. When I was on patrol my eyes moved around like a gun turret, swinging back and forth, up and down, all the time. Most of what we see, we pick up in our peripheral vision anyhow.

While we were resting, the point man moved out to check the hootch. When he and the Vietnamese guide returned, they reported hearing snoring inside the dwelling. The Chieu Hoi thought the occupants were women and children. Three VC were due in the morning. "What are their jobs?" we asked.

"To ambush you green faces," he replied. Both the VC and the NVA called SEALs "the men with green faces" due to the dark camouflage we wore on operations. I have to admit we looked very scary even to ourselves at times.

Doc Bryant looked the guide dead in the eye. "Why didn't you tell us this before?"

"You didn't ask what their other jobs were," countered the Vietnamese. "To you they were only tax collectors and district leaders. They are soldiers, too." Doc shakes his head in grim agreement. There was nothing we could say in response, but the irony was not lost on us. We were here to kill men who were coming here to kill us! Our assessment of the enemy had short-changed both his abilities and his intentions. Now we knew we would be waging war against some serious players, up close and personal.

Dawn's first light broke, and the jungle's animals welcomed it loudly. Around the hootch the roosters joined in, chasing away the night's stars as if they were vampires fleeing the sun's return. The light rain that fell during the night cooled our clothes and bodies, and then the morning's heat began to grow. I listened to the steady bloop-bloop-bloop of fat drops of water cascading off the thick green leaves all around our hideaway. VC children began toddling outside the hootch now. Mom must have been preparing breakfast. Oddly enough, there were no dogs present. I was pleased about this fact, as dogs always sniffed us out, it seemed. The children sang little songs, playing as the scent of food began to drift across to us from the cooking fire. It was so peaceful, so calm, and so refreshing that I could hardly believe we were at war with these people.

But we were.

Our Viet informer relayed what he was hearing. Suddenly he became rigid, alert, tense, as he saw something we still couldn't pick out. Something—or someone—was moving toward the hootch from afar. We still couldn't see anything, but the former VC was nearly quivering with anticipation. Movement. Human movement! Suddenly Murphy's Law came into play. One of the children clambered over the dike and spotted us. She froze in fear, staring straight into our green-painted faces. No one moved. She knew what and who we were; VC parents told horrible tales about the SEALs, much like our own boogie man stories. The young girl began moving slowly backward, her eyes fixed on us. She walked in a trancelike state to the hootch and disappeared inside. Suddenly there was no noise coming from the building. It was deathly quiet. But no signal came from the women that might have betrayed us to the inbound VC.

The lead VCI stepped into view along the narrow trail. He stopped, testing the air like a hound. I could tell he sensed that something was not right. He moved forward, looking at the trail for sign. Then he squatted, rifle at the ready. Now came his first really serious mistake. The VC point man failed to check the sides of the dike. He had totally locked on to the hootch—tunnel vision, like I said. Gary Shadduck moved quietly, quickly, like a viper, toward the man. Both Gary and the Chieu Hoi popped their heads over the dike at the same time the VC did. I saw his skull jerk backward in shock, his eyes widening with recognition and fear as he came face to face with Shadduck. Gary was up on the dike then, bracing himself on one knee, his M-16 ripping off a solid burst. The Vietcong soldier was smashed rearward, his arms flailing as his AK went flying. A blood mist came off the man as the 5.56 caliber rounds impacted with furious velocity.

The other VCI had no time to do anything but die. Our Viet guide was right behind Gary, picking up his empty magazines as he dropped them from the rifle's well and reloaded on the run. Shadduck noted his newfound bodyguard's actions, and I saw him nod with approval. I'd moved to the hootch, and I saw our rounds striking VC bodies. Pieces of enemy clothing and flesh were torn away as our accuracy improved, and then it happened.

Time for me went into slow motion. When combat got

this intense and personal, as it normally did in special warfare, my brain had to get a grip on the action and did so by freezing things up, frame by frame. It was the only way I could make good decisions with the overflow of information being fed into my system through my senses. I watched as the Stoner came into play, its rate of fire so fast and powerful it literally lifted a VC off his feet and held him suspended in the air for several seconds. Doc Bryant let loose and knocked the man down with his own fire. The VC's head exploded, causing his body to arch painfully. He had been blown apart, and bits and pieces fell to the earth like rotten apples. I couldn't tear my eyes away from the legs, which were sawn off from the lower trunk. An arm was severed between the shoulder and elbow. This was no longer a man but a pile of meat.

The adrenaline was really pumping now. I scanned the shattered face and saw only one remaining eye staring off into the soft morning haze. But I was moving, racing to cover the hootch more closely so as to protect our rear area. The rest of the squad was engaging the remaining VCI, who were trying to flee the area. The tax collector collected over fifty Stoner rounds up his back as he made for the jungle's safety. His body took flight from the top of the dike, where our gunner caught him, and he went airborne into the river. With him went the money bag. The man's legs were still running as he flew like a demented bird through the air. But when he hit the water he disappeared . . . along with our party fund.

The other VC was more successful in his bid for life. We couldn't locate him or his body. Shadduck told me to get inside the hootch and locate the other Vietnamese. From the east end of the dike trail I blasted through the door without checking. Too much shooting was going on and too much was happening. I yelled for the woman and her children to come out of the bunker I knew existed; having a bunker inside one's dwelling was standard for Vietnam. As she did so, the Chieu Hoi entered and I ordered him to search the hole for holdouts or weapons; many of the more intricate bunkers had false roofs where a man could hide while others left. Nothing in the hole.

As we began to search the hootch the woman was dead silent. I caught her eyeballing the table when she thought I

163

wasn't looking, but I didn't respond right away. Instead, I kept looking for things that would clearly mark her and her family as VC. Then, without warning, I grabbed the table and overturned it, sending everything crashing to the floor. Her eyes opened wide, and her hatred of us poured out of them like hot lava. "Gotcha!" I exclaimed as I ripped a B-40 rocket launcher from where it had been wired underneath the table. I jammed the deadly weapon right into her face, but she didn't blink. I yelled for the Chieu Hoi and when he appeared, the woman nearly passed out.

"Wee-see, Wee-see!" he said, jabbing a finger at her: VC. The Viet told the woman we'd killed her husband, but she already knew that. Her composure slipped away, and she began moaning, then crying, then wailing. As an information asset she was worthless at this point. You could never shut a prisoner up once the crying began, never. We decided to secure the area, gathering up what we could and destroying what we couldn't. Many times we'd throw the enemy's body parts into the river to send a strong mental message to the VC or NVA: the Vietnamese people believed the body had to be whole in order to enter heaven, so we let them know we would do all we could to prevent this from happening if they opposed us. And, as I explained earlier, we left death certificates on bodies so the enemy would know who'd hit them. Another practice was to photograph the bodies, empty their pockets, and hit the trail. And of course we carefully searched all equipment.

We were just finishing our search when I heard an M-16 go off. Peering out of the hootch's door I spotted Gary down on one knee taking deliberate aim with his rifle. The missing VC was lying on the ground. "I got him!" exclaimed Shadduck as all of our weapons came up. The dying man was trying to cock his SKS rifle when Gary nailed him. He didn't stop, refusing to accept defeat. He fumbled with the rifle, and two loud rifle shots later he was dead. The mission was a success.

Time to go, before a reaction force could arrive. Our radio man, Don, called for the LSSC and told it to get in there fast. We were watching the hootch carefully to make sure the woman or her kids didn't take a potshot at us. Don advised the LSSC to "come straight in, we're now fifty meters or so west of where you dropped us off." Ten tense minutes later we were on the craft and backing out of the area at high speed. Mud was flying everywhere, and the weight of everyone onboard was slowing us down even more. I was soaked to the skin and covered in mud. I must have weighed thirty pounds more because of it. Finally we broke free and were in the river proper. The usual combat bantering started, and I noticed that Gary Shadduck was sitting real cool. He slipped a pair of sunglasses on and kicked back to enjoy the ride. "Real professional," I whispered to myself while watching him. Shadduck didn't let anything get to him. It was all in a day's work. The hard-core VC and NVA react the same way, I'm sure. I decided to learn everything I could from Gary so I could bring my people and myself home alive from this grim little war.

We fought well at Dung Island, and I recall a final note of our stay at Soc Trang. Christmas came around and the platoon decided we needed to let off some steam. Naturally, everyone told the world the war was coming to a halt due to the holiday, but SEAL platoons often used the relaxed atmosphere to really clean VC clocks, as they took the truce seriously. I never had a problem with this policy. After all, this was the nature of special warfare. I remember sitting in ambush waiting for a squad of drunken Vietcong or North Vietnamese to stroll by, weapons on their shoulders, totally confident the gringos would do what they were supposed to be doing, which was nothing. The result was one less squad of enemy troops to fight after the new year was rung in, courtesy of the U.S. Navy SEALs. Nothing was ever said or done about this practice, and the enemy broke the truce as often as we might have, but in their own way.

We chose the city of Can Tho as the site of our upcoming bash. We decided to throw the party in one of the better hotels, inviting half of every SEAL platoon in Vietnam. The eighth floor was ground zero, and on the night of the fiesta food, booze, and women were everywhere. No Hollywood director could replicate this scene on film. There were SEALs with beards, with earrings, and way-too-long hair. We were wearing camouflage fatigue shirts, foreign uniforms, Levi's, and all mixtures in between. All manner of arms were in great display, including horrific combat knives, handguns, and automatic weapons. Over sixty SEALs showed up in Can Tho, and within hours things were out of control.

As night fell and the booze flowed even faster, the furniture began getting rearranged, often meaning stuff was broken up and tossed out windows or into the cluttered hallway. Every blade on the overhead fans was somehow bent downward even as the fans were operating! When the food ran out, someone discovered a Vietnamese wedding down on the fifth floor. Food problem solved. Empty beer and whiskey bottles were dropped from the eighth floor down into the courtyard below, just to keep the waiters and other guests on their toes. Pretty soon, no one wanted to run *that* gauntlet! Finally the hotel's owners called the military police.

The MPs arrived with all the bravado and cockiness most cops the world over possess. This stems from primarily dealing with folks who are either respectful or afraid of the badge, and not necessarily the individual. The MPs raced up the stairs, en masse. The first one to arrive got a well-placed boot in the gut, which sent him back downstairs like an old bag of dirty laundry. Now the cops pulled their sticks, believing it was time to crack some heads and restore order. Big mistake. The first two cowboys had their batons taken away from them and were beaten about the head and shoulders for their transgressions. They joined their fellow officer at the bottom of the staircase. Now came the third wave, and on cue they were met by a barrage of empty whiskey bottles thrown with full force. Down the men went, clutching their heads and faces as the broken bottles opened them up.

"Every one of them guys is armed, but they haven't fired on us yet," said someone near me. The senior MP sergeant had stayed at the bottom of the stairs as his men got trashed, just watching the mayhem.

After the last cop hit the floor, the sergeant was warned by a surly, drunken voice from the top of the stairs: "Next time you guys try to break up our party we're gonna break *you* up!" The MP turned tail and raced to the desk, where he finally was told there were about a hundred SEALs in the hotel having a blow-out. That explained everything to him, and within minutes he'd ordered the entire block cordoned off to protect either us or the civilian and military population at large. The hotel's owner was no doubt considering suicide about this time, and I can't blame him.

For the remainder of the evening we gave ourselves over to increasingly more bizarre forms of emotional and physical venting. There was so much broken glass on the floor that to have gone without footwear would have put fifty percent of all those SEALs operating in Vietnam in the hospital for days. I remember seeing some men wandering around naked except for their guns and boots. The weapons were as much a part of us as an arm or a leg. To be unarmed meant to give up a fighting chance should a sapper or assassin make a play. Anytime after 2100 hours that night the VC could have obliterated us all, but they missed their big chance, or perhaps figured caution was the better part of valor.

The party went on all night and most of the next day. Scenes I remember are best left to one's imagination. Almost everyone who was there is probably married now, with kids, and vague memories of Christmas night in Can Tho. Better it should stay that way. My own value system has changed tremendously since then, and as I approach fifty years old I realize my own mortality as it appears on the horizon. Heaven and hell are not just abstract terms any longer. It was hell that night in Can Tho, but I was too young and too self-involved to realize it.

When the smoke cleared, we all quietly exfiltrated the city and headed back to the real war. MPs hold grudges, especially when their pride is hurt as well as their bodies. They wanted us bad, but on a ten-to-one basis. No matter, we simply headed for the naval base and caught rides back to the boondocks from whence we'd come. I remember our sixty-mile ride back to Soc Trang as being quite beautiful.

On New Year's Eve 1970 we were on Dung Island and the entire platoon was drunk, dead drunk, unforgiving drunk. It had been a rough day. The army finally agreed to attempt to land a CH-47 helo at our location, as we needed supplies and our mail, and we didn't want to travel two days by boat to Can Tho to accomplish the same. Unfortunately, Lenny Horst saw the big helicopter before anyone else and went to vector it in to our landing pad. About thirty meters from the tiny landing zone was our three-seat latrine. The platoon chief was suffering a terrible bout of the runs and was at the time sitting on the john, facing the river.

The huge twin-engine aircraft came in very fast, as was normal given our tactical situation. Sand was flying everywhere and in an instant everything not nailed down was blowing away helter-skelter. We were jerking the shutters over the windows of our hootch closed as fast as possible, catching a glimpse of Lenny as he pulled his diving mask on to continue guiding the chopper in. It came to a hover at one hundred feet. Horst was waving for them to land. No one was on the radio. The pilots were pointing at something Lenny couldn't see because of the furious sandstorm he was in. They had the picture right away, and it wasn't pretty.

As the massive airframe pulled another hundred feet of altitude, we saw what was happening. The latrine, with our platoon chief trapped inside, was under way toward the river. The incredible prop wash from the helicopter had uprooted it, and we could see the chief with his trousers still down around his ankles being tumbled without mercy inside the bouncing and rolling structure. Worse yet, the buckets holding our combined waste had spilled their foul contents all over the hapless SEAL. Horst took this all in as he watched Chief Russell spinning away. He knew he was a dead man.

Lenny waved off the chopper and raced for the platoon hootch. He grabbed his weapon, slung it across his back, and jumped on a little Honda 150 he'd picked up somewhere. In a minute he was out the gate and disappearing down the dirt road. The battered latrine came to a stop at the river's edge. Chief Russell stumbled out of the upside-down toilet, dazed but with a murderous glare in his eyes, which we saw even from our distant vantage point. Gone was the abject pain of tropical diarrhea. Straining to keep our faces straight, we watched as he stumbled the few remaining steps to the river and jumped in. When he came out Doc Bryant gave him a shot of something and we sat down and listened as Russell told us in great detail what he was going to do to Lenny Horst.

Much later in the evening—after the latrine was put back in shape—we had dinner at the Seabee mess hall and began our New Year's celebration. By 2230 hours every weapon in our arsenal, including every weapon in our Vietnamese

SEALs arsenal, was on the beach. We carefully put enough ammo aside just in case the VC elected to pay us a visit, then lined up at the river's edge. Every firearm we owned was aimed at the Dung Island complex sitting out in mid-river. At five minutes before midnight Gary Shadduck gave us our warning order: "Lock and load, guys."

At midnight we welcomed in the New Year by letting everything loose at the islands only 1,500 meters away. Red and green tracers looked like solid beams of light as they arced their way over to strike anything unlucky enough to be in their way. The full moon only made things that much more surreal. The local army advisers living two kilometers away from our own base called in by radio and requested a cease-fire. The two-word response sent back to their radio man was clear: Don't even think about entering our camp tonight, and the heck with your cease-fire! They never showed up. Smart guys. With our party at an end and the new year greeted in SEAL tradition, we retired and made ready to go back to work.

After all, there was a war on.

16

My Tho: Intelligence
Games

Early February 1971. With our war on Dung Island over, Victor platoon moved to Dong Tam, Vietnam. As with other operating locations, you did the best you could in a given operating area, then moved on. This Vietnamese base was also home to U.S. Ninth Infantry Division, the Vietnamese rangers, and their riverine forces. It also housed the Seawolf detachment, which supported us, and that made Dong Tam a very special place. The base was located a few kilometers west of the provincial capital of My Tho. The French influence was clearly evident in the appearance of the buildings and the streets. I'm sure it was a nice little town before the communists and the SEALs showed up. As usual, we were located next to the main river and I'd never seen so much waterborne traffic! In Vietnam the rivers were the arteries of life, linking the countryside to the cities. It was our job to see that the Vietcong and NVA didn't clog up the arteries.

Home this time around was a long, open bay barracks. The platoon was housed on the second floor; below us was the Vietnamese Navy administrative section. I could tell right off the bat they didn't want us anywhere around their turf and that there was little love lost between the SEALs and the Vietnamese version of our elite unit. None of us cared what the Vietnamese thought. They knew who we were and what we did for a living, and the matter was left at that. Until we caught them stealing from us.

One quiet evening Don Barnes and I were sitting on the back porch when we spotted a shadow moving around our fuel tank. We slipped into the night like ghosts, Don moving around to flank the intruder while I did the same from the opposite direction. Bingo! There he was, pumping our gas into five-gallon jerry cans as fast as he could. Barnes and I raced at the man, our booted feet thudding off the gravel so loud our thief looked up, startled, and then tried to escape.

Hit by both of us at a dead run, the Viet was smashed into the side of a steel container. The fuel tank in question sat atop it, gravity-feeding the vehicles Woody Shoemaker, our other point man, had taken such great pains to steal for the platoon. The little puke started to fight us, but I launched a haymaker deep into his guts that dropped him like a deflated balloon. Don and I held a quick conference about what to do with the little dirt bag. We decided to jam him into the small brig the Vietnamese kept near our own conex boxes. The air hole was only about a foot long and no more than eight inches wide, but we managed to fit our new "friend" inside. Barnes and I then began dancing around the makeshift prison, singing Indian war chants and beating on the metal bars. When the Viet seemed to tire of us we grabbed a smoke grenade and popped the spoon. No matter what he did to keep the grenade out, we managed to evade, and within seconds his cage was filled with acrid, choking green smoke. Although he'd put up a good fight, he wasn't very bright. Instead of going to the floor where the air was clean, he insisted on standing up, sucking down most of the smoke. He finally passed out, and we unlocked the door, calling it a night. The message sent was loud and clear: Don't steal from the SEALs!

The VC and their cadre were very strong in My Tho and this meant good hunting for us. They hadn't been hurt—I mean really clobbered—for some time and we were now experts in putting the hurt on Mr. Charles. There was an active Chieu Hoi center available to us, and the platoon elected to start its own agent network. The trick was to get the navy to pay for such a network, as intelligence gathering cost big bucks. The man for the job was our corpsman, Terry Bryant. Doc was easily the most mature man in the platoon. He was stable and an excellent judge of character, with common sense and courage. Medicine would be our ticket to good Chieu Hoi guides and informants. Since I was always heavily into the intelligence side of our operations it would be my job to do the paperwork at our barracks, which was also now our command center.

Our first task was to hire a principal agent out of the center, and Doc soon had a name. The principal agent would serve as the figurehead of the entire organization and would take the fall if our cover was somehow blown. Plus, we had to compartmentalize the effort for security's sake. Bryant would be the primary agent handler and I'd act as the case officer, but we needed a fall guy—known as a cutout—as a middleman. Enter the Chieu Hoi recruited by Doc Bryant. Our officers were chasing down money and blessings from higher authority in Saigon so we could pay informants, purchase supplies, and generally fund the cause. Digging through my goodie bag I found several old passes from my previous Phoenix tour. We decided to duplicate them for our own use. Although I was no longer in the Phoenix program, there was no law against using every talent we'd learned there to beat Charlie at his own game. Every day we weren't in the field we were working on the network. Doc would ply his medical skills at the Chieu Hoi center, making friends and influencing people while I created the organization's infrastructure.

Downtown a young Vietnamese boy came to our attention. His name was Charlie, and both of his parents had been killed by the VC. He was fifteen, spoke English fluently, and had guts as well as an ax to grind with the enemy. He soon became our number one source of downtown news, and he was a tremendous asset. Charlie learned where the VC hid in town, and he filled us in on what our own forces were doing when the Vietcong came to visit. We'd sneak Charlie onto the base at night by boat and teach him how to take clandestine photos of objects and people so we could begin building files. After a while we learned where the American intelligence types hung out and where they met their own agents. Since we often had intel trouble from both sides of the fence, we played both sides to our own benefit. Knowing where and how our own secret squirrels gathered their information allowed us to do likewise, which made our missions more successful and less dependent on the formal chain of command. Our job was to locate, identify, and neutralize the Vietcong infrastructure. We would succeed, no matter what we had to do to accomplish the mission.

We were developing our own information and then targeting the objectives without outside interference. This is fairly significant, and some might consider it rather roguish, but it worked. The problem was money, lots of it. Our officers came back from Saigon with a working fund, which we banked, but almost immediately the military bureaucrats got wind of something going on they didn't understand. One day a lieutenant commander no one seemed to know showed up from Saigon to inspect our operations. I was ordered to prepare a full-scale briefing for the intelligence officer, but Bryant and I were successful in persuading the old man not to allow any of our agents' names to be given. We would supply the names of hamlets and villages we had connections in, but no names. Why? Because we knew the cowboy from Saigon would steal them and try to use them for his own purpose.

One of the first things you learn about intelligence gathering is that the CIA can absorb any agents it wants. My tour with Phoenix confirmed this and I wasn't about to allow all our hard work to go down the drain. We would run our own network from start to finish, beginning with the Chieu Hoi center and ending up on the battlefield. I used butcher paper for the briefing, giving letters and numbers rather than names for our agents. The letter represented a specific district while the number was a means of tracking the agents in question. I never kept the actual names near the files, in case we were compromised. Dead agents do no one any good.

After the briefing, the Saigon commando asked for our agent list. "No way," Doc and I responded. To their credit, our officers backed us up and the visitor simply wished us well and departed. That night Barnes and I shared a bottle of rum and discussed how we were going to proceed. It didn't take us long to come up with a game plan.

With our principal agent in place it wasn't long before we were meeting with agent candidates. Our man was doing the screening for us, only providing the best and most trustworthy Chieu Hoi. Doc then interviewed each potential agent, keeping meticulous notes, which he then shared with me.

The cream of the crop were brought to our base for a full briefing. They were subjected to numerous questions, which were translated by our interpreter, Tran Van San, who is now a successful accountant in southern California. Tran did a superb job for us and I will always admire his courage. Without Tran we could not have analyzed and then confirmed or denied the information given us. True intelligence work means digging, digging some more, and then digging even deeper. When you find it, you know immediately or soon thereafter.

Now came the touchy part. We started inviting other intelligence organizations' agents over for meetings without their handlers' knowledge. Charlie was really earning his money by now, having hired a cyclo driver to pedal him around town picking up agents for our clandestine meetings. As the pedal cab made its way through the twisted streets of My Tho, Doc would jump in at a predetermined point along the route and, with Charlie sitting on his lap due to the cramped quarters, the two of them would interview the agent. It was a simple, reliable system devised to work with simple, reliable people. To my great satisfaction it worked. We relied on tradecraft principles that applied directly to agent contacts and meetings. They are also called personal meetings by those in the business. Whatever you call them isn't really important just as long as everyone involved uses the same lingo to make things work. And work is the bottom line.

Our organization was clicking along quite nicely now. Possessing our own intelligence network made us feel far more secure where operations were concerned, as we weren't at the mercy of the army or anyone else. Whatever they did give us we could feed into our own system to confirm, deny, or add to. The platoon was once again the master of its own destiny. Better yet, there were no politics involved. When we found a worthwhile target we could mount an operation against it without worrying about someone else wanting a piece of the pie. When that happened, things got screwed up. Men died because of such interservice bull, and I wasn't about to lose anyone just to enhance somebody else's career. Certainly our friends and allies knew we had something going, which made them far

174

more respectful. We knew what they did, but they didn't have a clue as to our capabilities.

Doc identified two men who were very promising. We sprang them from the Chieu Hoi center and brought them to live with us at our base. Having Chieu Hoi living with us rather than downtown gave us better control over them and let us get to know them better. Another plus is that if they lived with us we pretty much knew the people they spoke to. It worked for us. One Chieu Hoi was a former VC sapper, the other a former Vietcong foot soldier. Both became very adept at passing themselves off to the VC as nothing more than village folk, keeping their special passes well hidden to avoid being compromised. My biggest fear was of our agents being betrayed by infiltrators working deep within the South Vietnamese government. Everyone working on the ground in Vietnam knew this was a more than serious problem. I cannot count the times Americans and loyal Viets as well as other friendly forces were killed, captured, or wounded because of high-level leaks carried out by clever North Vietnamese intelligence agents. However, that was the GVN's problem to root out. At our end we could only enact the most stringent of countermeasures and hope for the best.

Finally we hit the mother lode. Doc came across a Chieu Hoi who claimed to be a Vietcong assassin. He told us about hitting a U.S. Army captain while riding past him on a Honda motorbike. Steering with his left hand, he fired into the officer holding a handgun in his right, or so he claimed when we questioned him about the incident. We ran his story past our regular intelligence channels and learned that a young army officer had indeed been gunned down in the manner described on the day the former VC gave us for the killing. Still, we were not convinced.

Doc and I found a little-used dirt road near the base and borrowed a Honda. We set up some man-sized targets, gave the Chieu Hoi a .45 automatic, a motorbike, and told him to show us how he did the captain. Without hesitation the man jumped on the bike, stuck the pistol in his belt, and headed down the road toward the targets. Blam! Blam! Blam! Blam! Four targets, four holes center mass. Doc and I looked at each other and nodded; the Chieu Hoi was hired. When he arrived back where we were standing, I noted the crazy look in his eyes. I knew we'd be okay around him as long as someone was armed at all times. Doc told him if he ever picked up a weapon without our express permission, he was a dead man. Message received.

Some may question our ability to work with the man responsible for the cold-blooded killing of a fellow service member, but throughout the history of warfare men have changed sides for one reason or another, becoming informants, counterspies, or guides and scouts. In Vietnam, the Kit Carson Scouts were former VC and VCI who had elected to throw in their lot with us and by doing so led numerous American units against their new enemy. Our assassin was an asset to our growing intelligence program. I despised him for what he'd done, but I also understood war. More than one G.I. had defected and become a combat adviser for the VC and NVA, so such things were no surprise. In any event, if the man ever indicated a desire to become a VC again, we'd terminate his employment on the spot.

Soon after joining the payroll, our Chieu Hoi turned us on to information about an American POW supposedly being held along the coast where the My Tho River spilled into the sea. There was a $7,000 reward in U.S. currency for a live American prisoner of war being recovered or repatriated, and every SEAL in Vietnam wanted such a mission. Sadly, the military bureaucracy in Saigon also put its cold heart into such missions, but only in order to be involved should a POW actually be rescued. As we began preparing to launch a recovery effort every low-life oxygen thief in Saigon began poking his nose into the operation. Our platoon commander was nearly swamped with unwanted rudder guidance. People we'd never heard of were coming out of the woodwork and telling us how they would be controlling our operation from somewhere high above or far behind the SEALs on the ground. In my professional opinion this is why no Americans were successfully freed from prisons during the war. Instead of keeping their mitts off the men who knew how to get the job done, the brass injected themselves into the planning circle so loudly that security leaks literally spurted from command offices throughout Vietnam.

It didn't take us long to come to our senses. We would provide only what we absolutely had to in terms of intelligence and detail, and no more. My frustration level was exceptionally high but the job came first, so I put my personal feelings aside and got on with the mission.

We asked army aviation to provide armed Huey helicopters and slicks for the rescue, and they turned us down flat. The overweight aviation commander said, "Every time I turn my birds over to you SEALs, they get shot up!" Poor baby, I thought to myself upon hearing his lame-ass excuse. An American POW was being held under the worst conditions by the enemy, and this fat, lazy pig of a squadron commander was worried about property cosmetics. Naturally we went over his head, and two days later we were back in his office describing to him our exact needs and wants where "his" helicopters were concerned. The armed Hueys would fly support as our gunships with the unarmed birds ferrying in the raiding party and, hopefully, carrying out a live POW. Our next stop was the home of the Black Ponies, a detachment of fixed-wing OV-10 Broncos who could hang out at 10,000 feet, flying cover for the helos. These guys were real pros who never backed off a combat mission, and we needed their expertise to cover our infiltration and extraction. With the Ponies there was no fuss, no muss, when it came to laying on support resources.

At last the sickening bureaucratic battle was over. Every administrative puke in the country had tried to squeeze his way into this one, but we'd managed to shove the majority of them back into their holes, where they belonged. With nearly forty miles to travel, our party left My Tho in the afternoon, arriving at the district HQ at mid-evening. A borrowed coastal junk was waiting for us, and as everyone clambered aboard for the long ride up the coast, I began once again going over our intelligence briefing.

An aerial photograph taken of the target area revealed a large hootch, just as the Chieu Hoi had described to us. This was a good sign. I knew it would be important that we hit the site with total surprise on our side. The VC prized U.S. POWs and would rabbit as soon as they even sensed a rescue attempt. There could be no mistakes on our part. None, not one.

A navy swift boat kept in touch with our junk as it moved up the coast. The gooks would not expect us to come in from the sea, as most often we inserted either from a river or from the air. This would be the first time I'd infiltrated from the ocean. Every other mission had seemed to involve mangrove swamps and tons of latrine-smelling mud. We expected to find a lone guard somewhere on the beach, probably dreaming of a loved one while watching the scant moon and listening to the steady deep drone of the surf as it pounded away at the sand. If luck was on our side he'd have gone to sleep and we could infiltrate without a problem. If not, then it would be a foot race to see who got to the objective first. I was glad I'd worn my combat Nikes.

Coming ashore we spotted the tracks of someone who'd fled the area in great haste. The race was on! I knew we had over two kilometers to cover, and dawn was fast approaching. The raid party fell into formation, point man on lead, when our assassin suddenly took over point and began pointing out VC booby traps. He led us around them, stopping now and then to dismantle one that was impossible to avoid. His movements were swift, sure, and accomplished, even in total darkness. Couldn't argue with success. With time our most critical factor we moved rapidly, and just as the sun's first faint rays began to penetrate the jungle we spotted the hootch.

With security in place, we waited. No one was present around the dwelling—at least no one we could see or hear. There was no smell of woodsmoke, no sickening odor of human waste. Most of all, there were no animal noises such as those made by dogs, and dogs were almost always present at POW sites as an early warning system. But when the sun came up, our hootch turned out to be a clever mock-up. The large mound of dirt mimicked a Vietnamese jungle dwelling perfectly. "Here's your hootch, Walsh," growled the platoon commander. I couldn't think of a thing to say. Every hotshot photo interpreter in Saigon and elsewhere had given a thumbs-up to those aerial shots taken for us, and so had I. An overhead shot taken from an oblique angle would have clued us in. Such was not our luck. After a quick look around to make sure we hadn't been sucked into an ambush, we decided to turn the mission into a combat patrol. No sense wasting the day or the effort.

The trail was well used and soon we were padding along it looking for any sign of the enemy. Doc sent a signal up the file we were moving in. Someone was coming up fast behind us. I melted into the jungle, as did my teammates, weapons at the ready. Two VC appeared, both carrying rifles. At the last possible minute one of them spotted us and fired a panic shot. His buddy turned to flee as we hosed down his comrade. The wounded man scrambled into a nearby bomb crater where he covered himself with mud and oozed into the crater's wall. As hard as I looked, I couldn't find the man! Our assassin came up beside me and pointed to a spot in the water-filled hole. Nothing. Again he pointed and still I saw zero. Then the VC's nerves betrayed him and he moved just a fraction. We were on him in a heartbeat, dragging him from the hole and tying him up. Instead of freeing a POW we'd taken one, all ninety-some pounds plus a few ounces of bullet weight. The slicks were called in and we extracted immediately. Where the other VC went we're not at all sure, but the squad wasn't hanging around to find out. The pilots told us a press crew was waiting at Dong Tam, the district headquarters, for us. Those pretty boys in Saigon set up a media circus hoping to cash in on a POW rescue at our expense. The lesson learned was we would now present such missions as low-level VCI interdiction operations and then lay on all the support we could muster. Fighting the VCI was easier than fighting our own trophy hounds. At least you knew where you stood with the gooks.

Our disappointment at the failed POW effort soon faded in the rearview mirror. Doc and I were now calling our intelligence work a "class project," and we'd rented the top floor of an old French villa as a safe house for everyone when we were working downtown. It offered us a high vantage point for observation purposes, and we could, if necessary, defend it pretty easily. Those Chieu Hoi who were not allowed on base due to security concerns were brought blindfolded to our little home away from home in downtown My Tho. Our two senior Chieu Hois were now part of the platoon and went everywhere we did within reason. Charlie was superb at identifying all the notable players for us, the American intelligence types being the most predictable. One of our more devious efforts included taking clandestine pictures of American intelligence agents when they were partying with their Vietnamese girlfriends. Many of these men had wives back in the States. We used the photos when we needed leverage that one of these clowns could provide if he really wanted to. Most of the agents who couldn't keep their pants zipped understood our little insurance program very well, and they delivered.

The bars we frequented always had at least two exits and were often adjacent to the river, a handy location for a SEAL. I vividly recall one particular evening when two very drunk Vietnamese rangers decided to see who was the braver of the duo. One pulled a hand grenade from his pocket and placed it on the table between himself and his friend. He announced that whoever ran from the bar first was a coward, and then he pulled the pin, arming the deadly little device. Out the back door we went, and into the river. Charlie, who was with us, later told me that both men were blown to bits when the grenade went off. Not brave, just dumb.

After this I began carrying a mini-CS grenade so I could clear the area if we were trapped by too many drunken bodies from our escape route. A month later we were the target of an attack in another bar where we often met. The VC were finally figuring us out, and I'd expected them to wake up sooner or later, given the intensity of our operations in My Tho. As was most often the case, it was Charlie who alerted us to danger.

Charlie had managed to evade being identified as our agent. One night he slipped into the place where we were hanging out and informed me the VC were waiting outside, hiding behind small taxis and such, ready to waste us with automatic weapons fire when we left. Charlie was so scared his eyes were nearly leaping from their sockets as he described the setup. He was a brave kid to risk his life for us, and I've never forgotten him. The VC expected us to walk out the front, so I tossed the grenade out the front door and we boogied out the back exit. A twenty-foot free fall brought us into contact with the river's surface. Minutes later we'd found our boat and were headed back to base. Charlie spent the night with us, and the next day we cleaned out the downtown villa, feeling its usefulness was now over. Doc and I later found out some of the guys in the platoon had been bringing their Vietnamese girlfriends upstairs while we were away. Huge security breach, but there wasn't much we could do about it now.

I learned a great lesson from this. Guys who think with

their penis are the easiest to target and then kill or capture. Sex is a terrible weapon but one that works nearly every time. Even the best operators and agents make often terminal mistakes because they have a lady friend on the side. In 1983, one of our own SEAL officers was assassinated in El Salvador for just this reason by guerrillas. Good guys, bad guys, it makes no difference. Dumb means dead, anyway you cut it.

At last we got a break. Information came in about a VCI regional command post located in the northernmost reaches of our province. Hitting such a target would be like taking down a battle management staff hosting one- and two-star generals. This was one we had to do right or not at all. Somehow the Vietnamese Police Special Branch got involved and our security concerns went right through the ceiling. If our own second-guessers in Saigon could screw things up, how much more so could our allies?

Another major challenge was combat logistics. Our helos would have to fly us up to the objective, then turn around and come right back for fuel. Total time? Ninety minutes. If we ran into serious opposition from the VC, those ninety minutes would be our death sentence. Something had to be worked out and we all knew it. As was our habit, junior enlisted men actually ran the operations in the Teams, so point man Mike Wood picked up the ball and ran with it. The first thing we learned was that even one fly-over for a visual reconnaissance would tip our hand and blow the mission. Switching to Plan B we used the newly issued pictomaps, which were a combination of a photograph of the area and a map. Terrain features were highlighted and all coordinates were in 1:50,000 scale. I believe these are the best maps for combat anywhere in the world today. I only wish we'd had the kind of navigation systems that are available today back then.

Rather than play with the army this time around we went to our Seawolf aviators for helo support. We waited, though, until the week prior to mission launch, because we wanted to ensure the operation was a go before pulling everyone in behind us. The entire platoon—fourteen SEALs—would be hitting the C&C site. Each squad had a mission and an individual objective. The terrain was typical, a wide open area with little or no cover surrounded by jungle, paddies, and dikes. No vertical intelligence photos were available to us because raising such an issue would alert the pogues in Saigon to our little party. My squad was responsible for taking down the communications hootch, where we believed most of the high-ranking VCI's bodyguards would be located. Another squad would hit the VCI themselves. Capturing senior VCI alive was a very tough job, but we'd give it a try.

D day would be a daylight assault. Our tour was coming to an end, and no one wanted to be shipped home in a box. It was decided we'd do some serious practice, so a huge bunker near our living quarters was selected for close battle drills and entry techniques. Weapons were cleaned and tested, intelligence checked and rechecked, radios primed and readied. The atmosphere got heavy, we all wanted this one to go down in a big way, our last bit for the war effort before heading back to Coronado. I was even more intense than usual. So much work had gone into our entire effort at My Tho that this had to be the payoff.

During the helo ride, Doc and I kept staring at each other with that "we're in for it now, and we may even die, but boy, we're having fun!" look that SEALs get when they're going to war. We didn't care about living or dying at this point. It wasn't an irresponsible attitude, but one that was cultivated among the best of the breed so the job could be accomplished. You don't go to the Olympics with a maybe-I'll-win attitude; you go to win regardless of the opposition arrayed against you. That's how we fought the war, no mercy asked for and none given.

The Huey pilot was a natural at his craft. He came in low and fast and knew how to read a map. I could tell he'd done his homework as we skirted tree line after tree line in order to mask our approach. The sun was at our backs, and suddenly we were on target. The compound exploded into view and we were still moving at full throttle, making the helo an impossible target to hit. The entire area was a VC stronghold, and I noted gun position after gun position as we blasted past. I saw the entrance to the main hootch and caught a glimpse of a woman standing in the door. Her hands were over her eyes trying to blot out the sun's rich glare as she attempted to make us out. When she finally recognized the choppers she disappeared into the dwelling's dark interior to give the alarm.

Looking quickly over at Terry I got the same message I was trying to send him: There's a lot more bad guys on the ground than we thought. The rush of the wind made speech impossible, and the ground was coming up fast beneath the rapidly descending helo as the pilot prepared to land. I saw a man rushing from a hootch, an AK-47 in one hand and a huge rucksack in the other. Woody Shoemaker and I were halfway out of the Huey now, standing on its skid ready to leap off as soon as we were close enough to the ground to do so safely. With his left hand wrapped around something inside the helicopter's cabin, Shoemaker began firing his Stoner with the right, bracing the weapon's bucking butt-stock against his hip. The running VC's head was split dead down its middle as a stream of 5.56 copper-jacketed steel zipped through him. Brains flew all over the ground as the body collapsed. Great shot, I thought to myself. We were off to a super start on this one!

Two more men appeared at the hootch's door and split up as they made a run for the jungle. Both were armed, carrying packs and wearing NVA uniforms! VC we expected, but North Vietnamese regulars? Nope, just our luck holding as we sprayed the two with automatic weapons fire. One man went down, and I was so close I actually saw the look of surprise on his face as he plowed into the dirt. He died in place, and we turned our attention to his buddy, who was now hiding behind a dike. Every time his head came up Chief Russell and I sent rounds at him. Our Viets were yelling for the man to surrender, which he wouldn't do. The Viets finally began shooting at the trapped soldier every time his head popped over the top of the dike. Gunfire was everywhere, and I spotted the problem. Our SEAL squad inserted on the VCI hootch, which was the primary target. The other SEAL squad inserted on the communications/security force hootch. Across the 800 yards-meters of open, flat ground we saw the entire VCI security element engaging the other SEAL squad. Everyone on both sides was on line, facing each other, and all were firing while advancing. From our position it looked like something out of the Civil War. No one was giving ground, and the sound of gunfire was overpowering as the two sides engaged. One VC soldier was shooting at the advancing SEAL squad with nothing more deadly than a handgun of some sort. No SEALs had gone down, and we observed our other squad continue the advance on the VC squad. The enemy held his ground but was flanked, and within minutes our side had blasted them off the face of the earth. "What are they doing now?" I asked myself. Souvenirs! The other squad was ignoring post combat security and grabbing trophies from the dead even as we were still battling it out with our holdout VCI! What a way to fight a war.

Our attention went back to the task at hand. Inside the hootch we saw two very pretty women. It turned out they were NVA nurses, both of them striking. Rushing the large hut, we found a frail old man who was left sitting in a daze. We secured the area. The remaining enemy soldier was finally killed, his body dragged back to where we could comfortably search it. Then one of the most bizarre things of the operation took place, and I was center ring.

The moments after intense combat are the most precarious. Anything can happen as you are often totally beyond rational thought. Suddenly we had three dead VIPs at our feet and a squad of hard-core VC beginning to rot in the morning sun. The air was alive with electricity as we realized our success. Better yet, no one on our side was either dead or wounded. The two female prisoners were absolutely lovely, and clearly afraid for their lives as they realized who'd taken them. Our Vietnamese cops were jabbering a hundred miles an hour with the Chieu Hoi, who were helping search the dead men's belongings. It was an unreal situation just barely in control, as at any time the VC could hit us with a platoon, a company, or even a battalion for all we knew.

A SEAL suddenly grabbed one woman's shoulder and gave her a leer that needed no interpretation. Everyone got quiet as the unspoken message was sent around our small circle. The nurses understood immediately what was being considered by at least one of us, and the terror in their eyes was abrupt. I tried to break the spell by saying, "Hey, we don't need this" to my teammate. Without batting an eye he jammed his weapon into my belly before anyone could react. I froze. To this day I believe he would have killed me over that woman and his desire to rape her on the floor of that stinking VC hootch. I stared into his glazed eyes. "You gonna kill *me* over a VC whore?" I asked. The words sank in and he slowly lowered the rifle, allowing the woman to shake free from his grasp. Inside I was shaking, knowing how close I'd come to meeting my Maker.

The helos were now coming in to extract us. The women were put on one bird with the PBS cops and we decided to stay on the ground. After all, the Seawolves were inbound with their firepower and we wanted some more of the VC. Once our prisoners were safely delivered, we'd take the next chopper out.

While searching the dead we pulled apart the first man's rucksack. It was full of NVA documents marked TOP SECRET. There were biographies, maps, charts, battle plans, and VCI supply and travel routes all the way up to regional level. A real prize! Our Chieu Hoi then told us we'd bagged two generals, one a two-star. Generals seemed to be my forte, I thought to myself just as the jungle erupted with gunfire.

Main force VC had finally arrived from their holding area and as they began to break out of the tree line the Seawolf gunships came on station. The new 3,000-rounds-per-minute mini-guns went to work, and I watched rank after rank of enemy cannon fodder turned into salad as they were engaged by our pilots. When the extraction slick came in, we climbed aboard, shaking and smiling.

We'd pulled it off!

At Dong Tam the captured documents were taken from us immediately. The Saigon cowboys were on site as soon as word finally leaked out as to what our target was, and they were highly upset! The material never stopped in Saigon, we later heard, but went straight to the intelligence spooks at the Defense Intelligence Agency for analysis. What we'd captured shut the entire VC infrastructure down. It would take them two years to recover enough to rebuild their organization. A nice little piece of work in anyone's book, and you can't argue with success.

As we shut down our projects we began to realize how much trouble the war effort was in at home in the United States. Had our efforts, our sacrifices, been worth it? I believed they had been. Targeting people as we'd done on our own had proved successful. We'd learned a lot from this experience, and I was in the Teams for the long haul, Vietnam or no Vietnam. My own career had been richly enhanced, and I could proudly claim to have killed three important enemy generals. As a professional, this was all the reward I needed.

In retrospect, though, I never did hear what finally happened to the two NVA nurses at the hands of their countrymen. I hope history was kind to them.

17

X-Ray Platoon

Three-quarters of the way through my tour at My Tho I took some R&R and visited with X-Ray platoon at Ben Tre. I had a few friends there and visits with other platoons were rare enough as it was. Like us, they were located beside a main river, and since it was only a thirty-minute flight by helo from Don Tam, I decided to drop in and pay my respects. When visiting other SEAL platoons in Vietnam it was understood you brought along your combat gear. More than likely you'd find yourself on a combat operation before any socializing took place, kind of a weird way of welcoming you aboard. It also allowed your peers to see what you were made of and what level of operator you were. The SEAL community, like all other special operations forces, is a small one. Word got around, both good and bad. If offered a chance to run with a squad from X-Ray platoon I'd jump on it. To beg off would have indicated a serious problem in my attitude, and I had no such problem when it came to war fighting. Ben Tre would become a major turning point in my professional life. It was here I made the decisions that formed my career path for the remainder of my time in the navy.

Mike Collins was the platoon commander, and Ed Jones was the chief warrant officer. They'd done a tour together at Can Tho with Phoenix. Their activities there were regional in nature, and whenever those of us assigned to the program gathered in the city for business, Mike and Ed had their hands full. All Phoenix matters were handled before lunch, and we spent the rest of the day and night terrorizing the town as only SEALs could terrorize a town.

I recall one such meeting where six or seven of us were trying to check into the hotel in town. The young Vietnamese desk clerk was nasty, which just provoked us even more to give her a hard time. When she'd confirmed we were with the PRU she'd said, "No more rooms for you PRU guys" as if we'd accept this and go away. Bill (not his real name) took his briefcase and smashed it hard into the desk's polished surface. The young woman appeared to go into shock at the violence of the act, and stood there beginning to tremble. We understood her reaction, as we'd each seen it a hundred times or more when the "men with green faces" appeared from nowhere to capture and kill their enemies. Bill began undressing in the lobby. No one said anything, our faces deadpan as he slipped his clothes off. Finally he was nude and both Vietnamese and American guests were fleeing the lobby in a panic. High-ranking U.S. officers strolled past us, ignoring Bill as they tried to go about their business. Our teammate then opened his briefcase, took out a change of clothes, and began dressing. The desk clerk got the message, and rooms suddenly became available. I guess you just have to know how to talk to people.

That same evening the hotel was raided by both Vietnamese and U.S. military police. We heard later that "someone" had been spotted on the establishment's roof test-firing a silenced Smith & Wesson M-76 submachine gun at the stray cats living in Ben Sum Ouy alley, next to the hotel. Apparently a few stray rounds had found their way through the windows of a whorehouse across the street and the residents and guests were complaining. We felt the atmosphere created by too many cops in one place was not at all restful so we "checked out" on the run. Naturally the MPs figured we'd come down the elevator and leave by the front door, so they posted all their manpower in the lobby to await our arrival. Wrong! As was always our practice we did the unexpected and left by the rear stairwell, knowing how predictable the cops could be. By the way, the M-76 was a great little weapon.

I thought the world of Mike and Ed, especially Ed. We'd attended training together in the Cuyamaca Mountains where the instructors, for some reason, had given my teammate a bad time. I never knew why, as he wasn't a troublemaker, although he was somewhat outspoken. Ed was black, and a good man in every respect. It became my habit to confide in him, and I could count on him to shoot straight with me in return. Jones would tell you the things you didn't want—but needed—to hear about yourself. He was a sea daddy, the kind of man every young sailor needs to show him the ropes. I've tried to pass along much of what Ed Jones taught me since those early days of training, as a tribute to one truly remarkable SEAL.

X-Ray platoon suffered over 150 percent casualties during their tour at Ben Tre. This meant over half the men were wounded at least twice, and some were killed. No one in X-Ray platoon went unscathed during that tour. When I was operating at Soc Trang the X-Ray platoon was ambushed while inserting. Frank Bomar and a man named Ritter were killed by direct AK fire moments after stepping ashore. The VC had correctly predicted the most likely insertion point for a SEAL operation, and they had planted a submerged 500-pound command-detonated mine in the river meant to blow any small craft to bits. As the SEAL squad prepared to come ashore the mine was fired but failed to detonate. Despite this, the VC opened up with everything they had and Ritter took four AK rounds across the chest. He was dead before he hit the ground. Bomar was hit by a single round in the right femoral artery. The bullet severed the artery and sixty seconds later he bled to death. Not a good day for the good guys.

I was in Can Tho reenlisting for another four years of navy life when the bodies were brought in, and it was a sobering reminder we were not invincible. Either X-Ray platoon was really hurting the gooks, or they'd become too predictable in their operations. It turned out the latter was the case and the VC were hitting back . . . hard. It cost us two good men, but the men in the platoon learned their lesson.

Now I was in Ben Tre, seeing good friends and getting the chance to see how they operated. My first concern was how they were gathering and evaluating their intelligence. Ed and I disagreed over their modus operandi, but this didn't affect our friendship in the least. On my first evening in town we launched an operation using an MSSC, or Medium SEAL Support Craft, to patrol the main river. I noted almost right away that the map being used to navigate was inaccurate, but no one in the platoon seemed to give this much thought. Their tactics were flawed, and by the time we reached the infiltration point I knew we'd been compromised long ago. Regardless, the platoon boss gave the order to go in and so we did. The objective was a dry hole . . . although I wasn't at all surprised.

It was obvious why they were having problems. Sometimes it's more difficult to recognize one's shortcomings when you're so close to the subject and perhaps personally involved. This might have been the case with X-Ray platoon. Doc Barnes, my radio man and near constant companion, was along for the ride to Ben Tre and was picking up the same vibes. We decided to concentrate on the platoon's intelligence guys in an effort to upgrade their capability. The next operation was going to be a rough one, and we decided to go along and see it through.

X-Ray had found themselves a Chieu Hoi who claimed he knew a VC demolition factory located some distance from Ben Tre. The target was said to be situated on the upper reaches of a secondary river. The VC informer said he was unable to find the factory at night because he couldn't navigate. "Yeah, right," I told myself. Barnes and I, with our combat senses, could smell this one beginning to stink immediately. A VC who couldn't travel through the jungle at night? I'd never met one, nor had any other SEAL I knew. I was invited to interrogate the Chieu Hoi, as the intelligence guys had been students of mine during their training at SBI just months earlier. It was a psychological advantage I exploited to the max. This was one Chieu Hoi I didn't trust one iota, but in the end, my feelings made no difference.

Mike Collins listened to what I had to say, then listened to his own men, then ordered us to insert the next afternoon. "Here we go again," I told Barnes. I hoped history would not repeat itself where X-Ray's luck was concerned.

We could not have asked for a prettier day in which to operate. The sun was bright, winds were low, and the water was calm. Clint Majors, a recent graduate of both BUD/S and SBI, was running point. I thought a lot of him and still do. Our selected insertion point was a mystery to me. It offered no distinguishing feature whatsoever. Normally, this is a good thing; it means the bad guys probably won't set up on it waiting for Navy SEALs. But this time around I was getting that little feeling that told me this was going to be a bad day. We were going in over a riverbank roughly ten feet high, and its 45-degree slope would have been a real nightmare under the best of conditions.

The take-charge attitude I'd been slowly fostering as a SEAL took over. "Clint," I yelled, "get over that hump as soon as you can! I'll send an automatic weapon to back you up!"

Ed Jones flashed me an angry look. "Who's running this operation?" he asked as we neared the riverbank.

"You are, Ed," I responded, "but an automatic weapon makes sense, doesn't it?"

Jones motioned for the automatic-weapon man to move forward so he could scamper up behind Clint once we touched shore. Ed knew I'd been working with Majors as a point man, so he didn't give me too much smoke for offering the advice. I think Clint was secretly happy with the suggestion, as it would have been pretty lonely on the other side of the massive mud wall with just a rifle as backup.

The patrol scrambled onto the bank quickly as our boat nestled up to it as firmly as was possible. No contact meant we could get on the trail immediately, and within a short time we'd located the objective: a small cluster of hootches, all of which appeared to be deserted. I asked Ed to set out security while Clint and I moved forward to check the huts. "Watch out for booby traps," I warned Majors. Our Chieu Hoi was wandering around, and I motioned him to get down beside Jones. He didn't move—at least not right away. With a fierce shove I sent him headfirst into the ground, his face sliding across the coarse earth until he stopped just inches from where Ed was positioned.

Clint and I entered the empty compound. We found strong evidence the place had once been used as a demolition factory by the VC. Vast amounts of various explosives and their components were still present. We moved everyone into place once we were certain there were no enemy troops about, and we began gathering up what we could. I told the Chieu Hoi I was on the verge of cutting him up like a Texas steer. Ed restrained me, but the agent was convinced he would die at any second. Fear of me would keep him honest, I hoped.

Once our rucks were full, we burned and destroyed everything else. We recalled the boat, and the driver told us he'd just passed a squad-sized bunker on his way in. "Looks like the Alamo," he offered. After a quick conference we decided to locate the bunker and blow it in place using some of the captured demolitions. Might as well make a clean sweep of it so the operation wouldn't be a total loss.

We reinserted from the river near the bunker's position. After checking it for booby traps and snakes, we entered. I was always concerned about snakes, as the enemy often wired them up as living booby traps. If you missed one and he bit you, well, it was a bad way to die. More than once I used a small stick to swat at entrances just to see what might swat back. The hand of God was upon me, as never was I hit by one of these foul creatures.

The bunker was huge inside. There were firing ports, cooking areas, and sleeping quarters. Oh, for another claymore pillow trick! But the idea was to blow the entire complex, so that was what we did, using a time fuse and as much explosive as possible. The whole thing went up like a textbook problem. They'd built it well, but we blew it better. Time to go home and have a few beers over this one.

As we were leaving I noticed the boat was so heavily loaded now that we were having problems getting under way. Just as we seemed to be picking up some speed Doc Barnes saw a man stand up on the shore and fire a B-40 rocket right at us. Doc was just yelling a warning when the round struck us in the flank. We came to an immediate stop, dead in the water, a sitting duck for the second rocket, which was already on its way. I watched it strike the river's surface, ricocheting off the water and heading into the jungle rather than our crippled vessel. When it exploded, the shrapnel came back at us, zipping and cutting through the air with deadly intent.

I was at the bow, watching the port side as security when all this took place. The first blast lifted me off the deck, blowing my weapon clean away. There went my precious Stoner into the river. I was heading that way myself, but a radio cable wrapped itself around my throat as I flew past it, keeping me out of the water but not doing anything for my attitude. Shock was setting in from the unexpected attack, the fury of the blast that had nearly killed me, and from nearly strangling to death while flopping around the deck like a hooked fish. Clawing my way to a more secure position on the boat I looked at the horror the B-40 attack had brought us.

Thick, acrid, clinging smoke filled the boat's guts. The driver was peppered with bits of B-40 steel, his torso and crotch bleeding profusely. Bodies were strewn all over the back deck, so many packed so tightly together you'd step on someone no matter how careful you tried to be. Then I saw McCarthy. His entire right cheek had been blown off his butt, and what was left was actually cooking! He was conscious, and that blew me away as I looked into his pain-filled eyes. Ed Jones managed to grab the big .50 and began emptying its lethal load into the VC position. They actually ran! It was their worst mistake, because we would have been history had they stayed and kept up their fire. The ambush had been a good one; they just didn't follow through as a well-trained force would have.

As the coxswain got the vessel moving again I yelled over at McCarthy, trying to beat the growing sound of the straining engines as they picked up speed. "Mac, can you hear me?" I asked the wounded SEAL.

"Yeah," he slurred back groggily, "what happened?"

"All your grenades exploded, and you don't have an ass anymore," I explained to him as I crawled over to where he lay. "Hold still," I begged him. "Let me get the rest of your equipment off."

"Okay, Mike," he whispered back. "Just don't throw what's left of my butt away!"

Mac's grenades had been detonated in low order, meaning an incomplete detonation took place due to the B-40 rocket, which sympathetically set off the man's explosives when it struck and exploded near him. All the smoke grenades had gone off, filling the boat with their colored vapors. As we raced downriver toward safety, the smoke cleared and I could see the extent of the damage. Missing legs greeted me. Our Vietnamese interpreter had lost his legs, and I began looking for the Chieu Hoi. The rocket had struck the boat precisely where he'd been standing. It's shrapnel had gone through him and into the back of my head and neck. He'd taken the brunt of the explosion, lucky for me.

I found him lying against the inside wall of the boat. I picked him up, looking directly into his face. As he lay there dying, his eyes opened and he gave me a smile. He'd known about the ambush, and he'd led us into it with the knowledge he might have to be sacrificed. Pulling my Gerber fighting knife from its sheath, I buried it deep in the hollow between his throat and his shoulder. He'd die, all right, by my hand, for what had just occurred. Dropping the dead traitor back to the bloodstained deck I began tending to Mac. The boat was roaring along at full speed, and I was slipping into secondary shock. It was also my job to act as a backup corpsman but my world was swimming so badly that when I tried to inject morphine into Mac, I hit myself in the hand before realizing it. Ed Jones worked his way over to me and took care of Mac's pain with a quick shot even as I passed out next to my two teammates.

The coxswain radioed our condition and situation to our sister squad, which was waiting for us on the pier. I awoke before we landed, and still remember vividly the looks on their faces. Mac was first off, then everyone who was missing a limb. Walking wounded like me came last. I wanted a cup of coffee, for some odd reason. The platoon's leading petty officer was Lou DiCroce. Lou found me some coffee and then began doing what he could for the others. Army medics began tagging us, and it took two helos to get us all to the hospital. DiCroce came up to see me off, dinging me with the usual SEAL humor about getting wounded and having to leave the party. I remember pointing at him and jokingly saying "You're next, Lou." Four days later the boat he and Mike Collins were riding in was hit with rifle and grenade fire. Collins was killed, and Lou hit seriously in the head. He survived and is disabled today, but he's still got that sense of humor about him.

These two events brought an end to X-Ray platoon, perhaps the most hard-luck platoon to have served in the war.

On the flight to the hospital I began looking at the wounded men around me. Even though I was hurting, I'd been lucky. In my mind I began turning over the events that had brought us here. Were I one of the seriously wounded or maimed, my career would be over now. What skills did I have to survive back in the world? Sure, I had some photography background, but what good would that really do me? I took another look around. These guys were missing legs and other parts of their bodies. They were staring off into space, pondering—as was I—their fate. No one was talking; no one wanted to.

The future became more focused for me. The operation had been badly considered and flawed in its execution. During its entire duration up until we were ambushed, I'd been chomping at the bit to correct all the little things I noticed being done wrong. Good men, yes. Good leaders, sure. But this didn't translate as a good operation if everyone wasn't working together as a team. I decided then and there I wanted more control over my fate and the fate of my men. Yes, *my* men. No more victims, no more being a victim myself. Even as my head was throbbing and the back of my neck was driving me nuts, even with the now-dried blood of both Mac and the dead Chieu Hoi encrusted on my hands, I knew what had to be done.

I was going to become a commissioned officer, no matter what it took.

18

Ensign Walsh, Meet SEAL Team TWO

May 7, 1978, graduation day at Officer Candidate School, Newport, Rhode Island. I'd made it. The day was beautifully warm and sunny, a typical spring day in Newport, Rhode Island, and one made for newly commissioned naval officers. My mother, Margaret, and my brothers and sisters were there for the ceremony. Mom was beaming with pride. As a navy veteran herself, she knew what this meant to me. I'd brought honor to the family name by gaining a commission. Leaving the enlisted ranks is a big deal and it means a lot of things. Primarily, it says the navy system has acknowledged you have the capacity to lead men. But on the other hand, you're really very much on your own. Contrary to what is taught, preached, and publicized, the navy does not take care of its own. Some folks make it all the way to captain and still have trouble zipping their fly. Others learn how to build a wristwatch, but lack the capacity to wind it! I know, I've worked for these leaders.

As we were sitting in the auditorium waiting for the graduation ceremony to begin, I reflected on OCS and the last four months of my training. It was a long way from that hot February helicopter ride to the hospital, my friends' blood spattered all over me. Many of the men and women I'd gone to OCS with hadn't even seen a weapon fired in anger, much less killed a man. Too many of them seemed quite arrogant in their rite of passage from enlisted man to commissioned officer. Academically, I had not been impressed. The leadership classes were more a series of brainwashing sessions designed to intimidate the male candidates into thinking the women candidates were equal in combat skill and task accomplishment. Pure rubbish, as I'd been there and knew differently. But otherwise, I'd had a good time playing the OCS game.

I'd been to captain's mast, fallen in love with an innocent, beautiful brown-eyed girl from Seattle whom I should have married, learned to dislike Iranian officer students with a passion, and observed a system of double standards for the navy's men and women officers. But I'd become commissioned and was determined to conduct myself accordingly despite it all.

Thankfully, seven other SEALs had gone through with my class. We did what SEALs do naturally: organize, plot, subvert, control, infiltrate, spy, intimidate, and generally try to stay one step in front of the administrative pukes. What we hadn't counted on was the director of OCS, an old aviation captain by the name of J. J. McGrath. Captain McGrath was well read, well liked, especially by the ladies, and a guy who'd been there and done that when others were still playing in the grass. He knew SEALs real well, and he knew how to play the game with us.

My introduction to captain's mast had to do with the Iranian officer candidates. I'd become the regimental lifeguard and it was my friend Glenn's and my job to teach them to swim. Now, bear in mind that if it ain't sand an Iranian can't swim in it. The only saving grace to our program was the nurses' class in the morning, which was far more productive than trying to work with a bunch of conehead Iranians. No matter how hard we worked, only a handful ever got the big picture. As a group they possessed the worst attitude I've ever come in contact with. For example, they'd point their fingers at you at the start of every conversation and always preface each statement with "Hey, you . . . you!" We were off to a bad start with these guys, and it only got worse.

Every evening they'd come to the pool, jump off the diving board, sink right to the bottom, then bounce off the bottom until they safely reached the side. Glenn and I rescued at least one Iranian officer candidate a week from drowning, which got to be rather boring. To discourage their stupidity we took to bashing their knuckles with the lifeguard hook as they came to the side of the pool. They'd sink after a while, and we'd go rescue them. The message was "If you can't swim, stay out of the deep end!"

It didn't take long before we were both called up before Captain McGrath. Our accusers came strutting into his office like we were already dead meat. I sensed for the first time the political power these clowns had over the navy. They were arrogant to the max and held their heads way back so they could look down their noses at us. Then the sob stories began about how cruel Glenn and I had been. I was almost crying myself, listening to what a brute I was. The captain thanked them for sharing with him and asked they leave the office for a few moments. Then he lit into us.

We offered our side of the story. Although McGrath confessed he could understand our frustration, it did not excuse our actions. He told us what he planned to do to smooth things over, but made it clear if he didn't do it this way we'd never get back to the Teams. We agreed to his plan and with a deliberate wink, a wry grin, and a nod of the head he told us simply to take the heat that was coming.

The Iranian candidates were ushered back in, and the dog and pony show began. McGrath chewed us out loudly and with great emotion in front of them. He made us apologize to each man, to include shaking hands. I submitted, but did not surrender. When one of the arrogant students took my hand I squeezed it so hard that he came up on his toes in pain. His eyeballs looked like they were about to explode from their sockets, and I hoped inwardly that they might begin spinning like a deranged gyro compass. McGrath caught my act but said nothing. Just an old American custom, pal, and there wasn't anything he could say or do about it.

Checkmate, dirt bag.

The grinch inside me was a happy camper. After it was all over, the captain trashed the paperwork and told us to meet him at the officers' club the following Friday. We did, got drunk, and never heard about our nonswimming Iranian "friends" again. It was time for me to leave Newport and get back to the business I loved best, naval special warfare.

Being assigned to SEAL Team TWO was a dream come true. I had always considered it the model SEAL Team. For all the time I served on the West Coast I'd wanted to join the

East Coast SEAL family. The first character I met crossing the quarterdeck was Command Chief Master at Arms Knox, better known as Bull. He was a short, skinny, slightly built man but it was known he was extremely well endowed. Hence the moniker, Bull. Every morning he'd be on the quarterdeck looking over everyone who came aboard. If you needed a haircut, Bull told you so . . . including officers. He cut no slack and took no guff from anyone. If there is one thing I like in senior enlisted leadership it is consistency. If more officers practiced this same trait I believe we'd be a lot better off. Bull stayed on my case the entire time I was at Two, but we grew fond of each other and still communicate.

ST-2 was clearly run by senior enlisted men, and they held us all to very high standards of military bearing and performance. Each commanding officer who came through the group learned to trust their advice and judgment, and in my opinion, they made many a man's career. The mid-1970s and the 1980s were the best days at ST-2, after the Vietnam war was over. In 1983 all underwater demolition teams were redesignated SEAL Teams. The reasons were simple. By doctrine, UDT was limited to amphibious warfare. A SEAL command on the other hand could serve either a fleet or a joint commander, which meant a SEAL command would be able to fulfill traditional UDT missions and play unconventional warfare by charter. In truth, the standards set by SEAL Team TWO were the same standards used to forge all the new teams that have come on line, which says a lot for the East Coast influence.

My deployments with ST-2 were great in every respect. One of my favorites was with the U.S. European Command. This was a NATO deployment to Germany, Greece, Spain, Italy, and Denmark. Overall, it took four months from start to finish.

In 1979 the cold war was still raging. Terrorism was running rampant throughout Europe and the Middle East. The civil war in Lebanon was really getting hot, and SEALs were getting their orders to prepare for conflicts all over the world. After a brief stay in Germany, I found myself working the mountains of northern Italy with the Italian Alpini. These are some of the greatest ski troops in the world, and we spent a great deal of time mountaineering and checking an extensive system of weapons caches buried throughout the region as reserve stores in case of a Soviet invasion.

When I moved on to northern Spain I found a peaceful, lovely country with large farms and kind people. The Spanish Army was bivouacked at the base of the El Grado Dam, built with American know-how for the benefit of the Spanish people. Their engineers were interested in how they might blow the dam, if necessary, during wartime, so we conducted training in this area. Our classes spanned limited sabotage to the use of a man-packed nuclear weapon. It was quite a challenge, as the water depth is 350-odd feet, and the man-made lake is over eighteen kilometers long. I remember it offered great fishing, and ever since that experience I've always wanted to successfully blow a dam.

While I was in Spain I caught sight of a monastery located about five miles from where we were staying. A very elaborate affair that fairly bristled with antennas and the like, the castle-like structure was situated at the edge of a small, picturesque lake. The intelligence side of me just couldn't stand not knowing what this place was all about. The high-security fence surrounding it told me this was something special, and I determined to get as close as I could to learn at least something.

One evening I slipped away from our hosts and the platoon. My camera was with me for some picture taking, which I figured I'd offer up to the Defense Intelligence Agency once back on the East Coast. Wandering up toward the huge facility I met a Spanish captain, who'd moved up behind me. He called out my name, and sure enough he was one of our hosts. Turned out he'd noted my absence and tagged along, just to keep me out of trouble. He asked if I'd taken any pictures, and I replied I hadn't had the chance yet. I was pleased he accepted my word for this, and the fact he allowed me to keep my camera meant a lot. The two of us headed back to our site at the dam, with no words spoken about the heavily guarded lakeside retreat.

To this day I remain curious about that place.

Denmark was the highlight of the platoon's trip. We were going to the field with the Danish Fromandkorpset (Frogman Corps) and would be playing the role of terrorist-

200

insurgent for the planned exercise. The Danes have a long history of guerrilla warfare going back to World War II when they fought the Germans. Before the exercise got under way I made it a point to visit the resistance museum in Copenhagen. The implements of torture used by the Nazis on the Danes were on display, as were horrifying photos and testaments to Danish courage in the face of an all-powerful enemy occupation force. My tour reminded me of how important such exercises were, and that my Danish friends and fellow frogmen were not playing games. It was all the incentive I needed to do a good job for them.

We were introduced to NATO dry suits, under which we could wear our camouflage uniforms without them becoming wet. Being cold and dry is much better than being cold and wet, especially when you're on a military mission. Give me a dry suit any day of the week! We practiced close quarter battle drills with the Danes, who were forming their own counterterrorist unit at the time. The British, courtesy of the elite SAS, were the primary instructors, and no one group is better qualified. Finally we worked with the Danish Dog School, and I came away impressed with what they do with these fine animals.

Each of us was tracked and then attacked by one of the huge German shepherds, most of which are used to protect air bases. The dogs are highly disciplined and exceptionally well trained. One dog with the craziest pair of eyes was "reserved" for the new ensign—me. That dog hit me like it was in heat and I was its first love!

It was February and the snow in Jutland was three feet deep. At five feet four, I had some difficulty clambering through it, as you might imagine. Our squad was made up of four SEALs and three Danish frogmen. Just before we inserted into our operational area the local radio station informed the entire listening populace, as well as the Home Guard, that foreign terrorists were in the countryside . . . and that this was a drill. We had everything on us but live ammunition, and now we were the object of an areawide manhunt. Nothing like a challenge for a frogman, regardless of nationality.

Pulling us into a tight perimeter somewhere out in farm country I held a second briefing. If we were going to be terrorists we'd have to start thinking and acting like terrorists. "Okay, gentlemen," I said, "the first rule is that there are no rules." We then went to work.

Pulling operational funds from my pocket, I sent one of the Danes, in civilian clothes, back 80 kilometers to Albourg to rent a car. I had thought about stealing one, but the word had been put out to us back in the United States about ripping off cars in Europe during training exercises. Seems folks were getting a bit thin-skinned about this sort of realism, which I could understand. Renting a car was a better option, and certainly a terrorist, a real terrorist, wouldn't risk getting stopped on a routine check by the local police over a hot automobile.

"Everyone out of your uniforms and into civilian clothes," I then ordered. We'd packed civvies for doing in-close recon where military uniforms would be out of place, so this was an easy task to accomplish. Regardless of what has been published before, both the SEALs and the Green Berets had been playing this game for years all over NATO Europe and playing it quite well. Special Forces possessed an entire guerrilla warfare network throughout Germany, for example, and many of their operators had been conducting probes, recon, and other activities of NATO and U.S. military sites courtesy of the Tenth Special Forces Group. My own experience with Phoenix, including our in-depth training in southern California as both terrorists and counterterrorists, came into play in Denmark, making a mockery of recent claims that SEALs only recently learned how to sneak and peak, or act as effective counterterrorists.

With the Home Guard looking for a group of men in military uniforms, we knew their search pattern would be fairly predictable. They picked up our trail at the insertion point and were tracking us with dogs. The psychological effect of being hunted by a highly motivated and trained animal has its impact. If you allow your mind to become weak with fear it will unbalance your performance, and you will get caught. I fought the urge to flee when we heard the dogs barking in the distance, knowing we needed to put distance between us and our trackers as quickly as possible.

Now, you can outfight a dog and its handler, if such a tactic is to your advantage. First off, kill or disable the handler by either a booby trap or a precision rifle shot. Dogs like the ones pursuing us don't work for just anyone. They respond to the handler. Kill the handler, not the dog, and your primary problem is solved. Another tactic is to split a group up with one man going in one direction, the others going in another. The dog will normally scent on just one individual and attempt to follow that scent. While the "rabbit" leads the dog off, the main body goes about their business, linking up with the missing man later on at a prearranged point. How does he escape the dog? By hook or by crook, that's how. The point is not to panic, but to perform. You have to be pursued by dogs to fully appreciate the dynamics of this type of hunt. We were playing it as close to real as possible.

I elected to get us to a main road. A quick map check showed one close by, and the Danish point man moved out with a purpose. Once we hit the highway we moved onto the pavement so as to leave no tracks in the snow. Now we had a fifty-fifty chance, as dogs can't smell too good when tracking off of pavement, especially if it's frozen. As cars approached, the squad would throw itself just off the roadway, hiding until the danger had passed. It was nighttime, and most people don't look past their immediate front when driving in darkness anyhow. I was concerned about helicopters armed with searchlights, which are far more difficult to evade. We had to keep moving. With pavement under our feet and few cars on the road we made good time. Soon the barking grew muted as the dogs took a wrong turn at the highway where we'd broken out of the deep snow. It wouldn't take long for the dogs and their handlers to figure out what had gone wrong, so we picked up the pace and moved even faster.

Finally we found a summer residence community and burrowed into a tree line where we could hide and rest. The men pointed out there were already tracks and tire marks in the snow, so we decided there was enough traffic to mask our presence and set up the winter tents on the snow. I slept fairly well, and we broke camp before dawn. As the sun was coming up, the squad discovered a beautiful little cottage, totally isolated from any others. The Danes checked things out and confirmed this was a summer home, so we picked the lock and walked right in. This would be our safe house for the time being. I picked up the phone and called Sern, the Dane I'd ordered to locate a rental car. We needed to get mobile in a big way, and soon. The connection was made as planned, and after a few minutes of conversation to make sure he hadn't been captured and was being forced to ferret us out, I turned him over to the Danes for specific directions. Nearly all Danish frogmen speak English very well, but our location and how to get there was passed along in their native language for safety's sake. Late that afternoon Sern showed up with the rental car and the show was on.

Hals is the northernmost town on the Jutland peninsula. It's a small fishing village, not unlike those in Maine and Nova Scotia. The people are of hardy stock, the men having thick forearms and rough beard stubble on their faces. They all seem to favor a drab-colored hat of one sort or another, much like our own preference for baseball caps in this country. When we arrived I split the squad up into pairs in order to conduct a good recon of the town. The men were given enough money to walk around and partake in daily activities so they wouldn't stand out as having no business in town. I wanted them in the local bars, or food establishments, or shops, listening and learning. They weren't given enough money for girls and booze, as boys will be boys if you let them.

Each recon team was made up of one SEAL and one Dane. We'd stopped cutting our hair months before, as military-style hair and a healthy build is a dead giveaway in the civilian populace. We fit in pretty well with the fishermen, who surely looked like fishermen the world over. Tough, hard, and a bit on the wild side. My philosophy had always been if you're going to play the game, then play it all out. It is always the half-baked thought processes of those who consider themselves planners who get men killed in this world. You cannot plan an unconventional operation with a conventional mind-set. The administrative weenies, who have never experienced battle, much less pain, lack the ability to understand this. I have a little verse which I stored in my head, and it always seems appropriate whenever I deal with the conventional side of the house. It goes like this: "Those that can, do. Those that can't, teach. Those that can't teach, administrate." It's true whether you're in the military or selling life insurance. To win, SEALs have to operate freely and with only the bare essentials of command and control: when they can't, or don't, they die.

Our target was a ferry that ran from Hals across a river that flowed into the Baltic. After two days in town we were ready to execute our mission, and no one had picked up on our presence that we could determine. We were terrorists, so the plan had to be brutal. I wanted to sink the ferry with cars and people on board, and I wanted to use materials that looked as real as possible. The men rigged two charges roughly a foot square apiece using an aluminum window frame. The framed "explosive" would act as a breaching charge, blowing holes in both sides of the ferry. Meanwhile a rigged thermite bomb would detonate on one of the ship's fuel tanks. Burning at over 5,500°F, the resulting explosion would finish the job. By the time they were done with our training aids I had to admit that what we'd built looked as real as was possible. The stuff scared even me.

With the demolitions stored in the trunk, we piled into our rental car and headed for the docks. Sern drove, in case we were pulled over for a minor infraction by the local police. Casual interest would be our first hurdle if stopped, and our cover story was a simple but plausible one. Each man checked his Gustav, a silenced Swedish K model 9-mm submachine gun, a longtime favorite of both SEALs and Green Berets. We were carrying harmless smoke grenades as well.

We then took the ferry across the river, the opposite side being sparsely populated. Each man had his job to do and was well versed in getting the mission accomplished. The ferry only held about twenty cars, and we knew its schedule by heart. At 2330 hours we regrouped at the car and headed for the landing. We would be the last car on board for the final trip to Hals. The only other automobile in front of us had two lovebirds in it, and they weren't the least bit interested in us.

As soon as the ferry cleared the mooring we poured out of the car, weapons at the ready. One of the Danes shoved his K into the captain's back and began giving orders. The man knew this was an exercise, and there was a slight smile on his face as he watched his ship being taken by the dreaded terrorists. Still, I could tell he was a bit scared, as we were not fooling around or acting like this was all a good joke. I saluted the captain, and gave him a small hand gesture to let him know that everything was going to be okay. The lovers paid us little attention, preferring to go back to what they were doing before our little invasion. The men rigged the two dummy charges to the ferry's sides and the thermite charge to the fuel tank. We wrote the time of detonation on the walls for record purposes and then connected the firing wires for that final realistic effect.

As we came close to the opposite shore we warned the captain that a gun would be aimed at him at all times from a car at the landing, and he would be the first to die if something went wrong. With an audible *clank* the ramp came down as we docked. All of us were in the car by now, and we froze as uniformed Home Guard members rose up from hidden positions and aimed their weapons as the ferry. "Freeze!" I warned my men. "They haven't got any idea we're really on board." As Sern drove us off the boat undetected, the Home-Guard dropped their weapons and went back to their boring routine of waiting for us to show.

Big mistake.

Banging twice on the floor of the car we alerted our man hidden in the trunk. He flipped it open and began dropping smoke grenades out behind us, much to the stunned guards' dismay. The charges on the ferry blew, and smoke began flowing from its interior. It looked real, and it could have been. Despite their elaborate precautions, we'd successfully pulled off a terrorist attack right under the noses of the Home Guard!

Now the real work began. As usual, it had to be fun because we'd already proved our mettle down by the river. I spotted a uniformed Danish patrol moving down the main drag of Hals. "Gimme a smoke grenade," I ordered one of the men. As we passed by, I noted this was a mixed male and female military unit that was paying us no attention at all. I tossed the grenade at them, watching it land right at their feet. Nothing, no reaction at all.

"Hit it!" I yelled at Sern as the grenade went off.

"Huh?"

"Hit it!" I nearly screamed. The patrol was finally figuring out what had happened and starting to react to the smoke

swirling around them, and to us as the obvious source of that smoke.

Sern hit me. I mean, he really hit me!

"No, you idiot, not me! The gas pedal! Drive!" I yelled at him. The frogman figured it out and put the pedal to the metal. As we sped out of town I was making mental notes, one which included not using American slang with our allies unless I knew they knew what I was talking about. "Beer's on me," I informed everyone in the car.

Funny . . . everyone, including Sern, understood that command right away.

Later on that evening we listened to the radio to learn as much as possible about our attack on the ferry. By now the entire Danish National Guard was hunting us, so we ditched the rental car and bagged a Land Rover. Well, it was more like a Danish military Land Rover, which we'd "borrowed" the evening before our assault. With a second operation in mind, we took off for the next mission, which kinda fell apart when the vehicle's accelerator stuck to the floor and we crashed through a barrier at a Danish communications station that controlled Denmark's tiny naval fleet. Miraculously no one was injured on either side. Luck was against us this time as the guards released their dogs, which came at us with no mercy. I ordered a Dane to "take care of that dog!" when the first came flying, and he did . . . with an unsheathed bayonet.

Then Murphy's Law struck again.

We'd planned to mortar this station with some things we'd cooked up, which would leave the tube but not do any real damage . . . so we thought. With the attack dog dead at my feet, the Land Rover wrecked, the guard gate shattered beyond repair, and stuff getting further out of control, the mortar started raining rounds down and they actually exploded on target! I watched the first radio-radar antenna come apart, then the rest of them as we unloaded our volley of homemade rounds. By the time the smoke settled, the Danes had lost communications with their fleet, the Home Guard was ticked off about the dead dog, the Danish executive officer from whom we'd stolen the Land Rover was clearly upset, a farmer whose house we'd holed up in after the attack on the ferry was complaining that his daughter was no longer a virgin, and the car rental agency was in a high state of agitation as someone had found where we'd ditched the car and destroyed the vehicle after one heck of a joy ride.

But everyone else in the chain of command was happy with our efforts. I've always said there are those who will argue about the price of success, primarily because they are so insecure about how that success was achieved. So much for admin pukes.

I left SEAL Team TWO shortly after returning from Europe. It had been a wonderful introduction into the world of command. I'd learned a lot and realized I needed to develop my own style of leadership to be truly effective. As for the farmer's daughter . . . I never touched her, honest.

19

Special Boat Unit Twenty

With a tour of ST-2 now behind me, I was again breaking new ground. It had been decided somewhere in the navy that SEAL officers would serve tours of duty in the boat units, as they are commonly known. I'd gotten word of my impending assignment while in Denmark, so it was no surprise to find papers waiting for me back in Little Creek, Virginia.

The special boat units are made up largely of enlisted men and officers from the fleet. Their job was, and still is, to support operating SEAL elements with boat support consisting of surface small craft. They also operate independently of the Teams. They have a long and respected history going back to World War II, but it was in Vietnam that they really made their bones.

The boat units were known as Mobile Support Teams (MST) in Vietnam. The parent command Stateside was called Boat Support Units. These men have never really seen a high degree of recognition save from the SEAL community itself, but for many this is enough. Whenever we were in trouble, under fire, or needing support right away, these guys were the ones who saved us. Thanks to the MST and Seawolf helicopters many a SEAL is alive today.

Each SEAL platoon in Vietnam had an MST detachment assigned to it, usually a young lieutenant with five or six men. The relationship between the MST and the SEALs was close. They were an integral part of us, and we did everything together. Without boats, SEALs could go nowhere. The men who operated them were all volunteers from the fleet. Some were former river rats, sailors from the Brown Water navy that conducted combat operations throughout the riverine regions of Vietnam. The now famous PBR (Patrol Boat, River), was a thirty-one-foot fiberglass fighting platform from which we all fought and sometimes died. The tactics we used in Vietnam were gleaned from those conducted during the Civil War. Some things don't change, especially when they have been proven under fire.

I learned about small boats in Vietnam—how to navigate, read charts, pilot, and operate weapons systems. All this eventually led me to an assignment with the boat units. It was a good decision to have us in this capacity as it showed the special warfare community was maturing. Our presence as commanders further cemented the already strong relationship between SEALs and fleet sailors where such operations were concerned, and we needed that.

After completing the orientation phase I was assigned as an admin officer. This meant I was the legal officer, athletic officer, and several other collateral jobs, which every naval officer gets no matter where he is assigned—a jack-of-all-trades and master of none, so to speak. During this period the navy was suffering the aftereffects of the drug problem that had been running rampant in society and the military since the 1960s. The boat units had more than their fair share of dirt bags who'd been thrown away from every other major unit in the fleet. Still, I saw great promise in the good men who were there and resolved I would make my unit a better place during my brief time there. The problem was how to fix the drug problem, while still operating effectively.

Then came the Mariel Boat Lift.

Remember when Fidel Castro sent us all of his country's social rejects? Special Boat Unit-20, or SBU-20 was mobilized and sent to Key West to assist by patrolling the Florida straits, providing maritime security, and detaining Cubans for the Coast Guard. Although successful, there were problems with the operation. At one point an enlisted man beat up a junior officer in Key West, and I was the guy they sent down to find out what was going on. Drugs and discipline problems, I thought to myself. This was going to be a lot different from the Teams.

As the admin and legal officer I received my first insights into the navy legal system. They brought up the recalcitrant seaman who'd beat up his lieutenant, and one look at this clown told me everything I needed to know. He not only qualified as a Class A dirt bag, but as a bona fide oxygen thief as well. He had to be present for me to conduct his

Article 32 interview, which he was entitled to under the Uniform Code of Military Justice. I found him arrogant, and he answered every question with "yeah" or "uh-huh." A real cocky s.o.b.

Finally I asked First Class Petty Officer Darryl Bullinger how his hearing and vision were. Bullinger is a good sailor, one of the best I've met. He answered both were okay. Next I told our young pup to please sit down, which he refused to do. I casually walked over to him and climbed inside his comfort zone. I got real close, wanting to see what he would do. He was a big man, maybe six-one, lean, with a boxer's build. Everything said he could hit hard and fast, and he was alert.

I wasn't sure whether to knock him backwards or move in closer still, grab him, twist, and then throw him to the floor. This is basic judo, but few big men expect such a move from a smaller man. It works almost every time, but when it doesn't, you're in for a world of hurt. The office we were in was small, and if our bad boy was injured I'd have legal problems of my own. The problem was resolved for me when his right hand shot out toward me.

Grabbing it, I put him in a painful thumb lock, and led him to the chair. In true dirt bag fashion he began screaming something about assault, and then started in with stuff about racial harassment. It became apparent I needed to remind him that it surely appeared as if he had attacked me and that I had only defended myself. Bullinger's eyes were twinkling, but his face was as serious as stone.

In the aftermath of this incident I pursued the case all the way to court-martial. His lawyer fought hard, but she lost. It was then I discovered you had to visit anyone you put in the Norfolk brig every day to make sure he was okay. The only way around this rule is if the prisoner is moved to another location.

Oh, really?

I was not going to visit this dirt bag every day, or any day if I could help it. As luck had it, however, the former SBU-20 senior yeoman was working at the brig. After work one day the yeoman and I had a meeting at a local watering hole off base. He understood my problem. "How far away do you want this guy," he asked.

"Cleveland is nice," I answered.

"No can do, but Quantico is the next best place," he replied. The transfer cost me two six-packs of beer. The CO never did figure out how or why the prisoner went so far away so soon. I'm sure the marines in the brig at Quantico enjoyed their new playmate, and I never let on I knew anything other than that the case was closed.

After eighty-seven cases of nonjudicial punishment and seven court-martials, I had the legal end of things down to a science. But I wanted to drive patrol boats, not push paper or put bad guys in jail. Besides, the CO was at odds with me because we had fifteen men in the brig or in correctional custody. Commander Plumb was more concerned with cosmetics than substance, and I wasn't making his command look very good. Sure, we were short of men, but our discipline problem was ironing itself out with my approach. The more I learned about Plumb, the less I liked or respected him. He, on the other hand, didn't like Mustang officers like me. We were free spirits, and he was a product of the command establishment. I got little support from him, and the good men in his command suffered for it.

Then, finally, I was back at sea. The craft was a sixty-five foot MK III Sea Spectre patrol boat. Not the greatest patrol boat, but it got the job done. Pentagon commandos had designed the MK III, and it showed. An okay platform, but certainly not worth the money and time invested to bring it to life. Still, it was a welcome relief from Commander Plumb and his druggies.

We went to Cape May, New Jersey, to support the navy reserve exercises with the Mobile Inshore Undersea Warfare guys. These are the folks who protect the entrances to ports and harbors, and they must be ready to deploy anywhere in the world on a moment's notice. During the exercise I drove the patrol boat up on the rocks to avoid killing a man in a Boston Whaler who'd run up under our bow. It took only five and a half hours for the command engineer and his men to refloat the craft and get us back on line. Naturally, the bureaucrats at Commander Naval Surface Force Atlantic wanted my head to roll over that incident. When asked by the CO whether they would have preferred to see me kill the civilian in question, one of the cretins offered, "Well, it would have made prosecuting Lieutenant (j.g.) Walsh easier if he had." I responded that it appeared to me the wrong guy had gotten in front of my boat, and I could tell by the look in his eyes he knew what a slime sucker he was.

Heaven will be free of bureaucrats, thank God.

After this exciting exercise I headed for the naval station at Roosevelt Roads, Puerto Rico. There I was assigned the secondary mission of serving as the maritime security officer of the base. As on most navy bases, security was lax, especially from the SEAL point of view. I agree with those others of my peers who have opined that the navy does not take its own security seriously. We had a command in the service known as the NSCT, or Naval Security Coordination Team. It was designed to test the security of naval installations worldwide. This command was dissolved in October 1992 due to the reckless leadership of its first skipper. They had problems, big problems, and the problems got worse, but the NSCT concept was valid and remains valid today. Finding a sponsor in the Department of Defense is still out of the question, however. The problem in doing realistic security penetration operations is that the commanding officers of the bases being probed take the results too personally. They are concerned that their fitness reports will suffer; they *should* be concerned with finding and fixing the problems reported. The navy officer corps as a whole is totally fixated on the next fitness report. We are breeding a leadership class of gutless paper warriors more worried about how they can hang on to their jobs than about the national defense. Real leaders in today's military, regardless of service, scare people. The first thing a military bureaucrat wants to do is emasculate such leaders. Bureaucrats sleep better at night knowing that such leaders are not a threat to their pettiness and stupidity. Officers today refuse to take peacetime risks, and this means they will fail to take wartime risks when leading men into battle.

The NSCT program was nothing new. Special Forces had been routinely penetrating major U.S. installations, including NORAD, for years. They weren't even using special teams to accomplish their missions, but relying on the standard twelve-man A-team for which many such tasks were considered simply good training missions! Operational detachments from the Tenth Special Forces Group's two Stateside battalions were conducting full-scale urban operations in Providence, Rhode Island, and Fall River, Massachusetts, which were developing highly skilled penetrator specialists for larger, more intricate NSCT-type missions on behalf of the army. This was happening while SEAL Team SIX and Red Cell were slowly evolving in the naval special warfare community, and during a period when the army had already fielded Detachment Delta, Blue Light, FOG, and other subspecialty units in the field of counterterrorism and internal counterchecks. Again, the problem wasn't in the concept but in how the concept was executed. At Roosevelt Roads I essentially saw evidence of a very real problem, and in a portion of the world where nationalist terrorists were actually operating and had killed American service personnel as part of their campaign. No real progress was made during my tour, but I learned some lessons.

From Puerto Rico I took a two-boat detachment to Honduras, Venezuela, and then Panama. This was the summer of 1980. We embarked aboard the USS *Fort Snelling,* an LSD-30, an old but fine ship with a truly excellent crew. It was during this tour that my love affair with Latin America began. The Snelling would soon become an important part of my life as both Grenada and Lebanon steamed onto the horizon, but for this trip the LST was just a means of getting our little boats to the next stop.

My time in Honduras was a time of operating with the fledgling Honduran Navy. The base was located at Puerto Cortés, and it was pretty sad. We'd been asked to inspect the facilities and make recommendations. Our work was cut out for us. On the trip down from Puerto Rico I met Marine Gunnery Sergeant Roger Roll. He is one of two marines I've befriended during my career who were top-notch in every respect. Roll was an old recon marine who jumped, dived, and did every thing else that your garden variety SEAL enjoys.

At one point Roger took me to inspect the Honduran dive equipment locker. The building was ten feet long and maybe five feet wide. When we opened it up we stood there in shock at what we found. Roll went in first, then tiptoed out as I stood there silently with our Honduran escort. On the top shelf was all of the base's supply of C-4 explosive. Next shelf down? All of their blasting caps. Next shelf? Time fuse and blasting caps. Two more shelves lower? Scuba bottles filled with compressed air. In one corner stood the air compressor, and in the other were cans filled with gasoline. If this evil brew had been even accidentally detonated by a tropical lightning storm, the entire base would have resembled a B-52 crater. From a safe distance away, Roger and I explained all this to the Hondurans, and we were successful in getting them to employ a number of sailors in cleaning up the mess.

From Honduras we went to Venezuela and then Panama. A great country, Panama would also figure greatly in my career as a SEAL. The enormity of the Panama Canal captured my imagination not only as a military professional but as an American, too. A wonderful accomplishment that only this country was able to undertake and succeed at.

Once the operations in Panama were completed, it was back to Puerto Rico to drop off the patrol boats. I was moving to a new command back on the Teams. Being an operator, the prospects of becoming involved in what people were now calling high speed–low drag missions held great promise. I was fully qualified, blooded, commissioned, experienced in both conventional and unconventional warfare, and most of all . . . ready.

20

Dancing with the Devil

As I was ending my tour with the boat unit, we began hearing about a new SEAL command coming on line. Money was flowing in, and it was strongly rumored that SEAL Team SIX would be a no-holds-barred counter-terrorist unit owned and operated by the navy. My new assignment hadn't yet been carved in stone, so I decided to apply for an interview with SIX, which seemed to be right up my professional alley.

While their new facilities were being constructed, the boys at ST-6 were using several older buildings at Little Creek. The word was that the interview process was a real grinder as their commander wanted to have the first and last word on who was allowed to join the club. Even so, it was anything but what I'd expected.

The unit's founding commander was Richard "Dick" Marcinko. I didn't know him well on a personal basis, but we each knew of each other by reputation within the SEAL community. As I entered the building to meet with Commander Marcinko, I sensed something was wrong. Dick's office was filled with people, most just standing around making small talk. It was a large office, but still, it was highly unusual to have even one other person sitting in on such a meeting. Marcinko was at his desk, very professional-looking and demonstrating his position as a commanding officer simply by how he occupied his space. Invited to sit, I moved the offered chair off to the right side of his desk so as not to be sitting directly in front of him. Two can play the power game, I remember thinking.

As I sat, I realized what was actually taking place. This wasn't a serious interview, but rather a game dreamed up by Dick Marcinko for the benefit of his junior officers and men.

There were four or five SEAL officers scattered about the room, appearing to be casually chatting. I searched their faces and took in the looks each was forced to give when we made eye contact. Okay, so what's the story here? I asked myself.

Marcinko began with a series of casual questions, meant to break the ice. He wanted to know how I'd liked working with the boat unit, but quickly turned to why I wanted to join "his" organization.

"The work involved," I said. "It sounds exciting, low drag, high speed, that kind of thing." It was a standard answer to a standard question. Dick told me there would be no leave except for emergencies, and he asked if that would cause a problem. "Nope," I answered. How about marriage? "Nothing that would interfere with my job," I responded. I noted he checked that question off on the sheet laid out on his desk.

The commander then began rattling off about how much he cared about his men, but I noticed he also added how much he didn't care about how many backs he might have to break in getting the Team up to the standards he was demanding of it. I pointed out this apparent inconsistency to him, which went over as if I'd just pulled a wood rasp across the man's knuckles.

"Listen, Walsh," he growled, "I've already heard about you!"

"Fine," I said. "Then you know how I operate and how I see things."

In a slightly higher-pitched voice he countered, his shell of professional detachment beginning to fracture. "I don't give a crap about your 'better, faster, safer' way to do things, Walsh. The only way that flies around here is my way, you got it? You screw up in SIX and I'll rip that Budweiser off your chest, trash your fitness report, and throw you out into the street!" With that, Marcinko sat back and waited, his audience now suddenly very quiet and behaving much like a pack of wild dogs just waiting for the pack leader's signal to join in the fray.

Now I was pissed. My own voice rose several octaves. "So what you're saying is you don't want input from any of your junior officers, is that correct?"

"That's right," Dick shot back. "When I want your opinion I'll ask for it. Around here there's only one boss . . . me!"

I rolled my eyes at this one, and like two bull rhinos we began circling each other. The SEAL officers, loyal to their "club president," edged forward, hoping to feed on my carcass once Marcinko was finished with me.

But it wouldn't be me they would be having for lunch. "So what you want are clones, like these guys here?" I pointed to the small group, letting the acid drip off my tongue as I asked the question. It was clear I wouldn't be asked to join Commander Marcinko's boat crew, and in truth, I didn't want to at this point anyhow.

Before I arrived for my interview I'd done my homework about who's who in the initial roster. Most were steady customers of an old Teams hangout called the Casino Bar. Commander Marcinko had even held a number of informal meetings at the Casino, which I thought was about as unprofessional as anything I'd yet seen in the navy. Many of the early team members were the "ash and trash" of the other teams, passed on to Dick as a way of unloading the dregs of the command, so I suppose finding the Casino was a lot easier than getting to the base on time for most of the assembled throng.

When I told Dick this he fired right back. "It's my command and I'll muster it in hell if I want to!" he exploded. By now I was beginning to get bored with the program. There was no way I could work with this fruitcake and hope to survive the rigors of counterterrorist warfare. Dick had stopped going to war after his time in Southeast Asia. I hadn't. He'd done well on staff and in training, but I'd racked up a series of Navy Combat Action ribbons since pulling five tours in Vietnam, to include my advisory tour with Phoenix. Counterterrorist? Who was kidding whom here? I'd been a counterterrorist, and in some people's minds—many of whom were dead now—I was a terrorist as well. As I looked around again at the men in that room I wondered what proven ability any of those present could honestly claim in their new role.

At the same time I was greatly disappointed. It was evident the entire selection process for our newest command was personality-driven by one man. Sure, Dick

Marcinko was a unique character, but the Teams were filled with unique guys, many of them Dick's equal when it came to being enigmas. It angered me inside to realize this, but I wouldn't let Dickie and his lap dogs see this. I wouldn't give them the satisfaction.

Our meeting was now a battlefield, as hostile as anything I'd encountered when it came to flagpole politics. I knew of other junior officers who'd crossed Marcinko and whose careers had stopped dead in the water as a result. I tried to change tactics, questioning him one-on-one, waiting to see what other instant policy statements he'd issue on the spot. I like directness in people, but I wasn't getting it from Commander Marcinko.

During a calmer moment we talked about the aviation program and how everyone would have to learn to jump a square parachute for high-altitude pinpoint infiltration missions. Dick told me he was bringing in instructors straight out of the BUD/S program, putting them through his team's training program, and then jumping them on squares from day one. No problem there, I offered, but how would they ever be able to readjust to the Teams after a tour or two of being essentially rogues?

"Screw the Teams," Dick spat back at me.

Our voices began rising again, and I could tell this guy was into command by intimidation. I wasn't buying into it, and there were two hard-headed men sitting across from each other that day.

Dick swerved off onto another track, seeing he couldn't argue my point. Looking back, I now understand he was playing a very shrewd game.

Marcinko began lecturing me on how being the CO of Team SIX was more prestigious than being the group commodore. I was somewhat stunned at this pronouncement, and asked myself why this guy was going out of his way to say this kind of thing to me? His further description of the commodore as an administrative puke really angered me, and I became brutally direct. I held tremendous respect for Captain Lyon, who always had time to talk to and listen to his SEALs. Whenever I'd spent private time with the commodore I'd come away feeling as if I'd acquired something that made me a better officer and man. That Lyon was buried in paperwork was not his fault.

"I'll make up my own mind about a man who is an operator as well as an administrative officer," I shot back at Marcinko. "And I'll use my own judgment as to his abilities, which I greatly respect!" SEAL Team SIX's commander didn't take kindly to that kind of talk at all.

As we glared across the desk at each other, I realized exactly who and what Dick Marcinko was all about. He was laying it on the line that anything and everything that went on in his command was his and only his, period. It's been my experience that this is a position taken primarily by micro-managers who cannot work with people as people. This was an officer who wanted not individuals but servants, even lesser clones of himself, to do his imperial bidding. More than a few SEALs see Dick Marcinko as some kind of mythical UDT/SEAL god, but I'm not one of them. He was just a tyrant with a mission that afternoon, and our meeting was about to come to an end.

Marcinko was crowding the desk between us, and I truly believed we were going to get physical at any moment. That bothered me, as this was not how a professional senior officer conducted himself, at least in my book. He'd finished his pompous tirade regarding how His Royal Highness liked to see things spiffed up around the castle, so I went on the counterattack with a little speech all my own.

It went like this: "Well, sir, I came over here thinking I was going to have the opportunity to become part of a truly unique military organization. But what I've heard is that you're not concerned with military bearing, at all. Furthermore, if I understand you correctly, you don't give a crap about your men or anyone else despite the vigor with which you insist that you do. You don't want salutes, you want yes-men who will genuflect, kiss your ring, and then kiss your ass!"

There was a pause. I noticed his officers were completely silent now, and probably in a state of shock at what they were hearing about their new leader and themselves. Then I continued: "You're not running a military organization, but a personality cult. And I won't be part of it!"

Now Marcinko came unglued. "You ain't ever gonna see the light of day over here, Walsh!"

His toadies were suddenly restless, and I could see them jumping me if Marcinko snapped his fingers and nodded. It was time for me to exit, stage right. "Gee, I'll lose a lot of sleep over not being able to play with you guys," I tossed over my shoulder as I headed for the door. A few of the officers were nodding their heads, smiling at some secret joke as I passed by. "But I'd fit in a lot better if I were a brain-dead moron like the rest of your band," I added. I like to think they got the message.

Stepping back into the sunlight, I drove any thought of SEAL Team SIX from my mind and walked away without a backward glance. Marcinko's command would become an embarrassment to both the navy and the SEAL community, once his dirty laundry was hung out for public viewing. He would end up going to prison, writing a book, and making a lot of money while bashing a great many good men along the way. In a way, it's really too bad, because Dick has said a great many things that I agree with, but methods of command and overall experience are where we surely differ.

Later on, as SIX was stood up under Commander Marcinko's rules of war, the battered bodies and personalities from his little experiment began showing up on my doorstep at the group headquarters. The constant pressure of SIX's program, with its emergency-leave-only policy and emphasis on working hard and partying harder with Marcinko as grand master took its toll on the sailors under his command. Alcohol problems were abundant. Many young men simply didn't know how to behave any longer. The lines crossed so many times that right and wrong were no longer easily recognized concepts. The reputation of that early Team SIX was impressive in many ways, but fatally flawed in the end.

I did my best to patch up the walking wounded of Richard Marcinko's ill-fated "special project," and I've always thanked my lucky stars that I chose to steer clear of the taint it left on far too many good SEALs who fell under its spell. Today the program has been cleaned up, and it's being run by strong SEAL officers who are as concerned about the men as they are about the mission they are expected to perform. To be an effective counterterrorist you must train hard, train consistently, and learn to think like the prey you hunt. But this does not mean you begin to behave like a terrorist or truly think as one does in your everyday activities. There is a fine line between the good guys and the bad, and in counterterrorism this line cannot—must not—be crossed. I chose to remain what I'd always been since becoming a SEAL, and that was a war fighter.

And war was just around the corner.

21

Grenada: War without a Plan

"For there will be four great loves in a man's life. For there will be horses and women and power and war."
—*Rudyard Kipling*

The platoon was deployed to Norway in early 1983, with most of our operations near the city of Narvik, which is located at the end of a 140-mile-long fjord. The city of Narvik was the site of a major German campaign during World War II, a battle so tough the Nazis issued a special combat medal to its veterans. During my stay I had the opportunity to interview an old resistance fighter who'd fought against the Germans. What I learned from him would later help me a great deal in planning my own operations in SEAL warfare.

Back in the United States we went into high gear preparing for an upcoming move to the Mediterranean known as a MARG deployment. The basic concept of these deployments revolves around a SEAL platoon being one of the components of a Naval Special Warfare Task Unit. The unit is attached to an amphibious ship as part of the squadron, which normally is made up of three to five ships. Our particular group was made up of the platoon, two special boat detachments, and a swimmer delivery vehicle detachment, or SDV. I was pleased to have an SDV with us, as it could be used as a ship-to-shore underwater platform to move SEALs around while they were doing their job. An

SDV is one of the most lethal machines in the SEAL inventory, and we need to continue to improve this program at every opportunity.

MARG 1-84 was finally ready, with my platoon assigned aboard the *Fort Snelling* under the command of "Wild Bill" Taylor. Our objective was Lebanon, and we'd been drilling constantly at our training camp at Fort A. P. Hill, near Bowling Green, Virginia. Nine new SEALs right out of BUD/S were assigned to me, and I went to extra lengths to ensure they were ready for the rigors of what I felt was coming. On October 17, 1983, we set sail for Moorehead City, North Carolina, where we were to pick up the marines. This accomplished, we were truly on our way.

Time at sea is time to think. I was having serious personal concerns over my failing marriage, which is the last thing anyone in the military needs to have to wrestle with during a combat deployment. There was nothing I could do, no way in which to affect what was taking place between my wife and me. Finally I simply shuttled all such thoughts to the back of my mind and concentrated on the job ahead. It was very difficult, but the men and the mission had to come first, as they always did.

On the night of October 20, I was alone on the flying bridge of the *Snelling* when I noticed the repeating compass reading a heading of 160 degrees true. Our course was supposed to be 087 degrees true. I left the bridge looking for Bill Taylor and ran into him almost immediately.

"Mike," he said to me as we met, "better get your boys ready. We're going to invade Grenada!"

I'd been training for operations in Grenada prior to ever hearing Bill's words. Using real world intelligence reports we'd been conducting photo reconnaissance missions at Patuxent River, a naval aviation test base on Chesapeake Bay. Our scenario, based on intelligence information passed to us, concerned the high possibility that missiles were being shipped to Grenada and being erected there by both Cuban and Grenadan forces on the islands. We'd also been briefed about the presence of Eastern Bloc military advisers being present in numbers.

Our mission was to penetrate the Windward Islands and conduct a special reconnaissance mission to ascertain the presence or absence of missiles on Grenada, photograph any such ordnance and plot its location, and get off the islands without being detected. The photos would be developed aboard a submarine responsible for our infiltration and extraction. They would then be sent directly to the Joint Chiefs of Staff who would be responsible for briefing President Ronald Reagan. If missiles were indeed present, we'd have a second Cuban-style missile crisis on our hands.

So Grenada was no surprise to me.

On October 19, Grenadan Prime Minister Maurice Bishop was executed by political rivals led by General Austin Hudson. Bishop, head of his political party, had forged strong ties with the old Soviet Union and Cuba. Austin Hudson had begun seeing the prime minister as "soft" in his views, so he had ordered Bishop arrested and jailed. A large number of citizens had opposed this move and a public demonstration had forced General Hudson to release the prime minister. Bishop had then attempted to use the same tactic to gain the release of a co-worker. He was once again arrested, but this time he got a bullet in the back of the head.

As unrest grew, the United States, primarily the National Security Council, expressed concern for the safety of Americans on the island, many of whom were medical students. Despite assurances from General Hudson that there was no danger, a noncombat evacuation operation was ordered at the Pentagon, with MARG 1-84 ordered to assist. Hudson was informed via diplomatic channels that an evacuation force was inbound to Grenada, but he was not told the Army Rangers were already on the island conducting reconnaissance. The army was assigned to rescue the Americans, but no one knew where the American students were located. It turned out there were three campus areas with student concentrations, but now General Hudson was claiming that the evacuation force constituted an invasion of his country.

Grenada was a grave concern for the U.S. intelligence community. In addition, the island was being used as a staging and training area for Latin American revolutionary forces like those that had toppled the government of Nicaragua in 1979. The airport on the main island was being expanded to accommodate the largest civil and military aircraft in the Soviet inventory, which meant some awfully large transports and fighter-bombers could come and go from Grenada without a second thought.

Another player in Hudson's government was Bernard Coard. His public relations campaign claimed that airport expansion was meant to improve the island's tourist economy. We weren't buying it, and U-2 spy plane overflights were gathering more and more information showing that tourism was the least of Grenada's intentions where construction was concerned. Coard's wife was also a real piece of work. Intelligence reports showed that she had personally slit the throat of a Grenadan woman who'd been tied to a chair, then watched her die. This was not a nice group of people.

No big picture was available to us. Events were happening as opposed to being planned. No one on the flagship knew what was going on. Messages flew back and forth until we were ordered to cease electronic communications between us. This caused problems right away. I placed one of my men on the fantail of the USS *Fort Snelling* where he listened to the BBC. They were a great source of information, and I was shocked to hear that our impending arrival at Grenada was being broadcast worldwide! A signal from the USS *Guam*, our flagship, alerted me to a meeting with the squadron commander. When I arrived by helo, Admiral Metcalf and his staff were already on board, and planning was now under way. Metcalf was commander of the Second Fleet and now became commander of Joint Task Force 120. His deputy commander was Major General Norman Schwarzkopf, then commander of the Army's Twenty-fourth Mechanized Infantry Division.

After being briefed by Captain Erie on my support requirements, he brought me into the war room where the battle staff was waiting. We began discussing our options. My duty, as I saw it, was to be on Grenada as soon as possible so as to collect and pass back good information on the tactical situation. The admiral was not at all aware of the special warfare capability he possessed via my platoon, and that was okay. I was used to finding out what a senior commander did or did not know and then educating him accordingly. Metcalf impressed me with his near-immediate grasp of things and his unique ability to ask the right questions at the right time. After speaking with the battle staff I went and briefed the squadron commander, gaining his total support for our upcoming operations. We were now

800 miles from the island and steaming at seventeen knots, not very fast if you're one of the big boys on the water.

I wanted to get onto the island in a bad way. Our CH-53 helos didn't have the equipment necessary to fly us in at night, nor did they have the navigational gear required for pinpoint infiltration. The platoon could go in by rubber raiding craft at a point about twenty miles offshore and begin gathering information for the battle staff. Admiral Metcalf said, "You mean to tell me if you were there right now you could be conducting reconnaissance for me?"

"Yes, sir," was all I said in response.

Metcalf began chewing his cigar and pacing up and down the flag bridge in frustration. We all felt it, but there was little that could be done. The staff rallied behind the admiral and we began planning our next move even as the formal mission statement from the U.S. Commander-In-Chief, Atlantic Command, or USCINCLANT, reached us. We were ordered to conduct military operations to protect and evacuate U.S. and designated foreign nationals from Grenada. Our objectives were to neutralize enemy forces, stabilize the internal situation, and maintain the peace.

Sounded like war to me.

Furthermore, our rules of engagement included use of force and weapons as might be essential to the accomplishment of the mission. We were to minimize the disruptive influence of military operations on the local economy commensurate with the accomplishment of the mission. Then we were to execute initial tasks readily with minimum damage and casualties. I believed, as did others on the bridge, that the rules laid down were too restrictive. Everything I was carrying with the platoon was essential, and I would use whatever was necessary at the time to get the job done. Also, not one of my men was worth losing over some worthless piece of real estate in the Caribbean. Not one. I determined at that very moment that we would get in, get the job done, and get out all in one piece.

Our options as a task force included assaulting the island using all-air assets; assaulting the island using all-surface forces; assaulting the island using a combination of forces. Pretty simple, but probably a real brain-buster for the boys and girls at the Pentagon.

On October 23, my SEALs and I were assigned the

mission of taking down the governor general's house and rescuing its principal occupant, Paul Scoon. However, there was a big problem here: we had no charts of the island onboard except the admiral's chart, which was dated 1895 and authored by the British! I was fairly comfortable with the Brit map, though, as they seldom did anything halfway, even back in the late 1800s. The army and then the marines came up with charts, but both were different. Oh, it was getting better with every waking moment. The problem was "solved" with the capture of a tourist chart printed by the Office of Tourism in London. This became the common chart for all services involved in the invasion. It was a good map, depicting elevations over which a grid system could be drawn. It defined the road systems and population centers, as well. Our planning continued while the Defense Mapping Agency got their act together and sent out accurate charts around November 2.

My roommate, Lieutenant Ron Gay, was the officer in charge of the assault craft detachment. He'd been planning to attend medical school after this tour was over and just happened to have a brochure from the school on Grenada with him. It offered us a map and lots of good information about how the island was laid out. I used Ron's map as my primary planning document and we made it a point not to tell anyone else we had it, except for the CO of the *Snelling*. I wasn't giving up my map to anyone.

I asked the squadron commander to have First Platoon, A Company, Second Marine Reconnaissance Battalion, be made a part of my assault force on the governor's house. The twenty-five-man detachment was aboard the *Snelling* with us, and I had observed the men with great care. They were good, especially their sergeants. The officer in charge was young and inexperienced but full of confidence. They were professionals and I had no doubt they would perform wonderfully under fire. My plan had the marines acting as a blocking force on the low ground, while we took the high ground and recovered Mr. Scoon and his family. It was a good plan, simple and direct. We didn't know a whole lot about the situation on ground, but then, who did?

Two CH-47 helos were available to me and I wanted them to air-assault the objective. Always on the lookout for more intelligence, I had two marine gunnery sergeants working feverishly to get our FIST capability on line aboard both the *Snelling* and the *Guam*. This would allow the theater intelligence center to electronically transmit secondary imagery to deployed operational forces on a pull-down basis. You only get what you ask for in the intelligence business, and in the field you gotta know exactly what to request. The marines did an incredible job for us, reading operating manuals even as they were wiring up the system. Gunny Zematis, who was on board the *Guam,* deserves special mention here.

As night fell on October 23, we were at the high end of the planning scale. The marines were confident in their ability to take and hold the low ground objective. We'd armed them with additional munitions from our own stockpile, including plastic explosives and LAAW antitank rockets. My SEAL platoon was likewise ready to go, with only eight hours left before we'd launch for the island. It would be a clean hit. My plan was to come fast and low on the helicopters, off-load on the double, killing anything or anybody armed and stupid enough to get in our way. Then we would secure the high and low ground, locate Scoon and company, and exfiltrate under fire if necessary. Both forces, SEAL and marine, were heavily armed, including M-203 grenade launchers and lots of bullets. Five tours of Vietnam had taught me how to plan a raid like this one, and I'd accomplished over fifty personal snatch missions while with Phoenix. It would be tough, but not impossible.

Then suddenly our operation was canceled. The squadron was ordered to move off the target and to the east side of the island. Grabbing a chart I noted the only thing there was Pearls Airfield. Bill Taylor called me in and informed me "the other" special warfare unit would be going after Scoon. What other unit? SEAL Team SIX, he said. Everyone on the bridge of the *Guam* was confused at the sudden unexplained change in plans. We would later learn the decision came from the chairman of the JCS himself. The army's Delta detachment would be assaulting Fort Rupert even as ST-6 was grabbing Paul Scoon. It was a political decision meant to get everyone possible into the game. By this time Dick Marcinko was out of the picture; his command never tested under fire. General John Vessey, the Chairman of the Joint Chiefs, wanted his knights "blooded," and Grenada was available. Not to be left out, Delta grabbed a secondary mission, the search for and capture of Hudson's gang of sixteen henchmen who controlled the government from Fort Rupert. Not exactly counterterrorism, but close enough for government work.

Delta conducted an airmobile operation onto the island, successfully snagging the bad guys and whisking them into protective custody aboard the *Guam*. They also went after the Richmond Hill prison but were driven off by the intensity of the defenders' gunfire. ST-6 elected to conduct a nighttime water parachute infiltration from 2,000 feet into the ocean. Their highly modified Boston Whalers would also be air-dropped, the operators swimming to these upon landing at sea. No one told the SEALs the ocean was running at ten foot swells, winds were high, and it was raining hard. Four operators hit the water, their chutes open, and sank straight to the bottom under the excessive weight of their equipment. Their bodies have never been recovered. The already mauled assault element managed to locate their boats, and then land at Saint Georges where they made a hair-raising foot movement to the governor general's house. Taken under fire by PRA, or People's Revolutionary Army, military forces, the assault team was badly outgunned, outnumbered, and surrounded. Nearly every man was wounded. It was every SEAL's worst nightmare coming true.

As the battle unfolded at the governor's house I requested, then pleaded, then begged for us to be sent in to pull our teammates with SIX out of the fire. We had the plan and the helos, knew the terrain, and were so heavily armed the PRA would never know what was hitting them. The answer I got was a resounding no. Instead, the marines were ordered to break through to the compound and pull our people out. I later learned that the reasoning behind refusing my request was military politics at its worst. The brass were mortified at what was happening with ST-6, but would have been even more embarrassed if "blue water"—or your garden variety —SEALs were used to save ST-6 from defeat. So much money had been spent on their training, so much heat had been absorbed, that the navy felt it couldn't take another salvo in the form of regular SEALs like us pulling off the mission while also pulling its elite counterterrorists off the bull's-eye. So in went the marines to save the day, the entire mission of rescuing the governor compromised so someone at the Joint Chiefs level could save face.

We couldn't have cared less about saving face. Our teammates were in dire straits and we had the means and will to come to their aid. When it comes down to it, everyone is a SEAL regardless of coast or team. It was criminal to keep us from launching, and good men were nearly sacrificed out of a lack of professional courage on the part of the navy's highest command structure.

With thirteen men I was running three short of a full platoon. The decision was made to use air assault and to move by water as well in the taking of Grenada. We were assigned to conduct a surveillance of Pearls Airfield in advance of the marines coming ashore. I briefed the platoon and we began preparing the *SeaFox* for its mission. The men loaded Zodiac F-470 rubber raiding craft onto the SeaFox, which would be our seagoing launch platform. This would be the first time the F-470s had ever been used in a combat environment. I knew we were behind the power curve. The rough seas were costing us time as Captain Taylor tried to get us into position roughly twenty miles offshore. Events were racing past us and all I could do was urge the men on.

Finally the *Snelling* was in position. As I was climbing down into the *SeaFox* the captain informed me that the marine barracks in Beruit had just been blown to bits by terrorists. "Why are you telling me this now?" I asked him, the boat below me bobbing madly in the heavy seas. Bill realized he'd pulled a boner of sorts, and I could tell he wasn't happy with himself. He'd only been trying to keep me up to date on events, as confused as they were. Captain Taylor was a good man and a good officer. I gave him a farewell and we cast off.

The winds had come up, and it was slow going for our little boat. Heading west toward Pearls we picked up three blips on the radar screen, meaning we had company. No one had told us about enemy patrol boats, but here they were, headed directly at us. We changed course, and so did they. Already we were in the escape-and-evasion mode and nowhere near the objective. Worse, there was no naval gunfire or air support to take out these bozos. It was war without a plan, and I'd never imagined it could happen to the massive military machine of the greatest country on earth.

At three miles off the coast and closing I ordered the *SeaFox* Patrol Boat coxswain to reduce our engine speed by 1,000 rpm increments. At the same time we slipped over each crest of the huge sea swells facing us, hiding in the troughs they made. We moved in a zigzag pattern, trying to generally head toward Pearls. The men broke out the LAAW rockets, just in case. If we were going to fight them I wanted it to be fast and furious. The advantage was on my side, as we were a small target, very agile in the water, and armed to the teeth.

After a few more minutes and some skillful boat handling, the enemy radar signatures became erratic and then finally disappeared. We'd lost them! The storm intensity was increasing, though, and visibility was near zero. At two miles off the coast we picked up the island on radar. The boat detachment had brought us exactly where I wanted to be, despite everything thrown in their path. The rubber boats were lowered into the water, and the men readied themselves for the next phase of the operation. The *SeaFox* would remain on the windward (east) side of the island, out of sight and out of mind. It was to return to the *Snelling* if spotted by any more patrol boats, and we'd take our chances ashore. Hopefully, Cobra gunships from the *Guam* would be available to assist with air support if and when the weather allowed.

Then it was showtime. At 1,000 yards off the beach I held the rubber boats in place, trying to see through the rain and gloom where our infiltration point was. Breaking out a pair of night vision goggles I scanned the darkness, knowing my objective was north of the airfield and roughly 1,000 meters off where we now sat. Suddenly I found what I was looking for. But there also was an enemy base camp with fires glowing and people moving all over the beach! Scanning southward I searched for a better spot to go in. More troops, lots of them, running like crazy and obviously geared up for someone to come ashore. There were men digging, lifting, aiming weapons, the whole nine yards. The chief and I kept each other up to date as to what we were observing. Nothing looked good, so we decided to send in swimmers.

I wanted the swimmers to find us a point where we could land. They could do so by making their way right up to the surf zone and working parallel to the beach, right under the enemy's guns. Standard SEAL tactics, but these guys were brand new to the Teams and this would be their first combat operation. We spotted a BRDM armored vehicle parked at the end of the runway. No one had seen us yet, but time was running so low I knew we'd have to insert right on the target to be of help to the waiting marines. The BRDM would have to go, so out came the rockets again. Two men would swim in with the rockets and waste the vehicle as the rest of us came ashore in the rubber boats. This would occur only if the crew spotted us.

It was not just a job at this point, it was a nightmare.

The signal for us to insert was a repeated Morse code red alpha. I watched the swimmers lying right at the water's edge while Cuban and Grenadan soldiers ran past them. Brave lads, they were, and I was proud of their performance. Each man held his position and remained undetected. My boys were wearing their camouflage utility uniforms, and these stood out every time the surf broke against them on the beach. With night vision goggles we could see everything they were doing.

In the back of my mind I was also concerned with being ambushed at sea. With Eastern Bloc advisers—maybe even communist special forces—on the island it was possible. Ever so often I'd scan the water behind us, looking for an enemy rubber boat making its way toward ours. How ironic, I thought, if we end up fighting our peers at sea. With how screwed up this operation had been so far, anything was possible . . . and likely. The squalls were huge black balls of bad weather moving at us with no letup. My always evolving plan was to insert on the beach in the middle of the enemy force, using their own foxholes and trenches. If we had to, we'd kill, silently and quickly. I wished for silenced weapons, but we had none. Knives and bare hands would have to do. In Vietnam I'd killed men both ways, and I knew my SEALs would be up to it despite their innocence. Fortunately the Cubans and Grenadans, decided to hit the base camp and get out of the rain. They abandoned their newly prepared positions and headed toward the end of the airfield, weapons and shovels over their shoulders. My prayer had just been answered. Thank you, Lord, I whispered to myself.

"There it is!" one of the men stage-whispered. The signal to insert. We hit the big outboard motor and went sailing in on the surf.

"Keep full power up till we hit the beach!" I yelled at the coxswain. There was no time to play it safe; we had to get in and get in now. The rubber Zodiac craft hit the sand so hard I went flying out of the boat, landing hard on my rucksack, upside down and with a mouthful of wet sand. My lower partial bridge popped out, never to be seen again. Welcome to Grenada! The wind was knocked out of me, but I forced myself to refocus and get moving. The men were ready, waiting, and wondering where their little commander had gone.

The BRDM fired up its engine and took off for home. Good, I thought, they solved my problem. We dragged the rubber boat into the tree line, hiding it as best we could. I began inspecting the fighting positions the bad guys had been working on. They were good, real good. It occurred to me they almost appeared to have been laid out with the Marine Corps doctrine manual in mind. Several months later I would be told by the CIA station chief in Beirut, William Buckley, my old friend from Phoenix, that our own State Department had notified the Russian embassy nearly seventy-two hours before D day that we were coming! In turn, the Russians passed on this information to the Cubans, who flew in a colonel in from Havana with an armload of U.S. Marine Corps documents regarding amphibious assaults. He took over the defense of the island, and it was his troops as well as Hudson's PRA that we were now facing.

There are some very stupid people working in our State Department, and I would love to put them under fire one day just so they could see exactly how many brave young warriors they were directly responsible for killing with their insane priorities and sterile approach to war fighting.

Wordlessly and without having to be told, the squad dumped the outboard into one foxhole and covered it with palm fronds. They were doing exactly what was necessary and doing their very best to remember everything they'd been taught at BUD/S. I heard a rifle bolt slam home, but didn't pursue it. Sure, they were nervous. I was nervous, for

234

goodness' sake! But we were on the beach in one piece and moving like a well-oiled machine. In this business, the single most important weapon is the individual enlisted SEAL operator. He is our true capability. Each man brings skills and an inner desire to win to the mission at hand. You can't describe the feeling I had deep in my gut as I quietly watched those fine young sailors go about their business despite the storm and hundreds of enemy troops just meters away. You had to be here, on that beach with a loaded weapon in hand, to get it.

Hunkered down and fairly safe for the moment, I briefed the men. Things always change quickly under such circumstances and such briefings are the norm. It's how you stay alive. Communications are the key, and everyone needs to know and understand what's happening. Our job now was to determine whether the marines could come ashore by boat or if they would be better off going in by helo. The air option was the best, given the seas we'd just crossed, but I had to be sure. By morning the sea could be picture perfect and the situation changed. The men were ordered to recon the beach and then return to our position with their reports. When they did, I knew the marines would be coming in by helo. With only three hours left, the signal needed to be given to the commander aboard the *Guam*. "Walk track shoes" meant vertical envelopment, or assault by helicopter. I sent it, got a confirmation, and then watched as the tiny lights of the helicopters well off shore began twinkling.

But Murphy's Law was with us, as always. For some still unexplained reason the Twenty-second Marine Amphibious Unit went ahead and ordered a large force of men into assault boats despite our signal otherwise. The rest of the marines came in by helo, less than a half hour behind schedule. Echo Company landed south of the airfield and took the objective by 0800 hours that morning. Overall, things went better than I'd hoped for, given the total confusion of the day. I would later be told that no one had advised the marines there were SEALs on the beach! A little communications problem, I suppose.

While waiting for the marines to make their attack I checked my men one by one. We were the only Americans on the beach, and we would take under fire anyone coming our way. I only found one man asleep in his foxhole, but pressed my .357 Magnum to his face and issued some reassuring words about how the war would be over for him if he didn't wake up and stay awake. That seemed to do the trick. A rather conservative manner of solving the problem I'll admit, but one that does not require debate or liberal interpretation!

At daylight we broke the Zodiac boat out of the tree line and headed out to sea. We'd just been fired up by an enemy antiaircraft gun, which had tangled with one of the Marine Cobra gunships, who had nearly blasted me when he caught me in the open checking out the PRA gun position on foot. When the AAA gun tried to take the Cobra on, the crew fired its rounds almost straight up in the air, where they reached terminal velocity then fell back to earth . . . right on top of our humble little holes in the ground. No one tells you about such things in training; you just learn as you go about your job and hope to survive the lesson. In the end, the marine helo finished off the gun emplacement with a burst of 20mm cannon fire right down the tube. A nice piece of flying, and great shooting.

While we were pulling off the beach some idiot on the *Guam* radioed me and asked if the surf was okay for a landing and if I would attempt one if this were simply a training exercise. The question was so stupid I couldn't restrain myself. I blistered the caller with more profanity than I care to recall. Later—it was always later during this operation—I was advised that my less than professional response had been monitored by every ship participating in the invasion. I was a famous man for a short period, but not very popular with the boys who were fighting the war safe and sound aboard ship.

The afternoon of the twenty-fifth of October was spent cleaning equipment while I was called back to the *Guam* for briefings on our next missions. The next morning we were ordered to the west side of the island where the rangers and marines were facing stiff resistance. For the next two days the platoon conducted three beach recons and several search-and-seizure missions at sea. Sleep was a premium item, and I was concerned my men weren't getting enough. Tired men make mistakes, and mistakes kill good men. It was my job to focus on the details while still keeping the broad picture in mind. Metcalf was sending us all over the island because we were delivering the goods and possessed the only assets available to do so on a constant basis. It was good old-fashioned blue water SEAL work.

After the last of the recon missions I found myself once again aboard the *Guam*. This time I was supposed to brief Major General Schwarzkopf on the flag bridge. He was an incredibly big man, and I noted how he dominated the bridge by size alone. At one point I was discussing options with Commander Butler, the commodore, and his staff within sight and earshot of our little conference. I was tired, my belly was empty, and my physical state reflected a man who'd been on the field of combat. The only clean thing about me was the .357 on my hip. I was on the razor's edge and trying hard to avoid getting caught up in the chaos.

"Hey, boy, come over here. I want you to look at this." Stormin' Norman was standing by the chart table and staring at me like I was a pet dog or something. The hair on the back of my neck stood straight up.

"Sir, you can call me Walsh, or Lieutenant Walsh, or just plain lieutenant," I said in my most professional voice, "but I ain't your boy."

Everyone in the room froze. The younger officers' mouths were hanging open, and a few older officers were likewise revealing their shock at my response to this arrogant army officer.

"Okay, sorry. Now would you please come over here and point something out for me?"

Schwarzkopf was a cool one, I'll give him that. He was starting to see how special operations forces could work, if used properly within the conventional matrix. I assisted him as requested, then went my merry way. If I'd been some spit-shined office pogue and spoken that way to the general I've no doubt he would have eaten me alive. But the man knew a combat officer when he saw one, having served as an adviser in South Vietnam, where he'd been decorated for bravery.

Thanks for cutting me some slack, sir.

It was all too apparent that no one from the Joint Chiefs on down fully understand how to use their special operations forces. We looked like we were falling on our collective swords, given Delta's one-for-two performance and SIX's outright disaster at the Scoon house. Me, I was as happy as a clam with the performance of SEAL Team FOUR, which our platoon belonged to back at Little Creek. No loss of life, no wounded, and successful mission after successful mission despite those canceled in between. Just a bunch of blue water SEALs getting the job done.

On the twenty-eighth of October we conducted a recon of Grand Mal beach for the embattled rangers and then began looking for one of the missing-student campus sites. We were suppose to find a way in by sea, if possible, and then secure the place and its unhappy campers. Eighty-second Airborne was still slugging it out with PRA and Cuban forces, and the rangers were no better off. I found a way in and was preparing to step off the *SeaFox* when the order came for us to abort the mission.

Abort? We were supposed to be conducting this war for the express purpose of saving American medical students. At least that's what the mission statement said. Now I was being told to take my SEALs and get off the island as quickly as possible without the very same students. Orders are orders, however, and we reversed engines and departed. It took the airborne another full day to break through to this same campus and save the students we'd left behind the day before. The army was responsible for making the big splash where such operations were of note, not the navy. Military politics again, with no regard to logic or life.

After six straight days of combat operations the platoon was dead tired, and we were rotating missions as much as possible so some rest could be given. My men were frustrated at not having taken the enemy under fire, but their job was to recon, to collect information, not to engage. They did a superior job under horrific circumstances. As their commander I was empathetic to their need as warriors to draw blood, but I was also proud they'd shown so much control and stamina in not doing so. Grenada was a major screwup for many of the units involved, but not mine.

No, sir, not mine.

22

Beirut, Lebanon

Grenada was over. The platoon capped off our involvement with a two-day mission on the neighboring island of Carriacou, where the primary missile sites were always believed to be. There was an impressive modern barracks area capable of housing over five hundred troops, and a radar site atop the highest peak, which was reported to be owned and operated by North Korean advisers. Admiral Metcalf said we could go after the Koreans and "do whatever you want," or we could take up several other missions he had in mind. In the end, the admiral needed to know what the one runway on the island held, so in we went, several hours behind schedule, as always.

Just prior to inserting on the island we watched helplessly as a small plane flew over our heads and landed on Carriacou. By the time we reached the airfield, all we could do was watch as some very hurried people loaded the plane and lifted off. To this day I believe what we witnessed was the evacuation of Eastern Bloc advisers, whose presence was a given, according to intelligence reports. When I reported the plane and its activities, my observations were discounted. I sensed an arrangement between the State Department and the Soviets to get their folks out of the combat zone before they were discovered and engaged, but I could never prove such a connection. We conducted some major patrols of the island, sent back situation reports so the occupation forces could do their job properly, discovered a white slavery ring from which none of the primarily European teenage girls wanted to be rescued, and then packed our bags and headed back to the *Snelling*. The end result was that our platoon was the first ashore prior to the invasion of Grenada, and the first ashore prior to Carriacou being taken down. Despite the beating special operations took over Grenada, the record has now been set straight.

Back on board the old transport we immediately made way for Lebanon. Our orders stated we were to make all due speed for Beirut to "relieve the beleaguered forces there." The bombing of the marine barracks had demoralized our forces badly, and replacements were sorely needed to keep our presence effective and looking good.

Metcalf asked me to create a threat paper while we were steaming across the ocean at full speed. Bill Taylor and I worked together on this, as our relationship was by now very good on both a personal and professional basis. The report, when completed, was sent over to the *Guam* for review. I'd concluded that Beirut was going into core meltdown politically. There were too many ethnic and religious groups at odds with each other over the city, not to mention the country. And they were all armed and very, very dangerous.

For final analysis we came up three primary threat areas to the task force. These were an air threat, a sea threat, and unconventional warfare such as suicide-swimmer attacks meant to damage or sink a U.S. ship. The commodore and his staff were not real keen about hearing this, as they were inclined to underestimate the people we'd be up against. It was the same mentality which almost got us badly bloodied in Grenada by Cuban military men and well-trained Grenadan forces.

As for the air threat, I pointed out that even a small civil plane could be a lethal weapon. If the plane was loaded with enough extra fuel, its impact and the resulting explosion could cause serious damage to an amphibious ship. And I believed the *Guam*—with its extra aviation fuel, helicopters, and other aircraft—would be the prime target. Our super carriers were over one hundred miles out to sea and therefore out of range for the average terrorist with a Cessna. A civilian airliner, such as a 727, would also make an excellent flying bomb and could be hijacked anywhere in Europe and then forced to fly to the Mediterranean. Such an attack could affect an aircraft carrier and any U.S. ship would hesitate to fire on a civilian airliner out of concern for passengers. It was a classic terrorist scenario, and one that certainly could have happened.

What surprised me when we discussed this was the

genuine shock among the naval officers present that such people could exist—people who would not only sacrifice themselves but kill hundreds of others in doing so. To their great credit they accepted my assessment and planned our security posture based on their new understanding of what we might be facing.

From the sea we needed to be concerned with five possibilities. First, an attack by rubber raiding craft. Such a vessel could be loaded with 300 to 500 pounds of explosives and thermite with a contact detonator. My audience wasn't sure exactly what I was talking about, so we built such a vehicle with what was aboard our ship. Needless to say, the point was made.

Such an attack could be launched by day or by night. Even under way a ship poses little problem to a moving Zodiac boat with a skilled driver. At night, with little moonlight, cloud cover, and a choppy sea, such an assault would be perfect for any trained special commando unit. I pointed out that the flake aluminum we used in the charge would cause an initial detonation temperature of 5,500°F., enough to ignite any fuel coming from a ruptured tank.

A merchant ship could also be used against us. It could be anything from a Douh to a pleasure cruiser, and this is exactly what happened in the Persian Gulf during Operation Ernest Will, which preceded Desert Shield and Desert Storm. We were already considering this type of threat to our ships in 1983. Essentially a merchant ship could be set up just like the Zodiac threat, but with far more explosive. It would also be harder to destroy. A merchant or pleasure vessel could also launch an small craft or swimmers, who could place mines on one of our vessels or simply blow themselves up once they reached us.

Our fourth scenario centered on the PLO or an Iranian-sponsored Hizballah group conducting a nighttime assault on a ship. Such boats are nearly impossible to see on radar, and the men who would undertake such an action are committed to success at any cost. They are well trained, well armed, and fanatical in their intent. If they could capture or kill a number of U.S. service personnel while attempting such an action, the media impact would be devastating.

Finally there was the tactic of using one's own picket boats against the fleet. We were using old, slow landing craft for picket duty. Should a Zodiac boat with a terrorist cell capture the crew of one of these, they could then use the landing craft to go after a second such boat. Soon the primary craft could work its way near a major target and take it under fire, perhaps using shoulder-fired antiaircraft missiles like the Stingers brought into Lebanon via Iran.

My thesis on the unconventional warfare threat was based upon intelligence reports that told us there were ten Syrian combat swimmers in Beirut. Their job, it was said, was to attack U.S. ships off the coast of Lebanon. I wanted the ships to always be under way so as to discourage such swimmers. The commodore wanted to know how close he could bring the ships to shore and I advised no closer than 3,000 meters from the nearest point of land. It is a little known fact that a swimmer cannot negotiate a current of even a single knot, which is a significant movement of water, and this is one of the many reasons why intelligence, planning, and physical conditioning are so important to SEAL people. We train as we expect to fight, and you can't fight one knot's worth of current when going after a ship under way.

Our rules of engagement were restrictive, but what else was new? Marines could not even place a magazine in the well of their weapons until their barracks went up in smoke. I proposed several options to the commodore, knowing full well the existing rules would probably prevail. I then informed the battle staff that my research told me all terrorist attacks up until that point shared some common denominators. All the attacks were preceded by extensive surveillance efforts on the part of the group involved. We needed a good countersurveillance effort to pick up the watchers and do away with them. Hard talk and some very critical stares were aimed my way from around the table.

With the threat in perspective I began the process of figuring out how to deal with what I believed was going to be a huge disaster. Although I was listened to and sometimes agreed with, there was still that friction between the special warfare side of the house and the entrenched conventional navy. Some of this had to do with one simple fact: we made them feel vulnerable even in their multimillion-dollar floating fortresses. A determined group of men, armed with light infantry weapons and a few rockets and possessing a simple rubber raiding craft with an outboard motor, could go up against a battleship and wreak havoc.

As always, it was easier to kill the messenger than to heed the message.

23

Lebanon: War with No Meaning

The platoon had more than proved itself worthy, but Grenada would be nothing like the nonstop confusion of the Lebanon campaign. What we encountered in Beirut was calculated insanity, the day-by-day destruction of a country, a culture, and a people by their own hand. Our own casualties were almost by-products of this war, brought about simply because we were foolish enough to be there and to think our presence made a difference.

One of the first people I linked up with after arriving off the coast of Beirut was William Buckley, the CIA station chief in Lebanon. We'd known each other in Vietnam, where he'd also served with the Phoenix program. Bill was a former Green Beret officer, which most people never knew. He thought like an operator and hated administrative pukes almost as much as I did. Flying in on a marine helo, I was met by one of his people and taken straight away to their safe house. We hadn't seen each other since Vietnam, and I didn't know he was the station chief, much less with the Agency.

When he walked into the room I was surprised as well as pleased. He'd changed a bit, but was still the same thin man I remembered from so long ago. Although dressed in a conservative suit, Buckley wasn't quite as erect as he'd been during those years with Phoenix, and he was pale and tired looking. The eyes were alert, though, and his greeting warmed my heart.

"I knew it was you when I saw your name on the message traffic. I've been following your activities for a while!" he said. After shaking hands, we exchanged polite jabs about each other's appearance, then complained about how difficult it was to work with the marine leadership in Beirut. I knew I was in friendly territory. Buckley remembered everything despite the passage of time. Before long we were down to business. "What do you need from us, Mike?" he asked.

What I needed was access to information and assets that the marines were not privy to, and were loath to provide even if they had it. I wasn't getting along well with them, primarily because they couldn't intimidate me into playing their game and reporting the same back to my chain of command. In fact, it was pretty clear the senior marine leadership under General Joy was out for my hide and would do anything it could to see it nailed up on the barn wall. Lebanon was supposed to be a marine show, but so far it hadn't been a very successful one.

"Mike, I know I don't have to make a strong point of this, but don't do anything that would embarrass the Agency," Bill told me. "All the tactical calls are yours, and don't lose any equipment."

"Aye-aye, sir," I responded. Then we shook hands. With Bill Buckley on my side and support of the CIA, I could now get some work done. I wanted to get us into the mountains of Lebanon where we could operate. The folks upstairs needed good escape-and-evasion networks set up in case we lost aircraft and had pilots on the run. Plus, the threat scenarios required that we be on the offensive with a good countersurveillance program. In other words, I wanted my own intelligence network, much like the one I'd had in Vietnam.

No one really knew what was happening in Beirut. People simply parroted what they'd heard from someone else, and I soon discovered that most of them didn't have a clue to begin with. Mr. Buckley gave me the bottom line from point of view of Israel, perhaps the most serious player in the game. The Israelis were putting their agents in the mountains and as far away as the Bekaa Valley, the stronghold of those enemies we were up against. Our allies were reluctant to reveal their intricate networks to us because of their fear that one day we'd be called upon to testify before Congress and would tell all, including the stuff that wasn't supposed to have been going on. I'd heard the same thing when working with our European allies. It bothered me that our military indecisiveness and political interference from Washington were resulting in our inability to be prepared for what was happening around us.

I was ordered to stay within the boundaries of the Lebanese Armed Forces, and off we went to do some sight-seeing. I found a high point outside the city known as Bayt Miri, where I could see about ten kilometers into the country when looking to the northeast. While I was there a small group of U.N. soldiers arrived, the usual hodgepodge of international military heroes. They asked what we were doing, being very polite, as my escort and I were in civilian clothes. For a moment I was whisked aside by Buckley's man and advised to be careful what I told the U.N. guys, some of whom were known to be passing information on U.S. forces directly to the Syrians. An Irishman and a Canadian were present and both of the slimeballs were standing right in front of me.

The Irishman tipped his hand, making hostile remarks about the impotency of the United States and how Lebanon was going to blow up in our faces. It was a direct reference to the barracks debacle where over two hundred marines had died, thanks to a fanatic and incompetent senior leadership on the part of the Marine Corps. The Irishman asked again what we were doing up on the height, now aware I was an American and very much interested in me. I ignored him.

After a few minutes we prepared to leave. I made a point of passing close by the U.N. traitor, whispering in his ear so only he would hear what I had to say. "I'm targeting traitorous bastards who work in the U.N.," I spat out with as much venom as I could muster. Then I locked eyes with him for just a moment, the message coming through loud and clear.

The day arrived for our first reconnaissance inland. This time I was accompanied by a Lebanese counterintelligence type who really knew his way around. His little car was equipped with everything needed to survive in the hills and mountains of Lebanon, including a secure car phone. The agency men carried secure Motorola portable radios in the breast pocket of their jackets.

I had the hardware. In the trunk were three LAAW rockets, an M16 rifle with attached M203 grenade launcher, and my trusty silenced 9mm Smith & Wesson. As an afterthought I'd snagged a Remington Model 700 sniper rifle. You never know when you might want to reach out and touch someone . . . Inside the car I had several hand grenades tucked neatly away in a brown paper bag; these I held on my lap. There were two other men with us, both with diplomatic IDs, which the Syrians respected and therefore allowed us free access. We were ready for just about anything.

Our mission was to plot the Syrian positions in the hills west of Beirut City proper and adjacent to the ridges west of the Bekaa Valley. Late in the day, after driving along a mountain road so new it wasn't on any map, we arrived. We stowed the car and moved to an abandoned stone house with quite the vantage point. I broke out the sniper rifle, just to see how long a shot it would be to the nearest Syrian target—over two thousand meters. I wasn't *that* good, and after all, anything I could shoot at was way out of range, and there's only one Carlos Hathcock. The Syrians never knew we were there. At times, I got close enough to read their name tags with the binoculars. The soldiers were sloppy, with unkempt uniforms and rifle muzzles pointed to the ground. These are indicators of unit morale, discipline, and leadership. Oh, they had the hardware, thanks to the Soviets giving them whatever they wanted just to stay in their good graces. But hardware is only as good as the people who use it. The Syrians aren't that good, serving more as a safe haven for terrorist cowards than a respectable military power in the region.

Our notebooks crammed with good intelligence, and the camera nearly worn out from taking so many pictures, we headed back to Beirut. There would be other trips, and it was time to check in with Mr. Buckley. Because I was now working hand in hand with the Agency, the by-product of our relationship being good info and solid assets which benefited the commodore, Captain Erie, we cooked up a code to keep the marines guessing, as they were constantly trying to shut me down:

Men

Lieutenant Walsh	Batman
Lieutenant Thompson	Robin
Mr. Buckley	Chief O'Hara
Commander Butler	Commissioner Gordon
CIA rep Mike	Joker
Captain X	Riddler
(still on active duty)	
Captain Erie	Penguin
General Joy	Mr. Freeze
Ensign Petty, Gunnery	Cat Woman (meant to
Sergeant Zematis	throw the marines off)
Marines, collectively	Egghead
Mr. Buckley's man	Alfred

Locations

Bat Cave	USS *Guam*
Gotham City	USS *Fort Snelling*
Wayne Manor	Designated target area
City Hall	U.S. Embassy
The Museum	Safe house
Batmobile	Any vehicle provided
Batcycle	Marine helo
Gotham City Bridge	LZ Oracle (helicopter landing zone within the city limits)
The Garden	LZ Cardinal
State Pen	BLT area (USMC battalion landing team bivouac area)
Morgue	MAU bivouac and office area

Our coordinate passing system was deliberately designed to give the marines a fit and buy us time. It did. Deciphering information takes time, and time is exactly what we needed.

Coordinate System

E: 1	B: 6	36SYC remains a constant
A: 2	N: 7	
W: 3	G: 8	
J: 4	K: 9	
O: 5	C: 0	

Code Words

1. Point of origin: distance and bearing from tower at map coordinates 36SYC 295544
2. Dates: subtract two for actual date.
3. Red Samurai: mission success
4. Romeo Foxtrot: I'm okay
5. Raindrops: anticipate requesting 5-inch Naval Gunfire Support (NGFS)
6. Hail: anticipate requesting 16 inch NGFS from USS *New Jersey*
7. Bowling ball: anticipate requesting laser guided bomb support
8. Fast movers: jets
9. Darts: rocket-assisted artillery rounds

Trying to break the code gave the marines fits, but it bought us time. I briefed the commodore in person and laid out the information we had so the aircraft carriers could brief their pilots on the lay of the land and the positions of the enemy. The pace was hectic, but the pilots loved us. Our first show was on the USS *Independence*, which would be launching jets on a regular basis. If they were shot down, we'd want to be able to get to them quickly. The pilots knew the importance of a good escape-and-evasion plan, but most of them weren't well trained in survival on the ground. I had many young men come up to me and ask what to put on a personal survival vest. I couldn't bear to tell them it was way past time to think about that aspect of their jobs, but I gave them what I could.

My SEALs, likewise, had matured. Gone were the high school antics that had driven me up the wall. They knew their jobs and took them seriously. I encouraged individual thinking followed by action. I told them that if a situation was extreme they were to handle it as best they could if there was no time to communicate with any officers. That kind of initiative is what being a SEAL is all about. They responded well to this form of command, having seen for themselves that Lebanon was burning down around us and no fire trucks were coming to our rescue. For example, in Beirut we were constantly at the mercy of snipers. My instructions to the men were clear: If any sniper from any position takes as much as one shot at us, "waste him immediately. Don't wait for permission to fire; you have it. I don't want to hear about it. Just do it."

They understood, and they carried out their orders. As in Grenada, not one of my men was worth losing over a piece of terrain that had no significance because we weren't serious about attaching any to it. The marines had sent enough of our young men home in body bags; there were no body bags on order for those under my direct command.

While all of this and more was going on, Yasir Arafat— who I think looks like Ringo Starr—was in Tripoli. I don't recall why he was visiting, but he was in town and was trying to get out of the city but having little luck. The French got involved, as they always do, and wanted to provide a vessel for Arafat to travel on. That's when the computer chip went off in my head.

Oh, no, not another brainstorm.

What if we used our SDV, or Swimmer Delivery Vehicle, to get inside the harbor to take photos and conduct a day-night recon? I asked. If things looked good and we happened to be there when Yasir Arafat got to the docks we could even take him out, if someone wanted it done. When I ran this one past the brass, I thought for sure they were going to lock me up. I saw interest in the idea of checking out the harbor via SDV, but no one wanted to touch the idea of blowing away Arafat. Then the planning stage began, and hard questions were put to me.

"Could you actually get Arafat?"

"What do you mean by 'get'?"

"Grab him, kidnap him."

"Sure, if I had Army Blackhawk helos, fast rope systems, and voice radio communications."

We kicked the thought around and even began preparing the SDV. The *Snelling* was ordered to steam slowly north toward Tripoli, but then we got the word to cancel the mission. Yasir Arafat had made it onto a French merchant vessel and was on his way out of Dodge City. Besides, Bob Hope and his road show were on their way to the Mediterranean, and our "number one priority is the protection of

Hope and his entourage." Ah, well, Brooke Shields is a lot better looking than Arafat, anyhow.

As everyone feared, one of our aircraft was shot down. Lieutenants Goodwin and Lang took a missile up the tailpipe and were being held prisoner. We made every attempt to recover them. I was ordered to the embassy, where I met with William Buckley. He knew right where Goodwin and Lang were at that very moment. The problem was the two pilots were being moved and I had only eight hours to get to their present location and pull them out.

I asked for a helo, and selected four SEALs to go with me. The plan was to get the best marine pilot—one with confidence and a huge pair of balls—to put us right down in front of the vehicle believed to be carrying Goodwin and Lang. They were going to be taken across the Bekaa Valley and into Syria—the same Syria that Mr. Clinton is so friendly with today. Buckley's information was accurate this time, he had a man on the inside.

I headed from the embassy back out to the *Guam*. Commodore Erie was immediately briefed. Then the Sixth Fleet got involved, briefed over secure radio. Instead of getting the go-ahead at my immediate level the decision began working its way up the chain. My window of opportunity was closing, and they were discussing whether or not to go after our people! Finally the decision was made not to do anything as "someone might get hurt."

Hurt? Someone was already hurt—two American fliers who had been blown out of the sky and were probably being beaten even as the commanders were jacking their jaws and scratching their asses. I went into orbit. I knew we could get there because I'd been climbing around the Bekaa Valley like it was my own backyard. I knew my men could, and would, take out the bad guys, following me into hell if need be. I knew I could grab the pilots before anyone realized what was going down, and I knew I'd kill anyone who tried to harm them. The argument got out of hand, and I was ordered back to the *Snelling* under threat of a court-martial for insubordination. It was a cowardly decision on more than one admiral's part, and I'd told them so.

Heading back to the *Snelling* I stopped by the embassy— well, they hadn't ordered me directly back to my ship, only back to it as opposed to staying where I was. In all, it took me two days to finally return to the *Snelling*. I linked up with Buckley, filling him in and hearing what he had to say. Bill was even more upset than I was. A journalist had brought him a picture of Lieutenant Goodwin, now a captive of the Syrians. He was sitting in the backseat of a car, handcuffed. Lang had already died and his body was to be returned by his captors. His injuries had been severe, but he'd been alive when I requested a helicopter and four SEALs. It was a sad day when Lieutenant Lang was brought aboard the *Kennedy*. I knew then we could have saved Goodwin, at the very least. But the commanders were too gutless to let us try. I suppose making deputy chief of naval operations seemed more important to them than trying to save a man's life.

By now the word was out about our presence in the mountains. The Syrians were on to me, and Mr. Buckley told me it looked like the marines had leaked the information. I found out later he was right. The plan was that had I or any of my men been killed during our forays for the CIA and the navy, the marines could then have said it should have been them conducting an unconventional warfare in Lebanon. And they were willing to bury me to prove their point. Sorry, guys, you missed.

Since the gloves were now off, I provided Buckley with some information, including photographs, that my men had compiled during their overwatch of the marine positions in Beirut. We'd spotted marines trading their spare uniforms for drugs, passing packages back and forth over the fence at night. We were conducting countersniper activities one evening near the airport when the drug dealing went down. I spoke to some agents with the Naval Investigative Service, and they found out that the Amal militia was bringing the dope in and taking marine uniforms with the American flag sewn to their left sleeves, out. I wanted to infiltrate the group of marines to get to the bottom of the program, and NIS was for it.

But, Murphy's Law stepped in once again. One of the investigative agents was a marine warrant officer, and he briefed General Joy, the senior marine commander in Beirut. Joy refused to believe the incident had occurred, but the marine brass apparently believed we had pictures, because our photos were confiscated, as were the negatives. I was about to refuse to hand the photos over to NIS when I was told, "You'll lose, Walsh. The prestige of the Marine Corps in on the line, and General Joy will push every button he can to burn you down if you fight him." I handed the pictures over, remembering Bill Buckley's warning that if I pursued the issue it would turn out badly for me.

Buckley set up an appointment for us to meet a week later. We were going to wrap up what we'd been doing and issue a report about what we had learned. The CIA station chief wanted all my notes, and he assured me that the commodore, Captain Erie, would be presented with a copy since he'd allowed me to take part in these and many other activities.

That meeting never took place. Bill was abducted the morning we were supposed to meet. His people called me on the secure phone and told me not to go to the station or anywhere near the apartments they occupied, except for one apartment. One of Buckley's most trusted agents met with me, and together we visited this lone safe house. I covered the door while the agent went inside and removed some valuables. Then we got out as fast as we could, weapons locked and loaded.

William Buckley was horribly tortured, then killed. His body was buried in an unmarked grave in Iran but was eventually recovered. He today rests in Arlington National Cemetery. My SEALs and I offered to mount an operation to free him, or at least recover him before the pain became too great, but we were stonewalled.

Even sadder than his death was his abandonment by the bureaucrats at his own Agency, except for William Casey. Buckley was an operator who got things done. He knew how to think, and he was mission-oriented rather than inclined to slice up the operational pie just to make people feel important. He went the extra mile for this Navy SEAL, from Vietnam to Lebanon. Bill Buckley didn't have to give me the time of day, but he wanted to see us accomplish our mission. The fate my friend met is one that would have befallen any of us had we been taken by our enemies.

Surely the hand of God was over me. Rest now, Mr. Buckley, and know you are not forgotten.

American and Lebanese people began fleeing their homes in February. Homeless families were everywhere, and being homeless in Beirut was a nightmare. Artillery barrages hammered the city day and night. People went out to buy a quart of milk and never returned. Car bombs blew up all the time, random violence beyond the pale. This was life on a daily basis, life in the decay of Beirut, Lebanon.

I was at Juniyah where I met some folks from the Lebanese navy staff. A Non-Combatant Evaluation Operation was in the works, and people were lined up outside the base, hoping to get out of the country. They were wretched-looking, and my heart went out to them, especially when I spotted one special little girl who was obviously shell-shocked. Her mother, an American, was three months pregnant. My orders were explicit: I was not to allow anyone on the Lebanese naval base until the State Department blew the official whistle. Artillery rounds from the Syrians were hitting the waters adjacent to the base, and no one had coordinated with the Lebanese commander about anyone using his base for an evacuation of American and selected foreign national personnel by the U.S. Navy.

I spoke with the CO, and despite the best efforts of the marine staff pukes assigned to sabotage anything I did, I won him over. By the end of the day he agreed to let us bring people onto the base beginning the following day. But one person just couldn't wait. Heading out the gate I found the little girl—her name was Melanie—and her mother. Melanie stole my heart and still owns a big piece of it. She was just three years old and already a veteran of war. I brought her and her mother to my quarters and made them comfortable. Melanie never said a word; she just sat there and stared into space. It took another day before we could get her to eat, and I took both mother and daughter to the base doctor for a routine checkup.

The mother, Mrs. Kazan, told me Syrian artillery had blown away their home and all their possessions. It was the same sad story of Beruit. When her husband, a Lebanese national, showed up at the base I was able to get him inside, although it took some doing. With the Kazan family now reunited, it was a very happy day for me. Mr. Kazan had nothing but a toothbrush and a pocketful of cash. The only way to protect Melanie and her parents was to keep them under my personal protection, which we did. A platoon of combat-blooded SEAL veterans is not a bad bodyguard detail to have on your side.

The unofficial word was given and the evacuation got under way. The entire naval special warfare task force was now at Juniyah helping to coordinate the project. I kept the Kazan family very close to me, but I spent a great deal of time on the radio talking with the flagship, giving them situation reports and then telling them I'd already taken some people onto the base. They told me to "get those people back outside the gate or face a court-martial, or worse." I told them I was the commander on the ground and I didn't like being second-guessed. The Kazans were staying, court-martial or no court-martial. The crush of civilians trying to get into the base was reaching dangerous levels, so I made another one of those career-killing decisions and ordered the gates opened.

The Lebanese CNO called me into his office. He sat behind his desk, ramrod straight, and really pissed off. He began yelling, then screaming and waving his arms. I'd never had my butt reamed by a chief of naval operations before, and I wasn't sure what to do, so I did what all SEALs can do very well—I winged it, then faked it, and if it looked as if the roof was going to come down, I'd eject. While he was blowing his cool I just sat there, one leg crossed over the other, looking far calmer than I was. I looked this character right in the eye. I told him I wasn't usurping his authority or anyone else's. Mrs. Kazan and her family kept running through my mind. I had grown tired of the indecision all the way from day one onward. Lives were on the line and the State Department was taking its sweet time in setting the evacuation in motion. Besides, Mrs. Kazan was an American, and this dolt was the proud citizen of a country going straight to hell. Screw him.

In the end, the CNO upheld my decision, and the Kazans and everyone else stayed inside the safe confines of the base. Lieutenant Ron Gay, my buddy from Grenada, and I talked about how to best evacuate the crowd of people piling up. The enlisted men were performing with all the heart and soul our young people have in them. They knew we'd stepped over the line, but that's what Americans, real Americans, do when the going gets tough and tough decisions have to be made. Ron and I figured we could get two hundred people on the main deck of an LCU, if each carried only two handbags. If the bloodthirsty Syrian gunners decided to begin shelling the beach we'd opt for three hundred people per boat just to get things moving. Murphy was ordered to stay out of our AO if he knew what was good for him.

By the third day Melanie was once again beginning to look like a normal little girl. She was bright-eyed, innocent, and smiling. She told me her name for the first time, and that was all this old frogman needed. I'd have gone up into the hills myself and brought war like the Syrians had never experienced it had they harmed one hair on this young child's head. When I picked her up she hugged me, and that hug was worth a million bucks. Situations like the one we were caught up in elicit the most basic of human emotions. I was trying hard to keep from getting an eyeful of tears. If it had just been Melanie and me, it would have been easy for me to let go. But with all my guys around, I had to stuff the tears back down inside and wait.

On day four the marines showed up, bringing Murphy and his law with them, as usual. No one told us they were coming. Here we were, trying to manage chaos, and now the marines arrived without warning, just to add to the nightmare. The major who was leading this group sought me out personally, informing me he was assigned to "take over the evacuation, and you're now working for me." I'd seen this clown around before and had him pegged as one of those admin puke, slimeball, back-stabbing knee-scrapers who infest our military from top to bottom. Only those who have nothing behind them but their rank fall back on the old "you work for me" drill, and I've loathed these greasy turdballs my entire military career.

So we had a little chat. It was a nice, private meeting just between the two of us. The conversation we had must remain private, as it was a special time for both of us. Afterward, he stayed away from me for the duration of the evacuation, after concurring that I did not have to work for him if I didn't really want to.

Once this was done the marines began organizing the civilians. I turned over all the records we'd made, and the marines, much to their credit, had the manpower to get the thing done correctly. My men were exhausted, and despite the bad blood between me and the marine leaders, my men never allowed resentment to affect their work.

The marine major sent me a note at one point asking that all the civilians report to his people to be searched for weapons. I liked the idea of sending notes, as we'd agreed earlier it wasn't necessary for us to conduct face-to-face discussions except in the most extreme circumstances. He had heard about the Kazan family and, in his role, requested their presence so he could search them. I sent back a note saying they'd been under my personal protection for three days now and I would vouch they had no weapons or any other bad things (like drugs they might want to trade for marine uniforms) on their person or in their baggage. I added that if the good major had a real problem with this, we could get together on a personal basis and "discuss" the matter.

I never heard anything back from Major Disaster on this one, and the Kazans weren't bothered anymore.

Later in the day it was time to put Melanie and her family on the landing craft. I grabbed a photographer and had him take a picture of us together. The last I heard, the Kazans were living in the Midwest and prospering. That little girl was my lifeline in the swirling, bitter, bloodstained war that was Lebanon. I had lost Bill Buckley, but I'd gained a great deal back through the heart and soul of Melanie Kazan.

I learned a great deal from the Lebanese experience. Those who are not moved by this kind of human misery have ice for blood. The words of an English teacher leaving Lebanon that day ring in my ears. "They like the blood," she said of those warring in Beirut. "It has been going on for one thousand years, and we are not going to change it." She had lived in Lebanon most of her life, and I believed her.

By now I'd served under fire in Vietnam, Grenada, and Lebanon.

24

This SEAL Takes a Lickin' and Keeps on Tickin'

When I arrived in Panama in August of 1984 I was the theater exercise officer for Commander U.S. Naval Forces Southern Command. NAVSO, as we called it, reported to the four-star, or commander in chief—that is, the naval component commander. The Southern Command theater covers the expanse from Mexico to Argentina, although this is changing, as in the grand scheme of things no one really has responsibility for Mexico. Shortly after I arrived in Panama the gossip mill ground into high gear. The commander in chief was General Paul Groman, for whom my co-author worked as well, although he was assigned to the army's Special Forces battalion on the Atlantic side of the country. I remember Gorman for a lot of things, but the incident that really stands out occurred on the night he said during a social gathering that the greatest threat to our national security was Mexico in the late 1980s. One of his staff—a disloyal s.o.b., to say the least—phoned up the press with that one. Gorman was right, of course, but by the time the Defense Department and the State Department got through beating him black-and-blue over his lapse in judgment, it was all over. General Gorman was forced to apologize publicly to the Mexican government for offending them. Ah, for the good old days of Black Jack Pershing.

My fourth night in Panama I borrowed a car and cruised the streets of Panama City so that I could get to know my new home. When I'm in a new area, I like to drive around late at night when traffic is light and I can see things. At one stoplight a tall, very lean black man came up to the driver's side of the car armed with a dull fillet knife. I didn't see him until the last moment, and his quickness showed me he was a master of roadside robbery. I had the window down, and was only lightly armed. Four of my personal weapons, all handguns, had come into country with me. (I'd taken such things through airport security systems before; it really isn't all that tough if you're trained well.)

That evening I had my trusty .380 automatic tucked under my right leg where I could get to it easily. As the would-be robber got to the window I kept my foot on the brake, grabbed him with my left hand, and jerked him inside the car. With my right hand I grabbed my .380 and rammed it into his left eye. The eye went bye-bye, but he managed to hold on to the knife. He fell back out of the car, covering his now useless eye with one hand and wailing away. I covered him with the pistol, but he was a not a threat at this point. Leaving the scene, I went through the light and saw that a local cop had witnessed the entire incident. I decided right then and there that I wouldn't stop if the police came after me. He didn't appear to have a radio, and he wasn't going for his own weapon as I rolled by, so I declared it Miller time and called it a day. Sharing a beer with a new friend, Andres Otano, I filled him in on the incident. He was an old Latin America hand, and we remain buddies. Welcome to Panama!

Jumping into my work, I devoted all my energies to the tasks laid on my table. My marriage had been going downhill for some time, and I was now awaiting a divorce. My household goods arrived in Panama, followed shortly by my soon-to-be ex-wife. When I met her at the airport the look on her face told me everything. She was unhappy to see me and unhappy to be in Panama, and she was carrying a gift from "the other guy" to boot. No matter how tough you think you are, the human heart is fragile.

Personally, my bruised male ego needed some work. The remedy seemed to be a succession of very attractive Latin females, who somehow found out I was a single U.S. military officer with a good job and wonderful career outlook. Not thirty days after my ex went home the phone was ringing off the hook at the bachelor officer quarters. It was tough, but some one had to do it.

At the same time I decided to get back into free-fall

259

parachuting. I needed a good diversion of mind, body, and spirit, and the Special Forces guys had a jump club over on the airfield at Calsada Larga. I kept telling myself I was already a High Altitude Low Opening, or HALO, god, so I got the short course from the Green Berets. Up we went in a Cessna 185, and the first two jumpers went out at 3,000 feet. I asked the pilot for more altitude, as I wanted the longest ride possible. As the jump master leaned over me to spot the drop zone the worst thing a jumper can experience happened. My reserve chute deployed inside the aircraft and I didn't realize it immediately. As my eyes were drawn to the chute it was unfurling out the door of the plane, its control lines right behind it. I was seated, knees up, and facing the rear of the aircraft. I knew I had to get out of the plane and fast, so I dove for the door.

Too late.

The parachute caught wind and fully deployed, jerking me out of the compartment with full force. My right shoulder struck the edge of the door and was pulled out of its socket. What a ride! First I was upside down, then right side up. Then I don't know which way I was going except that it had to do with down. Time slowed, just like in combat. Somehow I popped my shoulder back into place, but I was going into shock. I saw the ground coming up fast, so I grabbed my right toggle to effect a turn. As I did this, I noticed about 30 feet of shroud line in my hand! Looking up, I saw that over 25 percent of my canopy was flat. The wind was pushing me across the earth at 25 to 30 knots, and all I could do was pull down hard on the lines and hope to miss the hangar I was headed for.

During my entire descent, two Special Forces colonels on the ground were watching me. When they felt I was within earshot they began yelling. "Hang in there, Mike, you're looking good!" Green Berets have a great sense of humor. I knew I was not looking good. In fact, I looked like crap, and they knew it, too. I watched the top of a flagpole coming at me. Always wondered what one of those looked like from up top. I didn't want to land on one of those things so I crossed my legs and prayed.

The flagpole broke my fall. Half the lines went down on one side, the other half opposite. I hit the pole with a loud *whack* and slid down to its base. When I regained consciousness I looked up and saw the flag of Panama flying. I knew then I hadn't been killed, and I surely wasn't in heaven.

The accident slowed me down for a while. A rib was broken, and I'd cracked up the right side and back of my body real good. A bone was chipped near my right eye, and the fall had damaged my right leg, which still causes me to limp now and then. Overall, however, I'd been lucky. I started reviewing my life at this point, and I wondered if God wasn't punishing me for something I'd done. Or maybe I was just unlucky, or maybe I hadn't paid close enough attention. All this time I was teaching myself how to walk again. Certainly the divorce was still playing with my mind, and I had to put that heartache behind me. My judgment was affected, and this affected my performance. There was a lot of healing that needed to take place.

I will call her Marina. She was the administrative head of the legal college in Panama City. The whole affair started quite innocently with a get well card from her to me. One thing led to another, and eventually this woman introduced me to some of the worst people I've ever met. At first I wasn't sure there was any connection between her and the affluent of the Noriega machine. But there was. She had been exiled to Venezuela for falling out of General Noriega's favor some time earlier, and she had many scars, some of them physical. When and why the general asked her to return to Panama I never found out. I almost wish he hadn't.

I wanted female companionship at that time but not a relationship. So I was easy pickings for her. At first there were no hard questions other than the usual ones a man and woman ask each other when starting up. She took me to a Panamanian congresswoman's house and introduced me around. Most of the women there were single, which I found interesting. When my lady friend, who was a lawyer, encouraged me to exchange numbers and cards with many of these women, I couldn't figure out what we had in common, but I played along and enjoyed myself.

The social-political situation in Panama was going downhill fast. Americans were being harassed more than ever before by the Panamanian Defense Force. Young sailors were being arrested and then planted with dime bags of cocaine by the PDF officers. They even tried this with me once, but I was hip to the program. I waited for the officer to get out of his car and as he was walking up to mine, I put it in gear and left him in the dust. Well, I kinda tapped him with the vehicle as I pulled out, knocking him to the ground but not hurting the scumbag too badly. I got his attention, but he got my plate number. I sold the car to a master chief I didn't like too much, and he ended up being followed all over the place until the Defense Force realized I'd bugged out on them.

Marina began asking more pointed questions as things around the country worsened. Suspicious, I visited with the Naval Investigative Service who worked across the hall from me. My friend Ricky gave me the inspiration to continue the relationship. "Who knows, Mike? We may learn something interesting," he told me.

And learn we did.

Marina took me to a birthday party near the Marriott Hotel. One of Noriega's worst henchmen, a real cold-blooded butcher named Suarez, was celebrating his success at having lasted another year on the planet. He weighed at least 250 pounds and was as queer as a three-dollar bill. All of his boys shared this inclination, and I found the whole group interesting, to say the least. Suarez had been kicked out of the PDF as a young officer for sodomy. That was a tough one, as the PDF was a truly corrupt organization that lived off of bribes, murder-for-hire, and a host of other nasty occupations. The big guy must have stepped pretty far over the line to get dumped for his sexual activities, but then again, here he was working for Noriega anyhow.

Marina had been told to introduce me as a navy diver. I also asked her not to leave me with the crew for even a minute. When you're straight and you walk into a room full of armed thugs, most of whom kill people for a living, and half of them are making goo-goo eyes at you, you feel a bit uncomfortable, kinda like being the only whore at a prayer meeting. Ricky had said to find out what I could, so I did. When an opportunity made itself available I wandered into the boss's office and popped the lock of his desk with a letter opener. I was just pulling out a handful of papers when in came one of the big goons. He saw what I was up to and made a gay run at me. The poor guy didn't notice I'd broken into the desk—he was just *so* excited about patting my behind and whispering in my ear. We headed back to the party, where I disengaged from my newfound "friend," and linked back up with Marina. Everyone had a gun, and the guy at the front door was armed with an M16. The host, Suarez, never left his cell phone alone, ever. Where he went, the phone went.

After this party there were others. All of the people I met were dirty, but they were filthy rich, too. Marina took me to parties on the same street where Manual Noriega lived, and at one of those parties I almost got killed.

Cleo Walker was the dentist at the Panama Canal Naval Station. He was a great guy and a good friend. He's a large man, well over six feet tall, and when he smiles all of New York lights up. Cleo and I were invited to a birthday party of another female lawyer who lived four doors down from General Noriega in what is known as the Golf Heights area of Panama City. Not sure of the address, we ended up knocking on Noriega's door, quite by accident. A hand came out the door holding a cocked pistol, its barrel right between my eyes and some good Spanish curses made sure I was attentive. Seconds later the house across the street came alive and a bunch of big guys surrounded Cleo and me. No one wanted to hear our sad story about being lost, and Cleo Walker was advising me it was time to leave.

"Get moving, or we will keel you, gringo!" spat one of the guards.

Cleo told me later he was sure we were about to die when he heard that. Another guy started talking to me, and I realized he was an Israeli! "What the hell are you doing with this scum?" I challenged. Then we got into it big time. It wasn't professional anymore; it was personal. The goons could do us both in a heartbeat and there wouldn't be a thing anyone could say or prove. But having an "ally" standing by was too much for me to take. Hands were going for guns, but my .380 was already out, muzzle pointed at the ground. The Israeli was the only one without a weapon, and I told him Cleo and I really wanted to leave but I only had eight rounds in the gun and if shooting started, he would eat all eight bullets right off the bat.

Cleo was now near hysterical. It was the first time I'd ever seen a black man turn so pale. The Israeli said something I didn't understand, as my Spanish was still basic entry level. No one moved, so we began backing up toward the street. I shuttled us down to the right address and once inside we were told by the hostess that we'd run into Noriega's personal bodyguards. It was well known in the Southern Command that the Israelis were all over Panama, training Noriega's elite military forces—like Battalion 2000, which our Green Berets destroyed during Just Cause at the Paccoro Bridge. Further, Israeli agents and paramilitary people were operating all over Central America, conducting counterinsurgency training in Guatemala and even showing up in El Savador.

When we finally left the party a goon squad followed me back to my quarters on Fort Amador. Two days later there was a break-in, and then the harassment began. The PDF put a military police car right outside my door one evening, less than ten feet away. I was in uniform and inquired what they were doing there, and one of the officers cursed my mother in Spanish. That tore it. I headed back into the house, returning with my favorite .357 Magnum in hand. His eyes widened when he saw me coming, but before he could react I had the barrel jammed deep into his right ear.

Now we could talk like men because he respected me.

The American MP who was driving the Military Police cruiser was staring at me in shock. They were supposed to be making their rounds of the base.

"Didn't you hear what this dirt bag just said to me?" I asked him.

"I don't speak Spanish, Sir," was his stuttered reply.

"Well, that means all these PDF clowns must speak English then, right?"

The MP just nodded in the affirmative.

I looked at the puke all dressed up like a cop and told him clearly, in English, that I wanted an apology. "If you don't apologize, I'll blow your freaking brains all over this nice car!"

"Sorry," he stammered.

I called the Naval Investigative Service man who lived across the street to cover my butt. The joint patrol had no business being in our area, and the American MP wasn't smart enough to know he was being used to cover the PDF intelligence probe of my quarters. Things were getting weird, perhaps because someone was learning about my forays into the jungle where suspected drug labs were hidden as well as my intelligence work up in Honduras and El Salvador where we were fighting some very dirty little wars.

About three weeks after that incident my quarters were vandalized by men who witnesses said were dressed in PDF uniforms. That was a bit much for me. Marina was becoming boring with her cat-and-mouse game; she was very obviously a stooge for Noriega. Leaving Fort Amador late one evening I was followed by a single car. They were good, being so obvious that my total attention was on them and not on the two cars in front of me. After slamming on the brakes to avoid what would have been a spectacular accident, I found myself spread-eagled on the hood, PDF cops patting me down. My .380 was taken, and then a kidney punch put me down but good. They didn't waste any time blindfolding and restraining me. It wasn't until later I would find out the entire scene had been witnessed by someone at the post.

While I was in a holding cell, the fun and games began. They'd taken my clothes, which are always the first items to go when you get around semiprofessionals like these meatballs. No clothes means no dignity, and it is a tactic meant to soften you up for questioning. But I was a SEAL and this wasn't anything new to me. One beady-eyed little sergeant whom I'd seen around Amador rebroke my rib, and I began to understand this wasn't personal, it was professional. I was just a part of the Noriega terror campaign meant to bring on the gringos. This was taking place a full two years before Just Cause. I'd angered someone with my activities, and I had become a target.

They tried bouncing me off the wall, but that was pretty punk stuff and my silence only made them madder. They wanted me to scream, but when they tried other, more serious stuff and I still wouldn't yell, they tied me to the bars of my cell. Out came a rubber-coated club, which didn't leave any marks. They were careful about my head and face, so I bashed myself against the bars and brought up a good-sized lump. That little stunt earned me another kidney shot. One of the little creeps mentioned my broken rib and that brought back a conversation I'd had with Marina months earlier. She knew that I had broken my ribs and injured myself pretty good in my parachute accident. If she knew, the PDF goon squad knew.

The night went on and so did the abuse. I figured I wasn't going to be killed, and they were very careful not to leave bruises and other marks. My insides were very painful; someone who knew his business had taught these boys well. The final indignity occurred when one of the guards began shoving his riot baton up my rear point of contact. I remember being beyond holding a grudge or thinking of revenge. God, I prayed, just let me come out of this alive and I'll be a good boy forever. It was that innocent a prayer, just like the ones we say as little children.

When I returned to my quarters my vehicle was sitting in the driveway, the pistol in the glove compartment. All my ID was present, too. Naturally, the money was gone. I went to the clinic at Howard Air Force Base to be checked out. The senior medical guy on duty was a young second class corpsman, and when I told him I thought there might be blood in my urine, he gave me a blank stare. I left and went elsewhere for professional treatment.

Yeah, welcome to Panama, Mike.

General Manual Noriega spent December 19, 1989, on the north side of Panama in the city of Colón. Returning to Panama City later in the day by car he stopped to have a few drinks at the PDF Officers Club near Paitilla Airfield. In addition, he latched on to an old stand-by prostitute and prepared for a night of cheap pleasure.

Mannie, as he was known to his amigos, held total power in Panama. He grew up on the dirt side of the tracks in the capital and was a typical little street rat. Although not intelligent he was cunning. Noriega spoke from his gut and thought from there as well. He could read a man or woman with all the instincts of a killer, and he could order a man drawn and quartered with a single word. His survival instincts were razor sharp.

On a more personal level, he has eyes that reveal no emotion. They reflect unrelenting cruelty. When he was in power our eyes met only for a moment during a briefing we attended together. I felt I was looking at the devil himself. Noriega looked everyone over, then swung back to me and we locked into each other. Very few men have ever intimidated me, but he was a notable exception. He reeked of evil. There was no conscience, character, or courage in what I saw of this man. It was easy to fear him; he was that powerful.

When I'd first gone to Panama in 1980, Omar Torrijos was "el Jefe." When Omar spoke on the radio the entire country stopped what it was doing. Torrijos possessed exceptional charisma. He was a complete alcoholic and said to be impotent, but he was smart. Look how easily he tied up President Carter. The reaction of the people to Torrijos's words and voice was universal. I felt it, too, even though I did not then speak Spanish.

Noriega was, at that time, Torrijos's chief of intelligence. I learned from the crowd Marina introduced me to just how the Panama Canal Treaty came about. You won't find this story in the history books or anywhere else official. I confirmed the story with an old hand with the Canal Commission who'd been down there since Moby Dick was a minnow. Even today I ask myself why the United States govenment is so deathly afraid of telling its people the truth about this affair. Maybe it's one of the reasons we took down the country the way we did, and why Mannie Noriega is doing a life sentence here in the States?

One evening I was sitting in a bar frequented by U.S. civilians working for the Canal Commission. I spotted two PDF goons trying to act as if they were on liberty, their uniform pants and boots giving away the dress shirts each had on. Both were packing weapons, and they nursed their beers for hours but remained very alert. They were working, no doubt about that.

I saw one American in the bar make eye contact with the PDF. This was a personal meet and it was going down in front of me. On signal, one of the team went outside, and five minutes later, out went the gringo. I had moved around to where I could observe the action, and sure enough, money and packages changed hands in the car they occupied. I noted the plate numbers of both cars and slipped back inside the bar. I passed the information to Naval Investigations, and they sent an agent to check the place out. He was spotted right away and was lucky not to be killed. A real dummy.

The investigation brought the Canal Commission in

screaming, assuring everyone they were drug-free. That was bull; I knew what I'd seen go down. Some further checking revealed that when the treaty was negotiated the various U.S. federal agencies who all had bit parts to play in the overall scenario asked General Torrijos to "get rid of that scumbag Noriega" as part of the deal. Torrijos said he'd be glad to deal with any of his other officers—but not Mannie. Why? Because Noriega knew where all the bones were buried. He was Torrijos's Achilles' heel, as well as his deadliest weapon.

Mannie ran a little team of guys known to us as Fuerza Ocho, or Force Eight. They were an execution squad, pure and simple. The team was suspected of having decapitated Hugo Spadafora, an intellectual whom Noriega considered a threat to himself and the regime. Spadafora's body was found in a green U.S. mailbag just over the border in Costa Rica. First-class job, and with no connections to the country of origin. When Torrijos's airplane went down and he was killed in the crash, many believed Mannie had decided it was time for a changing of the guard in Panama. That has never been proved, but it certainly is more than possible.

Pineapple Face, as Noriega was known, was more feared than loved by his countrymen. His power was so great that his wife once kicked a woman to death on the dance floor of a popular disco and was never arrested. Mannie never fit into the high society crowd, though. The Union Club would never let him join because he wasn't from the right side of the tracks. This always irritated him, because the club's refusal to issue him a membership reminded him of the gutter trash he truly is.

Paitilla Airfield is a tiny municipal airport near the eastern edge of the city. It's not far from Old Panama City, the one the pirate Henry Morgan bombarded with his ships and then plundered. Paitilla is capable of handling smaller aircraft of the Learjet variety. The runway abuts a sheer cliff overlooking the Pacific ocean.

General Noriega was having a few drinks, feeling up the woman he planned to dominate for the evening when Operation Just Cause got under way fifteen minutes ahead of schedule. Mannie was a wanted man. A U.S. grand jury had indicted him for drug smuggling, money laundering, and other assorted crimes. Noriega had also been doing a brisk business with Cuba. Castro's fishing fleet always tied up at Vacamonte and was notorious for getting U.S. goods through Panama and into Cuba. The fleet also brought in Cuban weapons, which then went north to Nicaragua. From there they crossed the Gulf of Fonseca where my co-author, Greg Walker, was working as a military adviser, and landed in El Salvador or Honduras. It's a fact, well documented and part of the reason we finally decided to take Noriega out.

The general also bought and sold intelligence. He had spies, good ones, everywhere. There were over eighty-seven U.S. officers in the Southern Command who were providing classified information to the Noriega machine. Their names popped up on lists taken from Mannie's own house during the invasion. I nearly got a copy of that list, but the opportunity slipped away. These traitors were providing an accurate picture of all U.S. military activities not only in Panama but throughout Latin America. This information was put on the open market, sold to our friends and enemies alike for the right price.

Noriega also charged a fee for allowing the United States to bring in troops from countries like El Salvador for specialized training. In the mid-1980s the going rate for sniper courses was $250,000 per class! Not a bad business, as many of these courses couldn't be conducted in places where the war was hottest. As a soldier of fortune, Mannie Noriega made Robert K. Brown look like an amateur!

Greedy and always wanting more, Noriega once found out an aircraft of his had come back from Colombia loaded with cash. He wasn't told about the flight and didn't get his cut, so someone died as a result. It was simply a lesson in business manners.

Operation Just Cause would be the first time U.S. special operations forces were integrated in support of the conventional battlefield since Grenada. Over four thousand operators would see combat in Panama. One of their missions was chasing the wily Noriega around the country until he finally gave himself up. In *At the Hurricane's Eye* by Greg Walker, an accurate account is given of the disaster that befell the SEALs assigned to flatten the tires of Noriega's Learjet at Paitilla airfield. I was intimately involved in the planning of our effort in Panama, and I opposed the Paitilla operation from the moment I read about it.

Four good men died at Paitilla, and many more were wounded. I'd recommended several other options in taking the airfield, or rather, keeping it from acting as an escape point for Noriega. I knew Paitilla, inside and out. The commander who sent his men on this insane mission failed to heed my warnings even though he had asked my advice about the impending assault plan. Worse, other SEAL officers who knew better should have stood up and fought this fool's endeavor alongside me. It was easier to sign off on the paperwork than to make waves and possibly upset a smooth career progression.

Men died, some possibly from friendly fire, and the blame was cast upon the survivors rather than on the leadership. Never had our SEAL community been so devastated, so bloodied, as on that single night in Panama. And for what? A lousy airplane tire. Since when has it taken forty-eight SEALs to punch a hole in a tire?

In the spring of 1990, Commodore John Sandoz briefed Admiral Carter and his staff on the SEAL community's involvement in Just Cause. Although totally responsible for pursuing a flawed plan that resulted in the death of his men and the near failure of the mission, Sandoz failed to mention even once the dead and wounded at Paitilla. Two SEAL officers who'd served in Panama and who knew the truth, sat through the briefing stony-faced.

Some months later Sandoz would spew the same story to an audience of several hundred SEAL and UDT veterans at the annual Fraternal Order of UDT/SEAL reunion held at Little Creek, Virginia. I was present, then serving as the organization's national president. It gave me great pleasure when the assembled group literally booed Commander Sandoz off the stage as he once again attempted to ignore his role in the needless waste of our teammates' lives at Paitilla. He had asked for advice and been given it. He had requested my signature on his bogus plan, and I had refused to be a part of the farce. He had reassigned me in an attempt to bury me in the weeds because I wouldn't play his silly games, and now the hens had come home to roost.

But there is no joy in my heart, as part of me died at Paitilla that night, as well.

25

Ecuador: An Emerald
Jewel of a Country

"Walsh, you get to take your pick: terrorists, drug runners, subversive Jesuits, or the marines."

"I'll take the marines, sir, the only good guys in the whole pot."

Ecuador is truly a magnificent country. The capital of Quito is 9,000 feet above sea level. It would be my base of operations while I was in-country.

As usual, what I was up to was not a pleasure cruise. Our job was to assess the terrorist threat, the strategic security, and the physical vulnerabilities of the country's key installations and then recommend ways to fix what was broken. Our survey party was made up mostly of intelligence weenies from the 470th Military Intelligence Battalion in Panama. Most were very full of themselves and terribly arrogant. Only one man stood out as an operator, and that was Colonel Margarita Cruz. I liked him right away as he had been responsible for the capture of Che Guevara in Bolivia some years earlier. A former Special Forces team commander, he'd done a fine job of running Fidel Castro's lap dog to ground and then seeing him buried. The sad fact of Che's revolutionary life was that his only victory came about in Cuba. Everything and everywhere after that he met with failure. In Bolivia, he'd broken every rule as published in his own book on making guerrilla war, and the Green Berets with their Bolivian rangers made him pay for it.

While we were all hanging out at our hotel, Cruz taught me how to spot the drug runners and dealers. He pointed out a nicely dressed Latin woman who'd come in on the flight after ours. I watched as she linked up with her husband, fresh in from the cocaine labs. The colonel noted her diamonds, mink coat, and host of bodyguards. Turned out the drug runners' families lived elsewhere—some of them in the United States—while the men worked the labs turning white paste into hard currency. Instead of going home to Mama they simply brought her down south whenever the urge to see the wife came over them. This kept them out of the United States where arrest might take place, plus it protected the families from rival drug lords.

Just how good Cruz was really didn't hit me until after I'd returned to Panama. He'd gone back to Ecuador and retrieved a roll of film taken of the entire American party, including pictures of me. Someone had made us and spent a great deal of time photographing our mugs for the record. From such photos target folders can be made, and target folders normally lead to long-range visits from high-velocity rounds. Thanks, Colonel, wherever you are today!

My interpreter for the Ecuador trip was Chief Petty Officer Juan Acosta. We were old friends from the patrol boat units, and Juan was now stationed at Rodman Naval Station, in Panama. My Spanish was still a bit rusty, plus it looked better if "they" thought I was helpless in the language and always accompanied by an interpreter. You never knew what might be said when he wasn't around and I was looking ignorant. We worked with the Ecuadorian counterintelligence folks whose headquarters is located west of the city on the eastern slope of the mountain smack dab in the middle of a San Antonio style barrio. The people who lived in this neighborhood knew exactly what was in their midst.

The streets were so crowded we were forced to park a block away, and I saw someone begin taking our pictures from a house across the street as we made our way toward the headquarters building. Juan and I hung back a bit from the rest of the gringos, who were bunched up big time and just waiting for someone to heave a hand grenade at them. My survival instincts were on red alert, but theirs certainly were not.

Once inside, we were greeted by guys dressed as if they'd all attended "Langley University." A two-star Ecuadorian general showed up, and the meeting got under way. The Sendero Luminoso, or Shining Path guerrillas, in Peru were running amok, killing villagers males, females, and children in their quest for total revolution. Since Ecuador shares a border with Peru, the military was concerned that the guerrillas would spill over into their country and start making life more difficult. I figured their worries were well justified.

In addition to the boys from Shining Path, there were other terrorists working in Ecuador, and drug runners and subversive political types were closing in on Quito itself. The counterintelligence arm of the military was working toward rooting these elements out, and the general was, in my mind, a good man in this respect. But, by themselves they couldn't get the job done, and so in came the Americans to advise and assist. General Galvin, at the time commander in chief of the U.S. Southern Command in Panama, told me to be absolutely candid with our hosts. He said they had real problems and needed real answers to them. Message received. I'd do what I could to provide solutions.

First off, the Libyans were providing the funds necessary for subversive activities in Ecuador through their embassy in Panama. For example, the Libyan terrorist bank would cough up $500,000 dollars U.S. to finance a political kidnapping. This covered a safe house to hold the victim in, phones, cars, weapons, and surveillance equipment, among other things. All was paid for in cash to avoid tipping one's hand or leaving a credit card trail. Now, none of this information ever seems to reach the American news media and therefore the people, primarily because very few networks bother to cover Latin America in the first place, and if they do, they send the rubbish of their reporting staffs down, because reporters who really sink their teeth into good stories run the real risk of ending up dead. Few American journalists today have the courage to do their job properly, and not many of them cover the Latin America beat.

A hotbed of subversive activity was the university campus, where printing presses were spewing out tons of materials contrary to what the government wanted to see. Their method was to send in the troops like the Gestapo to arrest students, smash equipment, and generally screw up the works, which only created more unrest and greater determination among the radicals. This manner of doing business accomplished nothing, and soon the newspapers and propaganda would be on the streets again, published from a new location with a new staff. I'd fought the best in the business—the North Vietnamese and Vietcong—and compared to them the revolutionaries in Ecuador were minor league, although certainly dangerous. I advised the general to allow the presses to keep publishing but to have his agents infiltrate the scene and begin following the trail in both directions. He liked that idea.

As always, the State Department had its hand in things all the way up to the elbow. I told the Ecuadorians—being very candid, as per my orders from General Galvin—that I considered the State Department and its personnel, who are collectively referred to as "political queers" by those who know them well, to be my personal enemy. To me, they are as corrupt and useless as the Federal Emergency Management Agency, or FEMA, the VA, and the Social Security Administration, government agencies that feed off of American taxpayers with little regard for any of us, either as individuals or as a group. State always handicapped our efforts wherever we were in Central or South America, crying over American leftist students who stuck their noses into the affairs of countries other than our own, using economic and military aid as clubs to beat down those trying to maintain some kind of order other than a communist one.

The State Department also only wanted good publicity, publicity that flattered them. Very self-serving buncha geeks. We couldn't kill terrorists unless there was an actual hostage situation in progress, for example, because if the word got out, it might look bad. My opinion was that you should kill terrorists before they start killing innocent civilians. If you do it quietly and quickly with little fuss or muss, no one but their own kind will ever miss the bastards. Terrorists are a distinct breed of international criminals, and they should be treated as such. Of course, the liberal crowd will denounce this thought, but then most of them are so well protected by men and women with the courage to live and work on the streets that their becoming a terrorist target is highly unlikely.

We round-tabled other methods and means of ending the subversive threat in Ecuador, and I hope those present made it happen. I gave the Ecuadorians a precis on the Phoenix program, suggested some modifications that would bring it up to date, and I clearly stated how a similar program could work for them in their own country. My credibility level rose to new heights after this. It was my way of helping out our allies, but not by raising their profiles any higher than they already were. It gave them plausible deniability should any State Department queers come nosing around, and this was something everyone involved knew was important.

After this, it was time for me to head for the subversives' paradise—Esmeraldas.

Before describing my adventure in paradise, though, a word about Phoenix in the 1990s. The program as developed and applied during the Vietnam War was the most effective counterinsurgency effort ever mounted by the United States. It worked, plain and simple. We were fighting hard-core guerrillas and even harder core political terrorists. I have studied communist doctrine on the goals and uses of terrorism; I have studied Marxist doctrine on the same; I have studied Chinese doctrine and how it applies to revolutionary warfare; and I have learned from my enemies how they think, move, and communicate. At Phoenix, we attacked the core. Identify the infrastructure, the movers and shakers, the ones who lead and give orders; then locate them. Once done, their removal from the scene cripples the much larger organization, making it ineffective, causing it to stumble and then fall. Our greatest successes in Vietnam came about when we turned VC and VC agents into agents for ourselves. Dead people are poor intelligence assets, and intelligence was the name of the game at Phoenix. Certainly the VC and NVA played the same game by the same rules as they possessed and fielded their own version of Phoenix, as thousands of dead South Vietnamese teachers, village chiefs, tax collectors, relief workers, and so on would attest to if they were alive today.

The program has been exploited by cheap writers looking for an easy buck, as well as by serious political players acting out their own—or other much larger and more complicated —agendas. Phoenix worked, and because it did the VC and NVA intelligence networks leaked word about its existence to certain friendly assets in the United States and Europe so as to focus an anti-program eye on what we were accomplishing. It was a clever and effective counterattack against us, and it worked. Phoenix advisers became big, bad assassins picking on helpless, harmless little Vietnamese freedom fighters and innocent civilians. The newspapers loved it, and the antiwar maggots ate it up.

In the end, though, the communist counterpart to Phoenix kept on playing up until the end of the war when all the good guys left alive in Vietnam were sent to reeducation camps similar to the concentration camps developed and executed by the Nazis during World War II. No one cried out in opposition to our enemies' destruction of the South's infrastructure, now, did they?

A Phoenix-type anti-drug program would be effective, and so my decision was to share the means and ways with our allies in Latin America. It allowed them to take on terrorists, subversives, and other criminal bodies which, until then, had been running rampant. Again, one would be amazed at how many Vietnamese trainers, advisers, and cadres were operating in Latin America at this time. They were an effective lot while working with the Salvadoran guerrillas, as well as welcome guests in Nicaragua and Cuba. You never heard about this stuff on the evening news back home? Neither did I, and there was a reason for this blackout.

Many Americans who travel abroad to do the kind of work I was charged with see things from purely an American perspective. But to be truly effective you have to understand what the other guy thinks and sees, and why his perception is the way it is. Lots of questions must be asked, and answers absorbed whether you like them or not. When we as Americans are in someone else's country we are bound by its rules, laws, social considerations, and culture. It is arrogant to think or believe otherwise, which too many of us do, with the result that all over the world we are thought of as the "ugly American."

I work toward gaining the perspective of those I'm dealing with. They are the ones who have to live with the solutions arrived at. I can always pack my seabag and go home.

At Esmeraldas I had to deal with the fact that Juan was my interpreter, a Peruvian by birth, which caused some of the Ecuadorians to believe he was a spy. The young navy officer whose men seemed always to be dressed in civilian clothes and packing weapons under their jackets was a real bozo, and I finally ended the inane argument by making him read Juan's U.S. military ID card aloud. That ended the discussion about loyalty and we got on with business.

The purpose of our trip to Esmeralda's in the first place was the concerns our Ecuadorian hosts had regarding overall port security. We went right to work to help them solve the problem.

For an entire week we covered this port town, looking over every aspect of its physical security with respect to attacks by guerrillas or terrorists on the primary facilities. I taught my counterparts photographic intelligence gathering and we hit pay dirt in every area we went after. One highlight was the Jesuit priest who was the political power in town. He made it well known he didn't like our presence in town, nor did he approve of the intelligence types we were working with.

What piqued my curiosity was the huge oil tankers that pulled up to the offshore pumping facilities in order to take on crude oil. The process takes about three days, and more often than not passengers or crew from these ships would come ashore, landing at a tiny pier off the beaten track at the port. There was no customs inspection, and all kinds of strange people were getting off the launches with big duffel bags and disappearing into the crowds. We decided to pick out one such individual and follow him around to see what was up. My counterpart agreed. The two of us by now were fast friends and respectful of each other professionally.

Our boy was a tall European man with steel in his eyes. He was no more a tanker monkey than I was. We followed him to the taxi stand and then to the monastery where the unfriendly Jesuit priest held court. Ah, the connection became somewhat clearer at this point. The European was an intelligence agent for the other side and was providing our priest with up-to-date reports on what was happening in his sector of the woods, including us. I'd made sure that we snapped a photo of the visitor while he was at the port. We set up a customs station that doubled as a clandestine photo booth, taking pictures of every s.o.b. who climbed off the barges.

Now it was time to deal with the Jesuit.

Our team found a high point overlooking his church and living area and we established a twenty-four-hour surveillance of the site. I'd taught the men the ABC method of conducting such an operation, and they'd caught on real fast. Finished with Surveillance 101, Juan and I advised three eight-hour shifts to watch over the priest while conserving our limited manpower. For some strange reason my counterpart wanted to visit with the Jesuit, and took two men over to the monastery to do so while Juan and I were in town.

When they returned I was told I'd been targeted by the Jesuit. Within a few days all sorts of weird things began to happen around me, and the protection level rose dramatically. I brushed this off as part of doing business, and we went back to work on the renegade priest. He was trying to tie me up, make me worry about my own safety rather than what he was up to. It was time to go on the offensive and play the game my way. "Let's get to this Jesuit," I told my people, "and then watch what he does."

On a piece of paper I drew a large circle with sniper's crosshairs down its center. At the center of the scope was a stick figure of a man. Beneath this I wrote in Spanish "Target: Jesuit priest at Esmeraldas." Another label read "Friendly U.S. Navy SEAL: shooter." I added another little phrase, plus a smiling face and ordered the paper delivered to the priest. He knew who and what I was, courtesy of his European masters, and I knew who and what he was. Oddly enough, after he got my little message we didn't see or hear from him again.

People tend to believe Catholic priests and nuns are above such activities. Hogwash! Some are clean, some aren't. I take each on a case-by-case basis. My own experience, based on personal knowledge of the faith and a study of history, shows me the Jesuits and Maryknollers are the worst of the Western religious lot where political interference is concerned. I'd seen them in action since Vietnam when I ran into a Catholic priest who was running a hospital and supply point for the Vietcong. He taunted us, telling us he was bulletproof, that he couldn't be touched because he was a priest and could do whatever he wanted to, and for whomever he chose.

Wrong answer.

To this day I will not address any priest as Father. Reverend is as far as I will go. I don't trust them, and this goes back to my experiences as a little boy in Boston. In Central and South America we knew for a fact that many of the nuns and priests were up to their ears in direct support of guerrilla operations. In El Salvador, for example, a huge weapons cache was dug up in one American nun's backyard. International politics and a powerful church machine with enormous funding keeps their rocks and skirts clean, but when they end up dead I consider it the price of playing a very dirty game with some very tough customers on both sides. God bless the good ones, the ones who really care and seek to do the Lord's will. As for the others . . . Wear the name, play the game.

After fun and games at the port I headed to Guayaquil, another port city and home to the Ecuadorian Marine Corps. These were good soldiers whom the Israelis have been training for years. The program is essentially Israel's ranger course, altered to fit the needs of the host country. I'd fight alongside these young men and their officers any day of the week. When they become your friends, it is for life. My kind of people.

When all was said and done, I turned over an executive summary that pointed out the offshore petroleum pumping facilities were extremely vulnerable to terrorist attack and that any first-rate power could take them out if it was so decided. I hope this report had a positive effect and that things have changed. Ecuador is a beautiful country with many potential problems, both internally and externally. I'd love to go back, maybe even to have lunch with my buddy, the Jesuit.

26

Bolivia: No Place Else on Earth like This!

Bolivia was once a seafaring nation, and today, along with Peru, it is one of the key cocaine paste–producing nations in South America. Cocaine production is a $13 billion a year industry, and I share the view that our government's ineptness, deceit, and bureaucratic incompetence go hand and hand with the total corruption of the Bolivian government and military where coke is concerned.

Bolivia reminds me of Vietnam in many ways. Its jungle, however, is much more alive with predators, both man and beast, and less accurately mapped than Vietnam's was. The country lives on the water, and all life begins and ends at the water's edge. All the rivers eventually flow into one of four main rivers in the country, and that was how I planned to reach safety if ever my aircraft was shot down or crashed in the interior. Going with the water's flow will bring you to either a town or city within two days. For a SEAL, two days in the water is a luxury.

The corruption of the Bolivian military came home to me in several different ways. When Operation Blast Furnace was being staffed, I spent a fair amount of time going through the countryside on my own. Everything is reconnaissance, no matter what else they want to call it. I headed from Cochabamba at the 10,000-foot altitude toward Villoreal, a notorious drug transshipment point on the west edge of the Ichilo River. Puerto Villoreal is as close to Dodge City as one will ever get today. Every man and boy is armed to the teeth. It makes Los Angeles look tame.

My job was to survey the road system, scout for helicopter landing zones, ascertain the composition, disposition, and strength of the bad guys, and get out without being shot to death. After walking around Villorreal, I accepted the fact no one would talk to me because I was suspected of being from the Drug Enforcement Agency. I explained this couldn't be the case because my parents had been married, but they didn't buy that one. I figured out they hated cops but loved the military, for some odd reason. So I wore my dog tags and kept my military ID in my left breast pocket. Things got better from that point on.

At one hotbed of drug activity I ordered a beer and scouted the customers. Not a friendly eye in the place. Guns started coming out and being pointed in my direction, and push was coming to shove in a very ugly way. "Captain," I said as I poured my beer.

"Capitán? No DEA?" responded one man with a very big gun.

"Nope," I said. "Militaire." I chose this term because I was a bit nervous and could not for the life of me remember the correct Spanish phrase. They bought it.

We had a nice chat, enjoyed a few beers, and then got the heck out of there. If I'd been a drug enforcement bozo who thought he could throw his weight around I'd have been turned into Swiss cheese and dumped out the back door for the hogs to eat. My driver, a good little guy in his own way, was scared to death and hated driving me around the country, because of incidents like this one. Along the roads I saw piles of cocaine paste drying everywhere. It was the only economic opportunity for the people living in the hinterlands. They knew it was wrong, but they had little choice but to go along with the program or die. A tough place to be, but then, Bolivia is a tough country to live in anyway.

Once, while I was waiting for a flat tire to be changed during a trip away from the city, a group of enforcer dirt bags showed up. They were armed with state-of-the-art weapons, and their intentions were less than honorable. Was I DEA? "Nope." Was I the police? Again, nope. Was I military? With my positive response to this question the big smiles went all around and the big boss put his gun away and ordered his boys to help fix the car! My driver had to go wash his pants out in the nearby stream as he'd lost control of his bowels when the gun barrels zeroed in on us and the bolts went sliding home. After Operation Blast Furnace, which occurred several months later in Bolivia, we would have died on the spot, as any American—military or civilian—became a wanted man. Operation Blast Furnace was the first time that U.S. military personnel, helicopters, and a limited number of troops had conducted a combined operation targeted against Narco-Trafficking.

On my last trip into Bolivia we had an exercise going that combined the Bolivian armed forces with our own. There were unseasonable rains during this period and the U.S. base camp ran out of fuel and could not be supplied by air as the dirt runway was washed away. Before the exercise could begin, I had dropped off 12,000 gallons of fuel at the Bolivian naval station at Rurrenabaque, and now we wanted some of that fuel back. I loaded a truck with every five-gallon can I could find and made the trip via jungle road to Rurrenabaque, which is also where the Bolivian Marine Corps hangs its hat.

Arriving, I asked to speak with the army colonel in charge but met instead with the chief of logistics, a navy officer. He had every reason in the world ready as to why I couldn't get our fuel. First it was all gone. Then it was in the boats already tied up at the pier. My dirt ball alarm went off as I listened to this creep-in-uniform. I checked each boat myself and learned they'd all been fueled the week before. Facing the navy supply geek, I told him what I knew, then watched as his officer buddies lit out for parts unknown, leaving him to take the heat.

He was pissed and came at me swearing in Spanish and drawing a crowd to back him up. I could see his game, having watched it played out all over Latin America. Accuse some fool of a crime in public, whip the crowd up, and then see the poor slob shot down by "parties unknown" in the heat of the moment. Only one way out if I wanted to see the morning's sun rise, and I took it. Moving on him, I grabbed a handful of shirt and locked his arm hard up around his back. "You move the wrong way, you s.o.b., and I'll break it off," I whispered in his ear. He tried to drop his notebook, but I grabbed it and threw both him and it into my truck. Taking his gun, I drove out of the area fast and within minutes I knew where he'd sold the fuel. He spoke English, and I told him as we bumped along the road that I'd kill him if anything happened to me or the enlisted driver. My companion was a young army private who was in love with Navy SEALs—can't blame him there—and would have done the job himself had I asked him to. I was careful, knowing how enthusiastic our troops can be if they believe you've given the okay. I wanted our fuel, not this toad's life, so we left it at that and kept on driving.

Once back on our base the army logistics people ripped the Bolivian officer's story apart using his own notebook and their records. He was now hiding behind military protocol, insisting that this would become an international incident if his treatment continued as it was. In the end, nothing happened to the thief . . . at least not there.

I went back into town the next day with over sixty jerry cans, and got them filled up with the fuel he'd ripped off from the United States. While the cans were being filled I wandered over to a makeshift command hootch and listened to the conversation going on inside. They were all there, all the colonels from the day before who'd run away when I'd grabbed their fuel-stealing buddy. The discussion centered on how to get rid of a case of American army grenades they'd ripped off from somewhere. The grenades were 40mm types, the kind you shoot from a M203 or M79 launcher. I bulled my way in and walked right up to the group, each man drawing himself up to full height and trying to intimidate me.

"You guys may have walked off with our fuel," I told them, "but I'll be damned if you're going to shoot one of these at me or any other American!"

Not another word needed to be said.

They had pure, absolute hatred in their eyes for me. As I lifted the crate I knew my life was in danger from here on out. It seems someone, somewhere, is always thinking about killing me. Well, they haven't gotten it right yet, but certainly there's more than one little white cross in a field somewhere marking the final resting spot of those who've tried. Back at the base camp I told Colonel Bigelow, an air force officer I was assigned to, about the latest incident. He was nervous and in a tough spot, but I was honest with him. We'd caught our "allies" stealing from us twice now, and it would happen time and time again as the drug war was played out in Bolivia.

Later on, I learned from firsthand experience how deeply the Bolivian Navy was involved in the drug trade. They deny it, but they are. Just like the Bolivian Navy, The Salvadorans were so involved they were providing the boats paid for by our tax dollars to pick up and then deliver cocaine shipments dropped off their coasts and in the Gulf of Fonseca for a hefty piece of the action. That's what killed Lt. Commander Al Schaufelberger in 1983. This young SEAL officer assigned to the embassy as its director of security was just preparing to release his report on such goings-on when those involved put the word out that he was no longer a welcome guest in El Salvador. Yeah, the guerrillas made the hit, but it was the dirty officers in the military who set him up.

At the end of my tour I briefed Colonel Bigelow on where I'd been and what I'd done. This time he sat me down and asked if he was in trouble with anyone, good guy or bad.

"No, sir," I told him, "not that I know of."

"Michael," he said while shaking his head slowly, "you're a very dangerous man." I appreciated his comment but felt I had only been doing my job to fight the great evil of cocaine in our country's best interests. In reality, we were fighting a lost cause and being hampered by State Department's lies and by kiss-ass political considerations as well as by the corrupt nature of the power base in Bolivia.

In the end it's our young people who pay with their lives as cocaine continues to flow into America despite all the efforts made to see the mission accomplished.

27

Shoot, Move, Think, Communicate, and Survive

Ever since the Goldwater Nichols Reorganization Act of 1986, the United States has made great leaps forward in the employment, training, and financing of its Special Operations Forces (SOF). Although we constitute 2 percent of the total military structure, we consume only 1 percent of the total budget. With the present drawdown of conventional forces we are seeing a parallel drawdown of SOF forces. This is primarily in the reserve SOF community, and in my professional opinion, allowing this to happen is a critical error on the U.S. Special Operations Command commander's part.

The threat of nuclear war with the former Soviet Union has lessened, but I do not consider them my brothers. Their Typhoon submarines are still at sea, and all they need do is deploy to the Barents Sea, submerge, and then bottom out. From this point they can launch their missiles at us, hitting targets in the United States and giving us less than twenty-eight minutes from the closest one to detect, track, and then target—not to mention try to intercept—even one such missile. NORAD is being crippled, and I shudder to think of what may happen to us as this insane drive to strip us of our defenses continues unabated.

The Russians are long-term thinkers and planners. They have used the concept of Glasnost on three occasions since the May Day revolution to play out their game. We in the West have bought into it every time. They are still our enemies. The Russian bear may be dozing now, but he still keeps over one hundred divisions under arms and can march across Europe without much trouble, given the terrible state of affairs with NATO and the cowardly politics of nearly every country other than perhaps England and Germany.

The Clinton administration elects not to address the very real threat facing us today, more than likely because this president is incapable of doing so or unwilling to face it himself. The Russians are in bed with the Chinese, the Indians, and even the Japanese. Three of these powers have nuclear weapons, and we influence none of them to any great degree. In the Middle East, the Syrians are ready to go to war with Turkey over water. In addition, the Syrians have institutionalized international terrorism with support from Iran and Lybia. The North Koreans are developing nuclear weapons, and as the former deputy director of intelligence at a joint special operations headquarters, I can tell you of reading about this two years before leaving the service. The Koreans, the Japanese, and the Chinese are all pragmatic thinkers, and I believe they will put aside old animosities in favor of an alliance that would insure their survival if push comes to shove.

Eastern Europe and the Balkans are in such a horrible state of decay and death that I believe there is no answer and no solution short of total military intervention, which would likely bring on a confrontation between all and any of the above. It is a strictly European problem and they have shown us they have no guts in solving internal problems. Not one American son or daughter's life is worth the shame of war in the Balkans.

By the close of 1995 I fully expect to see a defense treaty signed between Russia, Japan, China, and India—a formidable alliance, and one centering on the rising threat of Islamic religious warfare the world over. The SOF community is the only one that can react quickly to low-intensity warfare. I am looking ahead to 2050, a viable target date in concerned circles.

SOF works best at the operator level. The enlisted ranks have always answered the call, regardless of the stupidity of their leadership and the idiocy of some of the missions. Even our Congress has stated that "the special operations forces of the Armed Forces provide the United States with immediate and primary capability to respond to terrorism . . . the military mainstay of the United States for the purpose of nation building and training friendly forces in order to preclude deployments or combat involving the conventional or strategic forces of the United States is our SOF capability."

I hope the political and conventional force commanders will put away their biases about SOF and its capabilities and mature in their approach to how we are supported and deployed. Without this rethinking of an old problem, I believe that SOF will only continue to be misused and reinvented as time marches on.

I have always put my best foot forward, whether I was deployed in front of a ship's commanding officer, an amphibious squadron commander, fleet commander, joint commander, and or foreign political and military leaders and dignitaries. Nowhere in the words SEAL TEAM will you find the letter *I*. No one man is so good he is capable of doing it all alone. No unit in the SOF inventory is so good that it and its capabilities are all that is needed under all circumstances. Every man in SOF is a thinking individual. But we train and fight as a team, and only teams survive. Individuals in this business, on the other hand, die.

28

My Testimony

"And ye shall hear of wars and rumors of wars. See that ye be not troubled, for all these things must come to pass, but the end is not yet."

—Matthew 24:6

When I was a little boy, and even well into my teen years, I had a recurring nightmare in which I was going to die of a series of bullet wounds. The dream was always the same. It was a violent end, with the impact of large-caliber slugs tearing into my chest and belly. I always woke with a start.

When I told my father about the dream he had no answer for me. What can a father say in a situation like this? If I ever have a son or daughter I will say that the future lies in God's hands. The appointed time for us to die is ordained by God on the day we are born, according to God's word.

When I came to the Teams my nightmare ended and has never returned to haunt me. I took this as a sign that I'd arrived on the road to my destiny. Facing the end is the easy part of life. Living, learning from my own experiences, from my own mistakes and the mistakes of others, and coming to grips with myself as a result, is the hard part.

As a Navy SEAL I fully expected I would never have to stand on the podium and make the much dreaded retirement speech. Down very deep inside me I believed my life would end in battle well before the admin pukes ever got to me. For my SEAL colleagues who have always wondered what made me so intense about living from moment to moment, always doing everything with so much vigor, perhaps this clears up the mystery somewhat. No one is more surprised than I to have survived over twenty-six years of combat. I lived every minute as if it were my last, because I firmly believed it probably was.

Of warriors, I believe certain things to be true. What I have learned along the way is priceless and cannot be bought in any form. Are true warriors made or born? I was born to this life, and I have done what God intended for me whether I realized it or not. In retirement, I know that life is not over for me yet. A second book is beginning. My true mission and destiny lies ahead. In my deepest soul my spirit tells me I will need everything I know to fulfill this mission. I don't know what it is yet, but when the warning order comes down, I'll recognize it. Gone are the anxiety, the apprehension, and the dreams of doom. It is difficult for a man of action to sit and wait. So now I am learning patience in the truest sense of the word.

Whatever is coming is right around the corner. Whether I survive or not is no longer important, mission accomplishment is. I have survived and prevailed, but what has changed recently is the thought of dying no longer has the terror it once had. Because today I know where I'm going.

Living with the Chinese mercenaries in Vietnam taught me a deeper meaning of life, which applies to my Christianity today. When I asked for a singular symbol, or mark, of a warrior they gave me instead four characters representing what they perceived a true warrior must have. The symbols represent being erect and brave, unafraid, dauntless, and uncompromising. I have made these characters part of my personal signature.

The Cost: I am often asked what the human cost has been in all of this. In human terms the price paid has been a high one. But the rewards have been equally valuable. I regret not having had children. It is an issue I could never resolve during my first marriage and one I have not pursued in my second. A son would have been a blessing. However, I have seen things and done things few others have ever experienced. Does one's family life suffer as a result? Certainly. Most marriages in the SEAL community suffer terribly. Those blessed with women who can cope with all the realities of special warfare are truly fortunate men, their women exceptionally strong and brave.

Combat: What is it like to be in combat? There is no one answer. Each man has his own definition, experience, and post-combat look at things. Combat is and does many things to us as individuals. Only the simple succeeds in combat. Human life is precious, especially the lives of one's own men. Combat brings out the very best and the very worst in us as human beings. From the warrior-sage point of view, armed combat is the people fighting to win, not the administrative forces that send them.

Personal Commitment: My new field manual is the Bible. If getting saved by Jesus Christ doesn't interest you, then you are truly lost and need not read any further. You have sealed your own fate. To reach heaven you must make a personal commitment. Once this is done, faith will see you through its gates. For special warfare people like me, such commitment is nothing new. We renew it every day, just to survive. I am happily seeing more and more of my peers in the SOF community turning their lives over to Christ, just as I have done. He doesn't want halfhearted decisions as He knows the decision is a difficult one. I've got no complaints. The price Jesus paid in His suffering to save us all makes anything I've endured pale in comparison.

I can no longer go through life ignoring God or His calling. I did so for such a long time, getting just enough rope to hang myself with. By the time I'd totally muddied the waters around me I came to Him in desperation. You don't go through life giving God the finger and mocking Him. Can you then expect salvation from the Creator without first asking for forgiveness? I remember seeing my leading petty officer dying in battle, completely uncaring that he was going to hell. Once the smoke clears, though, the arrogance we carry inside us returns to replace the very real fear that the prospect of dying alone and unwanted brings with it. I want Him to look me in the eye and then extend His pierced hand in welcome. To be cast into hell with no recourse is eternity's ultimate life sentence.

My deepest held belief is that Jesus Christ is the Savior of the world. His own words underscore this to me. I need not worry about anything anymore. No matter what happens He is in control. I have been through enough battles of one sort or the other to know there is no such thing as luck or coincidence. Too many times I should have died, but only came away scared or wounded. The hand of God has surely been over this SEAL, even when I refused to acknowledge it, when I believed I was so all-powerful that my fate was my own to decide.

My decision to follow Christ began in Lebanon early in 1984 when I was alone and troubled. My marriage was in jeopardy, my soul was empty, and I had no peace. I did all the wrong things for all the wrong reasons. Still, a voice kept calling to me despite my seeking not to hear its message.

That changed on Good Friday 1988.

I was sitting at home alone, feeling sorry for myself. I was bitter and angry over my recent divorce. I wanted to vent my frustration and anger in the only way I knew how. The television was on, and I'd been steadily downing a bottle of Yukon Jack. When night fell, something clicked inside. I'd never felt such rage before, a rage beyond all reason.

My heart was broken, and Satan, through the booze, was driving me to make all the wrong decisions. I called my old friend Rich Peters. He heard my story and said he understood my pain. He, too, had gone through a divorce. "Time to go, Mike," he told me. "Time to give it all up to Jesus. Frankly I don't think you're doing too well on your own." How right he was. God is truly a strategic planner as He brought Rich back into my life when I needed someone I could talk to . . . and who had the right answers.

I'd been going to church with Rich and his wife, Katie. Whenever the minister gave the invitation I resisted. Even when Rich jabbed me in the ribs. SEALs do not hold back their views when they know they are right. It was Good Friday, and Easter Sunday was right around the corner. I'd lived enough of my life with one foot nailed to the floor, running around in circles. It was time to commit.

On Easter Sunday 1988 I walked up that aisle. The minister's eyes grew wide. He could not believe it. But as a true man of God, he welcomed me. With every step I took my resolve strengthened, as did my commitment. I told the minister I was a desperate man and I didn't want to lose the battle for my soul. "I accept Christ as my Savior," I told him. I later learned it's not enough to know Christ. We must also follow Him and turn all of our internal anger over to Him. He has big shoulders. In doing this my battle was won.

It took a long time for me to get to this point. If you're

already a child of God, congratulations! If not, it is time to think about the future. The answer is not a SEAL trident on your chest or a wall full of medals or New Age hogwash or a best-selling book. God will judge us all according to our works and our decision to follow Him. No one is perfect. Once I was saved, I didn't stop sinning. My sins, the Lord knows, are great and they are many. But I have been forgiven.

I am today committed to Christ because I know in my heart He is the only one who will never desert me under fire. He demands a lot from me, more than any SEAL mission I ever undertook. I will not let Him down, and He will never desert me . . . nor will he desert you, for that matter. God doesn't offer us a smooth ride, just a soft parachute-landing fall in the end. The decision to become a SEAL is an easy one. It just takes work, guts, and an iron will not to quit. But the decision to follow Jesus Christ takes personal commitment, the faith of a child, and steadfastness against the slings and arrows of those who are frightened of such a decision. All you have to do is put aside your pride and ask Him in.

Best battlefield decision I ever made.

GREG WALKER, with over sixteen years Ranger, Reconnaissance, and Special Forces experience, now serves as a historian on U.S. special operations and units. His military awards include the Meritorious Service Medal, the Joint Meritorious Unit Award (El Salvador), the Army Superior Unit Award (El Salvador), and three awards of the Army's Achievement Medal. He holds both U.S. and Brazilian (SF) Parachutist Wings, the Expert Infantryman's Badge, and El Salvador's elite reconnaissance/sniper badges. Walker is a senior editor for the special operations journal *Behind the Lines* and executive editor of both *Fighting Knives* and *Full Contact* magazines. He is author of *At the Hurricane's Eye,* the true story of U.S. Special Operations from Vietnam to Desert Storm.